The Theatre Careers Handbook 2014-15

a (pro) directory

© Stage Jobs Pro 2014

This edition published 2014 by

Stage Jobs Pro
131/132 Upper Street
Islington
London N1 1QP

www.stagejobspro.com

A CIP catalogue record for this book is available from the British Library

ISBN 978-0-9556273-5-4

Set in Frutiger & Serifa
Designed and produced by Prepare to Publish Ltd
(www.preparetopublish.com)

Printed in Britain by
Polestar Wheatons, Exeter

Chapter One: Job Types

Chapter Two: Training

Chapter Three: Life as a Theatre Professional

Chapter Four: Putting On Your Own Work

Acknowledgments

We are very grateful to the following individuals, companies and organisations for their contributions to this book. Their insight and advice is invaluable to those starting out in theatre. Many thanks are due to:

- Claire Brown & Broderick Chow, Brunel University
- Natalie Brown, London College of Fashion
- Sharon D.Calcutt
- Mhairi Cassidy, Royal Conservatoire of Scotland
- Diane Cutlack & Thomas Willshire
- Richard Darbourne, Richard Darbourne Ltd
- Jennifer Deane, Brighton Fringe
- Sandra Exelby & Caroline Silk, National Association of Screen Make-up Artists and Hairdressers
- Karl Falconer, PurpleCoat Productions
- Elaine Faulkner, Theatre Alibi
- Andy Franks, Mountview Academy of Theatre Arts
- Gareth Fry, Association of Sound Designers
- Martha Gall, Stage Technologies
- Joanne Gemmell, University for the Creative Arts
- Luke Gilliver
- Hannah Griffiths, Royal Opera House
- Wendy Heron, Crown Recruitment
- Sean Holmes, Lyric Hammersmith
- Sorcha Hunter, The Place
- Lina Johansson, Mimbre
- Rebecca Keable-Crouch & Eve D'Aton, Soho Theatre
- Simon Lovelace, Crew Class
- Caron Lyon, PCM Projects
- Tamsin McDowell, Ambassador Theatre Group
- Huw Morgan, Get Into Theatre
- Declan Randall
- John Robinson
- Andy Rowley, Stage Management Association
- Lindsay Rule, Drama UK

- Ian Saunders, Association of Lighting Designers
- Jo Smedley
- Joe Stathers-Tracey, The Liverpool Institute for Performing Arts
- Andrew Sugg, Bourne Leisure
- Cathy Thomas & Amelia Forsbrook, IdeasTap
- Robin Townley, Association of British Theatre Technicians
- Teunkie Van Der Sluijs
- Robert West, Creative & Cultural Skills
- Lisa Whitbread, Stag Community Arts Centre

And lastly, a big thank you to the Stage Jobs Pro members who kindly shared their experience, talent and advice. If you're interested in finding out more about anyone featured in this book simply search their name on Stage Jobs Pro.

Foreword

 stagejobspro

© Noel Light-Hilary

Welcome to the second edition of The Theatre Careers Handbook. This book was produced in response to the demand for more information and advice about this exciting area of work from people just like you – and we're proud to produce a book which we hope will inspire and educate the next generation of backstage talent.

The Theatre Careers Handbook is brought to you by Stage Jobs Pro, the UK's number one theatre jobs website. Since our launch in 2005, we remain the only UK website dedicated solely to professional backstage, technical and theatre staff. Stage Jobs Pro was built for theatre professionals to share knowledge and advice and we have taken the same approach with this book, allowing those in the industry to contribute to its contents. With case studies, tips and contributions from key industry players and our very own members, The Theatre Careers Handbook really is the ultimate guide to kickstarting your career in the world of theatre.

I hope you enjoy it!

Phil Large – CEO
Stage Jobs Pro

Introduction

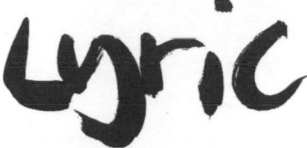

© Joe Dilworth

If you are reading this introduction you are probably considering a career in theatre. The best advice may be to stop reading now. Close the book. Walk away. What working behind the scenes in theatre can offer is long hours, low pay, pressure, uncertainty and constant deadlines.

If you are still reading you've passed the first test and I suspect it might be for you. Because what working in the theatre can also offer is true collaboration, collective creativity, surprise, change, lifelong learning and camaraderie. The very ridiculousness of the enterprise means we have to take it seriously. The seriousness of the intent means you have to laugh at it. And it is this mixture of hard work and fooling around, professionalism and make do, shared purpose and individual skill, that makes working in the theatre pretty unique.

Theatre matters. You will be working in an industry whose purpose, for all its frippery and nonsense, is to make the world a better place. That is concerned with the world we live in and presenting the truth of that world to our society in unexpected, challenging and thrilling ways. Unlike most art forms this cannot be done without the support and devotion and skills of many different people. Not all of these people may be artists but they are indispensable to the creation of art. This is a rare and rather beautiful thing and it is these moments of collective achievement that, on a good day, outweigh all the negatives I listed at the beginning.

We need people from all backgrounds to reinvigorate all aspects of theatre. I hope this Handbook proves invaluable in helping you to enter the profession and bring your own particular magic to bear on the world. Good luck.

Sean Holmes
Artistic Director
Lyric Hammersmith

Chapter 1
Job Types

Backstage

"No two days are ever the same and I get to meet so many different people, and learn something new every day."

There are a wealth of different roles available backstage, from Sound and Lighting, to Stage Management and Wardrobe. Some theatre professionals start out in one department and then move into new roles as their career develops, though there are just as many who stay in one discipline throughout their entire working lives. The beauty of a career in theatre means there are always opportunities to change direction, or learn new skills – you're in the driving seat.

You might already have a good idea of what area interests you, or you may wish to find out more about the different pathways and specialisms that are out there. Either way, we think you'll find this chapter interesting reading. Here we introduce the most common roles alongside Q&As with Stage Jobs Pro members to give you some insight into how they got into their current post and where they're going next, alongside great features and advice from leading industry professionals and organisations.

Lighting

"Being a lighting designer you are part scientist, part technician, part artist, part psychologist."

Lighting Technician
Lighting Technicians work with the Lighting Designer to implement the lighting scheme for a production.

We asked Stage Jobs Pro member Stephen Beresford the following questions about working as a Lighting Technician:

What is the most rewarding aspect of working as a Lighting Technician?
The best feeling I get while working on a production is show night. When the lights come together with the set, the sound, and the action, and the show is orchestrated to create a seamless and beautifully powerful moment. It's rewarding to watch that happen and know that I rigged those lights, that I programmed that cue.

What are the key skills required to be an effective Lighting Technician?
Safety: working at height, around electricity, and on busy stages. Knowledge of the working parts of the lanterns you use, and the technical specs of the theatre you work in. Keeping calm and assertive. Taking care of the space and the equipment.

Do you see your role as a natural step on a career ladder, and if so what is the next rung?
At the moment I work on a casual and freelance basis. I'd view my next step as either expanding my employer base further, or becoming a technician full time in a single venue.

How did you work your way into your current role?
I began by volunteering in productions as a technician while I studied 'English Literature and Theatre and Film' at university and in theatres during my holiday breaks. By the time I left university I had enough experience and contacts to begin technical work on a casual basis, and as a freelancer.

How much do you think networking helps towards landing a job in the industry?
Almost every piece of work I've had in the industry has been as a result of being connected with the right people. So yes, networking helps hugely.

Do you think you will be working in the industry in the next five years, and if so in what capacity?
If I continue to get work as I have been so far then I'd like to stay in the industry in the same capacity, or as a full timer. I might however find that I have to leave the profession to find a more stable source of income.

13

Please describe what a typical day working as a Lighting Technician might contain?

I usually work with a venue receiving a show. Therefore my day begins by preparing the space for receiving the company, then helping to get in and fit up the show. Answer and resolve any queries the visiting company have. Then pack down afterwards. More specifically it involves working with lanterns at height, maintaining and troubleshooting lanterns, and help with operating the lighting board.

Have you done any additional training courses to further your career?

I have so far relied on pure experience. However I would relish any opportunities to do further training.

How important is working for free at the beginning of your career?

I found working for free at the beginning of my career vital to gaining enough experience to work for money. Choosing the right time for this transition is difficult but it worked out well for me: I started a good schedule of paid work immediately after finishing my course at university.

Lighting Designer

Lighting Designers are responsible for the creative side of lighting – they design the lighting plot for performances.

We asked Stage Jobs Pro member Declan Randall the following questions about working as a Lighting Designer:

What is the most rewarding aspect of working as a Lighting Designer?

I think that one of the primary reasons that I do what I do is because I love being a part of the 'story-telling' process that is theatre. Being able to manipulate the medium which is light and use it to enhance the mood, support emotions, even trick the audience into seeing things in a certain way is great fun. It also means that I hardly ever have to wear a suit and tie!

What are the key skills required to be an effective Lighting Designer?

Being a lighting designer you are part scientist, part technician, part artist, part psychologist. Lighting design for me is a fusion of all these parts. You have to have artistic flair, but you also have to have a good understanding of what is required technically to see it through and realise your ideas. You have to be a 'people person' and good communication skills are essential.

Do you see your role as a natural step on a career ladder, and if so what is the next rung?
I could move on from being an LD and go into production management, or technical direction, but I love what I do, so for me, I am on my top rung.

How did you work your way into your current role?
I studied lighting and started out working as a technician in several theatres. It's the best way to learn – you get to meet other designers, you learn from them and slowly you start to develop your own ideas on what works and what doesn't. It kind of happened from there. It was a process – I did not just wake up one day and say 'hey, I'm a lighting designer'. It is years of hard work and relationship building.

How much do you think networking helps towards landing a job in the industry?
Networking is always important – you never know where your next job will come from, so talk to everyone and anyone. You never know who will 'know someone who knows someone who's looking for someone.'

Do you think you will be working in the industry in the next five years, and if so in what capacity?
I hope to be working in the industry for the next fifty years, ok, well the next thirty at least and hopefully always as a lighting designer. I can't help it – I love what I do.

Please describe what a typical day working as a Lighting Designer might contain?
This depends. It is really dependant on what stage of the process you are in. Some days you might have to be in rehearsals, others you might be sitting at home (or in the office) drawing the lighting plan, but once you move into the theatre be prepared for long days (fourteen to eighteen hours are not uncommon) where you will need to be – and be expected to be – alert and concentrating. You will start with a focus session in the morning, then have a rehearsal on stage in the afternoon and then start programming/plotting that night.

Have you done any additional training courses to further your career?
I studied lighting and lighting design, but I think that if I were to study further, some sort of personnel or business management courses would be good. It's helpful to know your way around the computer, so perhaps courses in PhotoShop or CAD too.

How important is working for free at the beginning of your career?
I still work for free every now and then! I am not sure that you should be

working for free as a means to build your career – I think that you should work for free if you truly believe in a project and want to give something back to the industry – you never know where the next piece of theatrical gem will come from, so sometimes you agree to 'help out' and who knows – it might be your best work ever.

Lighting Operator

Lighting Operators will set up and prepare lighting equipment before a performance, as well as operating the LX desk during it, often following the cues from the Stage Manager or Deputy Stage Manager.

We asked Stage Jobs Pro member Robb Mookhoek the following questions about working as a Lighting Operator:

What is the most rewarding aspect of working as a Lighting Operator?
The end result: the show, the audience reaction, seeing everything come together.

What are the key skills required to be an effective Lighting Operator?
Communication, the ability to work well in a team, willingness to work long and irregular hours, a sense of humour and problem-solving skills.

Do you see your role as a natural step on a career ladder, and if so what is the next rung?
I do indeed see my role as a natural step on the career ladder, and the next rung would be the Production Electrician role.

How did you work your way into your current role?
I started off by doing a theatre course in sixth form and then organised work experience in a local theatre. I was then offered work at the theatre, which I did whilst studying for my diploma. I then decided to go on to drama school to continue my training and to get more experience and skills.

How much do you think networking helps towards landing a job in the industry?
There's a saying that I've heard a great number of times: 'It's not just what you know, it's who you know.' What a true comment. Networking is a huge part of landing a job in the industry.

Do you think you will be working in the industry in the next five years, and if so in what capacity?
I'm certain that I will still be working in the industry in the next five years, and hopefully on touring productions.

Please describe what a typical day working as a Lighting Operator might contain?
Breakfast, the most important meal of the day. Arrive at the Venue, meet the in house team. Be briefed by the production electrician. Unload the equipment. Rig equipment. Lunch. Fault find/repairs. Focus. Update focus and pallets. Check Cues. Operate the Show.

Have you done any additional training courses to further your career?
ETC Ion & Eos Training First Aid Training Pyrotechnics Training.

How important is working for free at the beginning of your career?
You have to start somewhere, but you also have to earn a living. I do think it's important to do a little free work, as you don't know who you could meet.

Electrician

The Electrician is responsible for rigging and maintaining the lighting equipment for a production or venue.

We asked Stage Jobs Pro member Paul Beer the following questions about working as an Electrician:

What is the most rewarding aspect of working as an Electrician?
Being able to share skills and knowledge with others, and enhance and improve all aspects of the stage lighting required for a production.

What are the key skills required to be an effective Electrician?
The key skills are creativity, experience, knowledge of lighting/lamps/cables/electrical supplies to ensure a safe and operational lighting design and meeting the requirements of the production team and directors.

Do you see your role as a natural step on a career ladder, and if so what is the next rung?
I do see my role within lighting as a step on a career ladder. I always like to think there is room for self improvement, no matter the size of the production or performance.

How did you work your way into your current role?
By studying stage craft and developing a thorough knowledge of the electrical power, lighting and sound equipment used within performing arts. And most of all a lot of hard work.

How much do you think networking helps towards landing a job in the industry?
Networking helps a great deal within the industry.

Do you think you will be working in the industry in the next five years, and if so in what capacity?
Yes I do think I will be working within the industry in the next five years – and continuing to further my interests and skills in stage lighting.

Please describe what a typical day working as an Electrician might contain?
Rigging of lamps, focusing of lamps, plotting of lighting for the production to meet the requirements of the lighting designer/director, and meetings and discussions about the resources available.

Have you done any additional training courses to further your career?
Yes, general health and safety is very important. And the relevant training to use ladders/towers safely.

How important is working for free at the beginning of your career?
Very important.

Chief Electrician

The Chief Electrician arranges and organises the lighting equipment for a production, in addition to managing and overseeing other members of the technical/lighting department.

We asked Stage Jobs Pro member Garry Hoare the following questions about working as a Chief Electrician:

What is the most rewarding aspect of working as a Chief Electrician?
Seeing the component lighting parts of a production come from a CAD plan, to having equipment laid out and working, to hanging it in a venue and having a fully functional production. And free tickets to a lot of shows!

What are the key skills required to be an effective Chief Electrician?
As a Chief Electrician you don't just have to know about electrics, you have to have knowledge of all aspects of theatre as quite often you become inter-

changeable with other heads of departments. You also have to be a good communicator, with the ability to take on tasks alone or delegate them to the best available member of staff.

Do you see your role as a natural step on a career ladder, and if so what is the next rung?
I enjoy the role as a Chief Electrician. My next career move may be towards production management, but I am happy to stay put for a while.

How did you work your way into your current role?
I started as a casual Lighting Technician at the Crucible Theatre in Sheffield, which is where I learnt the trade from the experienced staff I was working with. From there I moved on to other projects and small scale tours, building on those experiences. I am currently Head of Lighting on a UK number 1 touring production. I think with the university options so easily available these days it's important to learn the theoretical skills, as well as the practical.

How much do you think networking helps towards landing a job in the industry?
This industry has always had a strong sense of networking. When employing staff for tours I always look down their CV and see which productions they have worked on – and who with. If I know someone I'll ask them for information on them. Networking also becomes important in terms of passing jobs between people. For example, I may be offered a job I can't do, so I will call a select group of people to see if they would like it. And the same works in return.

Do you think you will be working in the industry in the next five years, and if so in what capacity?
Who knows what is round the corner. I hope so. I am currently enjoying touring again so, I'll be out on the road for a few more years yet.

Please describe what a typical day working as a Chief Electrician might contain?
On a touring show, it really depends on where you are in the production process. If I am in the planning stages, I'll be working from my office at home (or on a train, or a hire company office) typically working out equipment requirements, drawing plans, budget management etc (typically two or three days of 9-5). In prep we would be assembling equipment, making up cable looms (taping cables together, allowing 1 loom to go to a lighting bar and not 6 singles), addressing lighting fixtures and ensuring we have everything together to go in to the production phase (typically 9-5 days). Production phase would involve putting the equipment into a theatre

as per the lighting plan, ensuring everything is working and programming the lighting desk (typically 9am – 11pm). During the show week, the Head of Electrics would be operating during shows, ensuring all equipment is working and is regularly maintained, ensuring consumable stock levels are kept to a set level, as well as man management of the electrics staff. Then every Saturday night, load the trucks and move on to the next venue for a Monday 9am load in. An in-house Head of Electrics would be very similar except they may not move onto another city, rather move on to the next show coming into their venue or the next show they are producing.

Have you done any additional training courses to further your career?
Rigging, First Aid (to paramedic level), Health and Safety, operation and maintenance of the majority of lighting fixtures on the market, programming and operation of most lighting desks.

How important is working for free at the beginning of your career?
If you can get paid for work it's great, but whilst you are learning it's important to get as much experience as possible working with a wide range of people.

Followspot Operator

Followspot Operators are in charge of moving a spotlight to follow an actor or highlight a piece of action onstage.

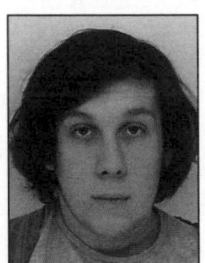

We asked Stage Jobs Pro member Sam Ohlsson the following questions about working as a Followspot Operator:

What is the most rewarding aspect of working as a Followspot Operator?
Being a key part of a team involved in creating fantastic shows for audiences. The effects added to a performance by the spotlight are essential for atmosphere creation and lighting key actions and performers.

What are the key skills required to be an effective Followspot Operator?
There are a number of skills required and they are a blend of technical skills and communication skills. You must have good knowledge of the equipment and have the ability to follow a script and instructions. Good communication skills are essential as clear contact between all members of the SM and LX teams is crucial for a faultless show.

Do you see your role as a natural step on a career ladder, and if so what is the next rung?

For me, my role as a Followspot Operator is only the beginning of a career in the theatre industry. I see my career progression moving further along the lighting path, becoming a Lighting Programmer and eventually being Head of Lighting.

How did you work your way into your current role?
Whilst studying the Stage Management and Theatre Technician course at LAMDA, a contact at 'We Will Rock You' at the Dominion let me know there was a vacancy for a Deputy Followspot Operator and forwarded my name to the Chief LX. After fulfilling the Dep role for two years, I was offered a permanent role when I'd completed my studies. From there I was made aware of a similar role at 'Wicked' at the Apollo Victoria and was offered and accepted the position there.

How much do you think networking helps towards landing a job?
Networking is essential, the more contacts you have, the more opportunities you may become aware of, and the more your name becomes known.

Do you think you will be working in the industry in the next five years, and if so in what capacity?
I will definitely be working within the theatre industry for the foreseeable future. My career is only just beginning and I aim to take on more responsible roles. I would like to be in a position of LX programmer leading to Head of Lighting eventually, whether that will be in five years time, who can tell?

Please describe what a typical day working as a Followspot Operator might contain?
When equipment requires maintenance or there are additional rehearsals, my day could start any time between mid-morning and late afternoon and go straight through to the performance. However for a typical evening performance I have to be in the theatre for 6.55 for the show to start at 7.30. The show closes around 10.30.

Have you done any additional training courses to further your career?
I studied the Stage Management and Theatre Technician course at LAMDA for two years. Whilst working on the Olympics I passed the Honeywell Harness Fall Protection Training and Safety Passport Alliance Training.

How important is working for free at the beginning of your career?
Working for free is one of the best ways to make a start in the industry. You gain experience of different equipment and different ways of working, but most importantly you begin to make contacts for your future career.

Careers in Stage Lighting

IAN SAUNDERS, ASSOCIATION OF LIGHTING DESIGNERS

The Association of Lighting Designers

Although the Association of Lighting Designers was started by theatre lighting designers, these days our members work in a many other places too, and they are not all lighting designers either. There are many ways of earning a living in stage lighting and many routes into these different roles. The one thing they all have in common though is that it can be hard to see any way in from outside. This article attempts to give some guidance to those thinking of a career in stage lighting, but it is not a complete guide – so if after reading it you want more information, do contact the Association. To start with, let's have a look at some of the top jobs.

Lighting Designer (LD)

As the name suggests, the Lighting Designer is responsible for the lighting design, that means the configuration of lighting equipment and the creation of lighting states (cues). On a large show, the LD may also be responsible for putting together the team of people who realise the lighting design – production electrician, programmer, specialist technicians, follow spot operators etc. On smaller shows however the LD is often expected to do lots of things like rigging the equipment and programming cues into the lighting desk.

LDs don't just find work in theatre. Live concert touring (what some still call Rock 'n' Roll), events and spectaculars (such as opening ceremonies for example), commercial product launches and conferences all make use of designed lighting – and so provide work for lighting designers and all the people who work with them.

Generally LDs need to have creative vision and a 'craft knowledge' of how the lighting equipment they use works. After all, they will be asked to come up with ideas in light, the rig plan that will make possible those ideas, to focus all the instruments, create all the cue states and communicate the way they should be played back each show, and stay reasonably sane. To do this work consistently well requires knowledge, talent and experience. To do it well at scale requires great organisational skills, and probably great selling skills too – someone has to be persuaded

22

to spend a lot of money before any LD gets a big rig to play with. There is no single place to learn all these skills!

Production Electrician and Touring Chief LX

Generally these are the people in charge of setting up and maintaining the lighting rig and all the associated equipment. They work on the larger shows, theatre of all kinds, concert touring and all the rest. They usually work very closely with the lighting designer and, on largest productions, may lead a big team. Often they look after the show for the LD, who may not come to every performance or date of the tour.

These men and women lead teams who build shows in a single venue, or for a tour. Touring a lighting rig means designing the system so that it can quickly be packed away in trucks, moved, and set up somewhere new – sometimes every day. The touring staff stay with the show and on some productions they may travel all over the world – though on a busy tour the tour staff may not get to see much more than the inside of a lot of clubs, theatres, arenas or stadiums.

"Live concert touring, events and spectaculars, commercial product launches and conferences all make use of designed lighting"

Most Production Electricians have at least some formal training. Many started their working lives as theatre technicians. Many touring chiefs started working at a lighting hire company before moving on to be touring lighting technician, and gradually gaining the skills to be in charge.

Lighting Programmers

Programmers (as distinct from operators) are usually only required on larger shows and, like the Production Electrician and Touring Chief LX, they will work closely with the LD. It is largely the programmer's job to make the lighting rig do what it needs to do so that the LD's ideas can be brought to life. Programmers need to have good computer skills, a logical approach, and a good eye so they can see the stage in the same way the LD does. Most programmers start as lighting technicians then become show operators, gradually developing the skills of programming.

Freelancing

Lighting Designers, Production Electricians, Touring Chiefs and Programmers are almost always freelance practitioners, running themselves as an independent business. This can be a lonely and stressful thing to do, which is where the support of an organisation such as the ALD can really count.

Theatre or Venue Chief LX and Head of Lighting

These job titles can describe a number of different levels of responsibility. In some cases, the Chief LX is little more than the head maintenance person, looking after the infrastructure of a building and having very little to do with actual shows. However in many more cases these are the men and women who really make it worth working in a particular venue – for the visiting LD and for the crew. They will usually have held a number of positions on the way to these responsible jobs – perhaps in the same venue, perhaps in different theatres or perhaps 'on the road' touring.

In the largest theatres and opera houses the Head of Lighting will be a very senior role, responsible for the quality of lighting on one or more stages and perhaps on the company's touring productions too, working with international lighting designers and ensuring their in-house and hired equipment is the best it can be.

"The Chief LX of a theatre with a long running high tech show will need to work out how to keep all the moving lights and video equipment working properly for every show, which is no small task"

This kind of responsibility is not really found in concert venues, as most visiting acts will come with their own lighting team.

The Chief LX of a theatre with a long running high tech show such as a West End musical may work for the production or the theatre. Either way, she or he will need to work out how to keep all the moving lights and video equipment working properly for every show, which is no small task.

Like all the other top jobs mentioned here, being a successful Chief LX or Head of Lighting requires a great deal of knowledge, and lots of experience.

Getting Started
So those were the top jobs – how might a person work to get there? Here are a few ways of getting started.

Lighting Hire Company
Lighting hire companies have become a good way to get started in many branches of the industry, particularly concert touring and events. Most lighting hire companies have some kind of formal or informal training scheme, and some now run apprenticeships. They also often have busy periods when they need extra help. One good way in for newcomers is to offer to work as a casual to prove that you can turn up on time and do as instructed. There are lots of people who have begun their professional lives in lighting in this way. Some stayed with the company, some went off to get degrees or other qualification, others branched out as freelancers once they felt they had learnt enough.

Most large scale lighting rigs, and many others too, are rented from a lighting hire company. Part of the job of the Production Electrician or Touring Chief LX is to negotiate the deal with the hire company and to lead the preparation of the rig at the company's base. The hire company staff can therefore have plenty of opportunities to meet and learn from these top practitioners.

Your Local Theatre or Concert Venue
Most theatres will have age restrictions on who can work there, but once you are eighteen there are often casual jobs to be had by anyone who proves to be keen and hard working. You need to be realistic and understand the kinds of show your local venue puts on. A professional theatre or concert venue is not going to let you walk in and light a show, or even programme one. Even so, just being good at pushing boxes can be valuable experience, and put you in the right place to meet people who can help you take the next steps.

Formal Training and Qualifications
The most widely known post 16 qualification in England is the Production Arts BTEC. Some colleges do this really well. If you are thinking of applying, remember that this is really only a first step into the lighting industry. Find out where successful graduates of the courses you are interested in have gone and be sure that you can get what you want from the particular course before you commit yourself. Remember too that the BTEC national diploma is not the only way to gain qualifications for your

next step, and that good A-Levels, or an apprenticeship may be just as valuable for you.

Graduate Lighting Person?
A degree will not make you a lighting designer, programmer or touring chief, but it can help you on the way, and it can also give you something to fall back on should you decide that 'touring' is not a job for your mature self. (It's worth mentioning that few lighting people work right through to retirement 'on the road', or even in a venue, for all kinds of reasons. A degree can help you start a new career more easily later on, should you chose that.)

One other important thing any degree should teach you is how to think, plan and reflect on experience. This is one reason why many graduates progress more quickly in their careers than non-graduates.

"Most lighting degrees are hard work – so if your idea of university is a few lectures a week and an exam at the end of unit, then you probably should be looking elsewhere"

Does it have to be a degree in Lighting?
No. The choice depends on where your interests lie and – these days especially – you should only consider doing a degree if you are pretty sure you are going to enjoy studying that particular subject for three or four years. Most lighting degrees are hard work – so if your idea of university is a few lectures a week and an exam at the end of unit, then you probably should be looking elsewhere.

A good vocational degree (in lighting or any associated subject) will offer you opportunities to try out a variety of professional roles within the safe environment of the institution. It should also offer the opportunity to experience the actual industry – on placement, or working evenings or vacations for professionals you have met through the course.

Most lighting degrees base their training on a theatre model, but don't be put off if theatre is not where you see yourself. Many courses have wider options in later years, (ask what these might be) and most areas of professional live performance value the discipline that theatre based training provides.

A vocational degree should teach you the stuff you need to know to practice safely too, and help you develop skills that will enable you to progress quickly through the industry, making the most of every experience.

What next
Doing some casual work in any sector of the lighting industry can help you decide if it is really for you. It can be a strange place – people often talk about stage lighting being a 'life choice' rather than a job. While that is immensely satisfying for many of us, it is not for everyone, so try it out before you commit.

Join the ALD, which means you will get copies of FOCUS 6 times a year. Here you can read about what all kinds of lighting people are up to.
If you still like the sound of working in stage lighting – give it a go. At its best it is a mix of art, craft and technology and is full of extraordinary people.

The Association of Lighting Designers is a professional body representing lighting designers working in the live performance industry in the United Kingdowm and many other parts of the world: **www.ald.org.uk**

Lighting Angles – The Different Approaches to Lighting Design

DECLAN RANDALL

As a lighting designer our work is often as varied as the requests and challenges that we encounter as we move from one project to another. This week we might be lighting a ballet, next we might be lighting an opera and perhaps after that a music video. Knowing the tools of your trade are extremely important, but an understanding of the craft of lighting and the art of light are also vital.

Every new show will bring with it its own unique set of challenges: a particularly tricky colour palette; minimal lighting angles available due to the geography of the theatre or the set design; a space not originally designed (or intended) for live performance; or perhaps the show requires you to use a new piece of technology that you have never used before.

It's this variation, and environment of constant change, that excites me and keeps my passion for lighting design alive. Over the years I have been extremely fortunate to work on some amazing productions with some incredible creative teams. I hope that the experiences I share below will capture and convey my love of light and lighting. Lighting design cannot happen in isolation – it is always a team effort and would not be possible without the hours of dedication and love for live performance that is shared with my fellow members of the creative team and the many wonderful production crews that we all work with.

Dialogues des Carmelites – an opera.
The opera is based on a true story – it's about the persecution of the Carmelite nuns during the French Revolution. The plot revolves around a central (fictional) character called Blanche who is born into the world in fear and seems to grow up to be someone who is always afraid. It was this shattered psyche and the opening scene where her carriage is attacked and the windows smashed that gave set designer David Farley the starting point for his marvellous design. The show opens with a projected image of the shattering glass (one which we used again, both as a negative image and later, red with blood) which were designed by final year student Chris Jackson. Both director Stephen Barlow and David wanted the stage to feel closed-in and threatening, and offer the audience a sense of the danger and fear that ruled her life. This was achieved by two sets of sliders and headers, shaped like fragments of the shattered glass, which would move

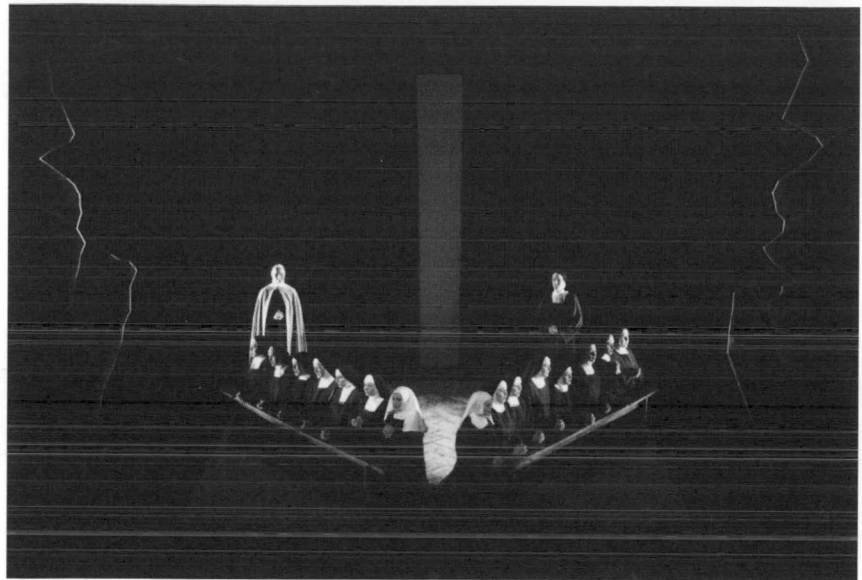

in and out to open up and close down the space and create the different locations within the opera.

The main performance area was a raked wedge which revolved as required to further change the location settings. I fell in love with the set the first time I saw it and knew how important the light would be to enhance the sense of fear and dread that Blanche felt and that the set created – and I just could not wait to get 'stuck in'.

Most of the scenes called for a specific light source, and even if these were not actually seen, they were certainly alluded to. As with any good piece of theatrical writing, light is inherent to the telling of the story. It is written that it gets darker and more ominous which adds to her fear and that flickering candlelight would cast shadows on the walls which would frighten her. Daylight and candlelight became the two main motivating light sources, but as she (Blanche) was living in a world that to her was full of fear, I did not want to use colours that were too realistic in suggesting the motivating light. For instance, I wanted daylight, but it needed to be an uncomfortable daylight – something that was just 'off-normal' and unsettling. The same applied to the candlelight – it was warm and flickering, but it was not a 'happy' or a 'cosy' warm. The other dictating factor was that Blanche's world demanded the light was fractured and broken. This again, ties in with the theme of the broken glass established early on in the opera. There were a number of cues that we created for

Blanche that would slowly fade in a gobo wash as she entered the scene, so that it was almost as if her mere presence was causing the light to fracture and break. Depending on the tone of the scene, these were then adjusted in intensity to become more dominant as her fear grew and then recede slightly as she was comforted, but never going away completely.

Macbeth – site specific performance

There are few words that can strike fear into the heart of any lighting designer quicker than the words 'it's a site-specific piece...' For a number of years, the Guildford Shakespeare Company has been presenting their annual production in the Holy Trinity Church on Guildford's High Street. This time it was Shakespeare's famous tragedy MACBETH that was to take to the boards.

With director Caroline Devlin and designer Sarah Bacon, we set out to create a production that made use of the church's wonderful architecture (including a Grade 2 listed Rood Screen) while still being able to retain a sense of the slightly supernatural world that Macbeth inhabits. To add to the joys that are lighting for site-specific works, it was decided that the main acting area would be in-the-round, with audiences seated on all four sides of the main stage, as well as using a smaller stage in front of the rood screen and a few guest appearances (by ghosts and pages) on the balcony. There were also a few smaller stages dotted around the space where the witches would appear. Large timber structures clad the fronts of our stages and came to be affectionately referred to as the 'trees'.

As with any site-specific work, the main problem is usually power, or the lack thereof. Of course, you can bring in generators and the like, but our

budgets did not really extend to that. Fortunately the church did have a 63A 3-phase supply which we were able to use. I was also very fortunate that both Philips and ETC were able to assist us – ETC with an Element console, and Philips with six of their new PL-1 Cyc lights. The other big problem when working site-specific is the lack of suitable lighting positions. Every now and then you get lucky and there is some sort of structure that you can rig from, but we had to make do with what we had. I decided that the bulk of the lighting for the main stage would have to come from a boom position, because it was easier to rig and cable and it meant that if I could rig them at a low enough angle I would be able to focus them in such a way that we could keep the worst of the glare out of the audience's eyes. The result of this was that most of the action ended up being slightly up-lit and I think this worked to our advantage. Whilst I did install some low voltage birdies around the edge of the stage intended for the 'asides' where we wanted a more unnatural feel, the balance of the general lighting also had a slightly unnatural feel to it as it was coming from a lower angle than we are used to seeing in everyday life. We had just about enough power to drive the twenty-four dimmers that I used, although we did not dare bringing everything on at the same time for fear of plunging Guildford into darkness. There were also seven re-plug circuits, all with A's, B's and C's, so the ASM had quite a job frantically repatching lights during the performance.

Le Nozze di Figaro – an opera
It was a dark and stormy night. Well, not really. But it was a Tuesday. The phone rings. It's Bridget Kimak, designer for Guildhall's production of Le Nozze di Figaro.

After a few pleasantries, we get down to business and start to talk about the set.

"You're going to hate me", says Bridget.

"Let me guess", I say jokingly. "Three walls and a ceiling?"

Silence.

"It's probably best if you come and take a look at the model".

So I did, and it was amazing. Director Martin Lloyd-Evans had decided to update the production and set it in modern America, Texas in fact. The set was essentially a floating white cube that would be dressed differently for the various locations. It was indeed three walls and a ceiling, and the upstage wall would also be a mirror finish for two scenes, but it did not bother me as it was simply beautiful. And challenging.

So we started to talk about the possibilities. Having recently been appointed to a new hotel, development, architectural applications and fittings were fresh and floating in my mind, so I set about looking at alternative (more 'real-world' ways) of getting light into the box. There were loads of discussions about how deep the box should be to accommodate the fittings, but also not wanting it to become too chunky so as to ruin the design aesthetic.

The one solution that I came up with was to make the two side walls into light boxes. That way, the light would come from the room, which was an important aspect of the design, but it would also mean that we could achieve a soft, diffused light as a base for some of the scenes which would be really helpful. We also created two channels for light fittings in the ceiling and in this we packed in a row of dimmable fluorescent fittings. I wanted to have two solid lines of line without any darks pots, as this added to the modern feel of the set and architecturally suited the design as we were able to align these with the door frames that were set in the walls on either side.

I am still a huge supporter and advocate for retaining the use of tungsten light in theatre, and this was no exception. Even though we had installed a load of dimmable fluorescent into the walls and ceiling, I added in another two rows of low voltage downlights into the ceiling. These were all in individual circuits and they doubled up as a warm light source, but also as specials within the box when we needed to isolate.

In addition to all the fluorescent and LV downlights, I also added some RGB LED ribbon into the side walls and the two light channels in the ceiling. This would allow me to shift the colour and mood of the room slightly to adjust for the moods and tones of each scene. Fluorescent can be quite a brutal and unforgiving light source (one of the reasons I like it) and the LED meant that we would be able to make it slightly more malleable and user-friendly.

Madam Butterfly – an opera
Set designer Yannis Thavoris' design for Stephen Barlow's staging was simple yet striking. It had been decided to stage the opera in Japan in the mid to late 60's and this (naturally) influenced many of the design decisions.

The biggest challenge for the lighting design was the cyclorama. The show was going to be touring to a number of different venues all ranging in size and technical facility and in some spaces there would be less than 500mm left for the cyc lighting.

I started my search looking for Japanese art and it was not long before I had hit on the lighting concept for the cyc. I was immediately struck by the watercolours. They seemed to have a softness that I found really interesting and the distinct bands of colour also conveyed a sense of time and place. I found a number of other references that I used as a basis for my design and the majority of the colour and angle choices came from these.

To achieve the watercolour effect on the cyc, I opted for two vertical cyc light positions and used PAR64s with scrollers on each side. We also orientated the scrollers through 90 degrees to ensure that the colour changes were running up and down as opposed to left to right, and these were mirrored about centre to ensure that they all moved in the same direction. I did not have as many units as I would have liked here so we used EXG lamps which gave us a wider spread and the coverage that we needed. The cyc needed to represent Butterfly's mood and echo the location at the same time. We needed a bright day time, a darker more ominous sky for the Bonze, romantic for the love duet and so forth. I also wanted to capture a sense of the smog and polluted air of 60's industrial Japan for both the realism and for the metaphor of how her world has been tainted by Pinkerton and her wait for his return. For Butterfly's entrance I opted for a jade green skyline using LEE 241. We were able to write several multi-part cues to get the cyc to change colour in a series of barely perceptible ripples, another extension of the watercolour idea.

We could use very little FOH lighting for the show as there was no guarantee that these positions could be replicated on tour and so the show was forced into a direction that actually suited the watercolour feel quite well. Seeing as the show was presented in a unique setting, we were not bound by any other conformities and as such this gave us freedom to express Butterfly's world in, well, a new light. The colours for the rest of the rig needed to link up with the cyc if it was to be believable that the sky was a part of their world. When we were creating a smoggy sky, the light quality in the apartment had to match that sense of dirtiness and conversely, the romantic blues for the love duet needed to be reflected in the performance area as well.

Light continues to fascinate me. The way it moves and dances and interacts with the performers. I count myself extremely fortunate to be able to do what I love for a living.

Declan's website is **www.declanrandall.com**.

We asked Stage Jobs Pro member Jamie Parker the following questions about working as a Sound Technician:

What is the most rewarding aspect of working as a Sound Technician?
Achieving a good, solid mix. There are a lot of factors to what we do, but the end result is one thing only, and that is for as many people in the audience as possible to hear a good version of what is happening on the stage.

What are the key skills required to be an effective Sound Technician?
Good ears, first and foremost. It's all very well learning equations and how to use the latest piece of gear, but actually making sure it sounds good is far more important than all of that. Interpersonal skills are also very important: if the performer or client doesn't like you or doesn't feel safe, you've lost the gig. Also, being headstrong and independent goes a long way.

Do you see your role as a natural step on a career ladder, and if so what is the next rung?
Perhaps, but this industry is quite vague in terms of career progression. I see it more as 'which direction will I take at the next roundabout'. It's all about grasping opportunity and being aware of where the industry itself is heading.

How did you work your way into your current role?
One of my most recent contracts was with Rambert Dance Company as Sound Engineer for their Autumn/Spring Tours. To secure that, I had to have previous touring experience, which I had through touring with the Harlem Gospel Choir, and numerous lower-profile theatre tours. Prior to that I had a multitude of roles, each bringing their own bits of experience, from corporate work to cruise ships to studio recording – it's funny how skills learnt along the way can suddenly be useful later in your career.

How much do you think networking helps towards landing a job in the industry?
A lot! If nobody knows who you are, you're not going anywhere. You need to be proactive, outgoing, and in the right place at the right time (which isn't a mystical art – see what's happening and be there!). Also this is very much an industry that works on who employers like working with, rather than who has the 'best CV'. If they like you, you're in. Simple.

Do you think you will be working in the industry in the next five years, and if so in what capacity?
Yes of course. As previously stated, I think trying to foreplan a career path

in this industry is asking for trouble. I intend to keep seeing where work is available, and follow that path. The industry is always changing – previous safe paths are now almost closed off, and new paths are opening up. Be vigilant and aware. Long term career plans are asking for disappointment as a sound technician.

Please describe what a typical day working as a Sound Technician might contain?
'Typical day' is a bit difficult to define in this career. However, in my most recent role on tour with the RDC, we meet the trucks at the theatre on day one, unload and I start rigging the sound system with my allocated crew, finishing at about 10pm. Day two is another early start for checks, run-throughs and first performances. The rest of the week is more relaxed, with later starts unless we have matinees. Then after the last show, we derig and generally shut the last truck at about 3am. Of course, a 'typical day' varies massively across the industry. Only key rule: be flexible, and forget any idea of 9-5!

Have you done any additional training courses to further your career?
Aside from a training day from Midas on their Pro-series digital desks, all my training outside of my diploma and degree has been on-the-job. However, I can see that at some point in the future, specific training would be useful. Currently, health and safety is a big one to have, especially for bigger venues. And other courses to broaden my knowledge – rigging for example is often useful.

How important is working for free at the beginning of your career?
I'd never do this, and think it is a bad thing for anyone to do. It harms the industry greatly – of course companies will abuse free labour, in favor sometimes of more skilled paid labour. I've seen it happen over and over. If you're in the industry, even at the beginning, you're still worth money. Don't accept 'but we're training you' or 'we'll start to pay you soon'. If you're there, you're worth money. And there are companies who will pay – keep searching.
Jamie's website is www.jamie-parker.com

David Gregory – Production Sound Engineer
Current Projects include Propeller's Taming of the
Shrew and Twelfth Night world tour (design)

What does your job entail?
My job entails working with a sound designer to get the best combination of equipment for a production with the budget, the time and staff available, which meet the needs of the show and the designer. Then I work out how that equipment is linked together and becomes a complete sound system, with the correct cables, A-D converters, microphones clips and stands, and how to install that show into the venue in the most efficient way possible, such as how the speakers can be rigged where the designer wants them, in a safe way. Essentially I look after the practical side of a production's audio requirements.

What's a typical day for you?
I'm freelance, and tend to work about sixty hours a week. I typically start work in the morning at a venue, wherever that might be in the country and work till 10:45pm. There tends to be four phases to each job: planning, the fit up, the tech and previews. Most jobs last seven to twelve days on site and pay tends to be £225 per day.

How did you get to where you are now?
I worked as an apprentice to a company for four years, and also shadowed a lot of people, which was valuable to gain the experience needed to start to talk to designers and engineers in the correct way.

What training exists to become a production sound engineer?
There are some great audio engineering courses out there. I have read about City and Guilds courses and there are theatre design courses such as Central School of Speech and Drama. I would say the best form of training for production sound is on the job. Working in a hires warehouse can be a great place to get familiar with the equipment you are going to use, and the people who will hopefully be your colleagues. I'm a person who learns from reading: John Leonard's 'Theatre Sound' book is a good read. Yamaha's 'Sound Reinforcement Handbook' is also a great reference guide.

What's the best thing about your job?
The variety – each production and venue throws up different challenges.

What is the most challenging aspect of your job?
The technology we use in our industry is rapidly changing, our field is

growing in size and standards are getting higher. Also, making productions happen with limited resources. Obtaining money for proper staffing is harder than obtaining money for equipment.

David is a member of the Assocation of Sound Designers. Interview reproduced with kind permission from the Association of Sound Designers.

Sound Designer

Sound Designers create a soundscape that enhances a production.

Emma Laxton – Sound Designer
Recent projects include The Physicists (Donmar), The Sacred Flame (ETT)

What's a typical day for you?
During the rehearsal phase of a show, I'll spend time in rehearsals watching, going to production meetings, organising hires, making sounds, and talking with the director. I'll make the sounds for a show in the rehearsal room, at home, in a studio or in the theatre. During the production weeks I'll be at the theatre 10 am – 10pm, though I may also have another show in rehearsal that will need attention – I have two shows in rehearsal at the moment. My job tends to be seven days a week, and often will involve working through holidays and fielding calls and requests from directors at all hours.

How did you get to where you are now?
I did work experience at my local theatre in Shrewsbury, and I got a followspot op job there from that and eventually became the technical manager! I went to Central School and did the Stage Management and Technical Arts course, I hadn't done any sound before but I realised the whole point of going to drama school is to learn the bits you don't know and to find out what you're interested in, so I choose to do sound for a term and really enjoyed that. I stayed on for another year to do the BA Theatre Studies final year and did a lot of work placements at Les Mis, Miss Saigon and the Royal Albert Hall. My tutor, Ross Brown, put me up for a sound op'ing job at the Royal Court – just a week long job – then they needed someone for the next show, and so on and eventually I became deputy head of sound there. I got an opportunity to design a show upstairs which was a safe environment to start in, and got to do more and more designs there. Eventually I decided that was what I wanted to do, so I went freelance.

How did your training help you?
There are working practises and a language of talking that I learnt at
drama school. It's been so useful to me as a sound designer to have been a
sound op, an engineer, to have installed sound systems and put radio mics
on actors, because I know what I'm asking for. You're always learning on
the job and you have to continuously adapt because different directors
work in different ways and require different things from you.

What is the most challenging aspect of your job?
It's not the design aspect of things – it's fighting my corner, whether that
be the budget or staffing, or to educate the other people you're working
with as to your value in the room and your needs to put equipment in the
set or auditorium.

Are you freelance, or employed?
I'm freelance, and most of the time I love it – the variety of venues, people
and challenges but it is tough, for example, if you injure yourself and you
can't work. There's also the insecurity waiting for your diary to fill up with
bookings.

What is the average pay?
I get paid a fee for a production, which often varies between £1k and £4k;
this is for plays. You are asked to commit non-exclusively to the rehearsal
period, which can often be four to five weeks long, and exclusively for the
two production weeks. How much you need to be in rehearsals depends on
the job and the director. Musical work pays more and often pays royalties
too, but tends to involve longer production periods.

What has been your favourite project to work on, and why?
Invisible for Transport, because of who they are and the work they want to
create. I spent a lot of time in rehearsals and really felt like part of the
company. They had a great attitude towards the way a piece of work
evolved on the road and employing the right people to make that happen.
The sound was integrated into the show from a really early stage and that
really paid off.

**What advice would you give for someone wanting to be a sound
designer?**
Take any little opportunities that come up: readings, studio shows, fringe
shows. The associate directors that I worked with at the Court have
become the next generation of directors and those contacts have proved
great. The fringe shows are great – the limits they place on you make you
think really hard about how to do things.

It's often directors that take you places, or set designers, who get brought into a project earlier than anyone else. It's all about networking and meeting people, and at the early stages it's not necessarily about your body of work, as much as about your ability to be part of a team and work well with people. You have to be able to talk to a director. Knowing QLab inside out is essential.

*Emma is a member of the Assocation of Sound Designers. Interview reproduced in its entirety with kind permission from the **Association of Sound Designers**.*

Sound Operator

Sound Operators operate the sound desk during the course of the performance, often following the cues from the Stage Manager or Deputy Stage Manager.

Peter Eltringham - Sound Operator
Currently on Chariots of Fire

What's a typical day for you?
Typically I'll arrive at the theatre at 6pm for a 7.45 show. I'll power up, check through the rig and make sure everything is working. This gives me a contingency time of 30-45 minutes in case anything isn't working. Once the show starts I will be playing in sound effects, mixing the occasional radio mic or float mic, which are either cued by the DSM or I do at a musical cue point. I finish as soon as the show has ended and I've powered down.

How did you get to where you are now?
I was interested in live sound when I was younger, but it wasn't until I did a school production of Les Mis that I got into theatre. I did the sound course at Central School of Speech and Drama and made lots of contacts there, which proved really useful when I graduated. One led to doing fit-ups at Hampstead Theatre, where I got to meet lots of sound designers and get my name known. From there I've got jobs as a sound operator, production sound engineer and as associate sound designer on a range of shows.

What's the best training for a Sound Operator?
Sound operating can seem quite a simple job, but that's only the half of it. Usually I am the only sound person in the theatre – a department of one – so when things go wrong, I have to fix it, fast. I have to understand all the bits of kit and how they work together. The last thing anyone wants is for

the show to go up late or even be cancelled. You have to have a good foundation in sound and the equipment used. There are lots of courses that provide this, though op'ing a show at a drama school is a good environment to make mistakes without theconsequences you'd face in real life. My experience at CSSD was great for learning the fundamentals, and things like the health and safety aspects of the job. But I've picked up so much on the job itself.

What is the most challenging aspect of your job?

Keeping concentration over two or three hundred shows is essential – you can't afford to make mistakes even though you're watching something that you've seen a million times before. You want to make sure than the 300th performance gets the same level of attention and diligence as the first night.

Are you freelance, or employed?

A lot of operating tends to be on a PAYE basis, particularly in the West End. Some places allow you to invoice, but it can be tedious to produce an invoice every week – which might take a month to be processed and paid – so often it's easier to be PAYE. The pay averages between £575 and £650 per week, before tax, for an 8-show week, Monday to Saturday.

How long does a contract tend to last?

Contracts tend to run from two weeks to a year long, but shows can close at any time and you're often only given two weeks notice.

What advice would you give for someone wanting to become a sound operator?

You need to learn about lots of things that aren't operating to be a good operator! Take any opportunity you get to learn a new skill. Build your contacts – one job will usually lead to another.

What other roles do you do apart from sound op?

Some people just op', and some do other things with their days. I do installation work, production sound engineering, and assistant and associate design work and fringe sound designs.

*Peter is a member of the Assocation of Sound Designers. Interview reproduced in its entirety with kind permission from the **Association of Sound Designers.***

Sound Manager

The Sound Manager is in charge of all aspects of sound in a production.

Tom Hares
Senior Technician – Sadlers Wells

What does your job entail?

The company tends to go for staff who can work in more than one role but who also have specialist skills. So I'm the only 'sound technician' and lead on that but do also assist with flys and sometimes with lighting when appropriate. Our theatre programme is normally a new show each week, normally from outside companies on tour, but also in-house productions too. Over Christmas and Summer, we tend to have a show in residence for a few weeks and we'll do a number of one day events and showcases over the year around the normal bookings.

I have to ensure that our in-house kit is maintained to a good standard and that I know how to operate it all, check incoming riders and source any kit that we don't have, often liaising with incoming engineers and rental companies to meet each others requirements. I have to book casual staff to meet any sound team requirements and then lead them from the first day of fit-up to the closing of the doors at the get-out. I have to be available to meet sudden changes in the needs of the show. And I have to assist with the general running of the department.

What's a typical day for you?

Prior to opening night, I will normally be assisting the visiting company's sound crew in setting up and preparing their kit and leading any casual sound staff we've employed for the show. During rehearsals, I'll be onstage learning the show. I'm not often at the desk as the visiting engineer will do that but I'm often the Duty Technician for the building – dealing with FOH clearance and any emergencies that should arise during the show (fire alarms and so on). I try and operate a show every so often so that I can keep in practice and I'll often shadow the operator on any show that is playing for a few weeks so that I can be emergency cover. Once the show is up and running, I'll be scheduling sound crew for upcoming shows, sourcing rental kit and generally checking audio requirements for upcoming shows – ideally we like to have the prep work for future shows done with a month in hand.

I also assist our Technical Director with the departmental finances so there will be an office day per week. This office day is sometimes spent on union activities as I'm the site rep and union branch secretary, and probably once a month I'll be offsite. This will either be looking after our offsite storage which I also have control over, or working on a broader project. These have included being part of the working group that revised the National Occupational Standards for Technical Theatre education and keeping up to speed on the 800MHz Clearance.

How did you get to where you are now? Was there (or is there now) training courses available?
I started at my local youth theatre during school holidays. While studying GCSEs I became interested in the technical side of theatre, particular lighting. After A Levels, I studied an HND in Lighting and Sound Design (a course no longer running) and worked alongside at the college theatre which did a fair amount of community theatre, so my paid work was running alongside my learning. I moved to London to study for a degree in Theatre Practice, specialising in Production Sound. After university, there honestly didn't seem to be much in the way of training opportunities. I attended a course run by Orbital Sound, and I got my ADTT Bronze award. I had also attended a pyro course but most learning was on the job and there was no certification for it. I worked freelance for a few years on a broad mix of theatre, corporate events and school support. This included freelance work here and when a new tech role became available, I applied and got the job. The sound technician at the time left after a few months and I stepped in to cover them. Since going full-time, training opportunities seem to be more prevalent though most have been through my employer so I now have vocational training in things like First Aid At Work, IPAF, PASMA, and IOSH approved courses – my most recent being forklift training. I've also been able to call upon my union contacts and have courses in employment law, the environment and earlier this year got a C&G in teaching.

What steps are there on the career ladder are there for you?
Within this particular theatre there aren't many actually. From my current role, there would only be the Technical Manager's position. However, I should be able to sidestep to any of the large national houses or companies if I want to continue in theatre. Or I could move across into a production company if I wanted to do less venue specific work and stay in the industry.

What is the most challenging aspect of your job?
Dealing with limited resources – the theatre is only so big, there is only so much time in the day, there is only so much money around.

Are you freelance, or employed? What are the working hours like?
I'm employed full-time, contracted at 40 hours a week though the average working hours tend to be 50 hours per week. Our programme means that

hours are concentrated near to the weekend and easier during the later week days. There is some flexibility if the show hours are less than contract and we are able to do office/maintenance work at hours that suit us.

What is the average pay?
Pay starts at around £22,000pa for a starting full-time technician. There are payments for learning additional skills and different grades so, with overtime, the salary is around £30,000 after a year or two of employment.

What advice would you give for someone wanting to do what you do? How does someone go about getting a similar job?
Start at the bottom and work up. You may find that you actually prefer to work in a different area than you initially thought. Do find a course to study but do make sure that you do additional work outside of the course to put it into context (and make contacts and earn some money). Maths and engineering are useful things, as are additional language skills – being critically able to analyse a play is probably less useful, though every skill will come in useful at some point. Once you decide on what you want to do, make sure that everything you do is geared towards achieving that (don't get really good at pushing flightcases unless that is your ideal job) but until you decide on that, do try out a broad range of positions. Even if you decide, for example, that being part of the stage crew is not for you, knowing the basics of the role helps in your job. The entertainment industry relies on cooperation and collaboration – you can produce a show on your own but it's a lot easier with everyone working together, and a lot more fun.

What has been your favourite project to work on, and why?
The recent World Cities Residency by the Pina Bausch Tanztheatr Wuppertal was something amazing to be part of – 10 shows across 2 venues in 6 weeks. All their shows are visually impressive (a mountaintop that pivots mid show to become a mountaincliff; a 5-ton breeze block wall that collapses at the top of the show and the show takes place on the rubble, or inside three 5 meter high earth mounds with live sheep being herded); and the company are a delight to work with.
*Tom is a member of the Assocation of Sound Designers. Interview reproduced with kind permission from the **Association of Sound Designers**.*

Sound No. 1, No. 2, and No.3

In long-running or larger productions, the sound team are split into Sound No. 1, Sound No. 2, and Sound No. 3. Sound No. 1 is the most senior position – they are responsible for managing the sound team, looking after equipment, overseeing budgets and scheduling. Sound No. 2 is responsible for managing sound and communication during the performance. Sound No. 3 works to assist the other members of the sound team.

Simon Sayer – No.1 Sound
Current projects include: Sound No.1 for We Will Rock You and supervisor on worldwide productions of We Will Rock You; also effects operator on the Olympics Opening Ceremony.

What does your job entail?
All the musicians' mics, the performers' mics, the sound effects: everything comes into the mixing desk front of house and I have to create a mix for the audience, and provide monitor mixes for the cast and musicians. Keeping a wide range of performers and musicians happy about how they sound to the audience and to each other requires a lot of diplomacy – a colleague once told me that the job is 20% is making it sound good, and 80% keeping everyone happy. My job is to make the show sound as it was designed to be, to maintain that quality over the run, and to make sure everybody else does too!

What's a typical day for you?
I normally go in for 5pm to do a sound check which is normally done by 6.15pm. Then I'll mix or supervise the show until 10.40pm when the curtain comes down. Sometimes we're needed in the daytimes for understudy and cast change rehearsals so we'll come in for that. We do a lot of outside gigs – TV appearances, etc – which often involve making backing tracks and the like.

How did you get to where you are now?
I did drama at high school, then got into lighting for A Level Theatre Studies, then did the Technical Theatre course at Bristol Old Vic. After graduating I worked at Birmingham Rep for three years in the sound dept, then got a job as No.3 on Les Miserables in London, then No.2 on Blood Brothers and so on.

What's the best way to train to be a No.1?
There are a lot more training courses out there now in theatre sound than when I started. After doing something like that I'd recommend getting

work at a Rep house to experience a bit of everything. Coming straight into the West End and sitting on a show isn't going to give you an all -round training.

What is the most challenging aspect of your job?
The mix of this show is very involved, with everyone on stage going hell for leather. We have to create the dynamics and sound of the show, whilst keeping the composers, the MD, the actors, the producers and, of course, the audience, happy. For a show like this, where the music is one of the principal attractions, it's paramount that the sound be first rate. It's quite a responsibility but not one that is often recognised.

Are you freelance, or employed?
I'm a limited company and I work on a freelance basis because I go and work on a lot of other projects. A lot of people work on a contract, increasingly on a 'buy out' basis, which is where you get a set fee regardless of the hours worked. I think most No.1s get between £850 to £950 per week on a buy out. The hours are typically a 40 hour week but it varies- if we're teching it can be up to 90 hours. Contracts tend to be for a year to start with, then open ended as the show runs, with the usual two weeks notice period if the show closes.

What has been your favourite project to work on, and why?
Recently it was working on the Opening Ceremony of the Olympics which was an amazing experience. We also put We Will Rock You into Las Vegas, so I was out there for 9 weeks. I produced the German and Spanish cast albums which were great fun. I really enjoy the variety.

What advice would you give for someone wanting to become a No.1?
Once you've done some training outside the West End, do everything you can to try and get a No.3 job. Be nice to everyone, get on with everybody and as soon as you can try and get on the desk, do some rehearsals. Once you've done that, the hardest leap is to go from being a No.3 to a No.2, to get the opportunity to prove that you're good enough to start mixing the show and take on that extra responsibility.
*Simon is a member of the Assocation of Sound Designers. Interview reproduced with kind permission from the **Association of Sound Designers**.*

Zoe Milton – Radio Mic Technician
Current projects include Glyndebourne Opera Festival; NT Live broadcast of The Curious Incident of the Dog in the Night-Time

What does your job entail?
There are two phases – getting the show on and running the show. Getting

the show on is the hard part and will often involve installing and programming the radio mic system and liaising with Wardrobe, Wigs and Design to integrate the microphones, transmitters, in-ear-monitors into the show. I'll often start at 10 or 11am each day and work until 10 or 11pm. Running the show is a process of recreating what you set up consistently each night. Radio mics need a lot of maintenance. I'll start at 5pm on a show day.

How did you get to where you are now?
I started off doing concerts on Sundays and working in Am Dram. I went to Uni in London and applied for a Dep' job on Blood Brothers. From there I got work on other West End shows.

What's the best way to train to be a Radio Mic Technician?
The main skills you need for my job are people skills. You need to understand other people's processes – actors, stage management, etc – so you can work most effectively with them. A technical/stage management course is ideal for this – I've seen a lot of good people coming out of Guildhall. My Uni couldn't afford radio mics or digital desks so I didn't have any training in these when I left, but I learnt about them on the job.

What is the most challenging aspect of your job?
I'm the face of the sound department onstage – when we're putting a show on, people can get very stressed, and it can be difficult to explain to performers why they need to wear a radio mic and why we can't necessarily give them the foldback they want.

Are you freelance, or employed? What is the average pay?
I mostly work on a freelance basis, but a lot of the longer running shows work on a PAYE basis. I like the freedom and variety of being freelance, and being able to make my own hours and choose my jobs, but I don't like having to take care of the financial side of things. A freelancer might work for between £225 and £300 per day, whereas on a West End show a dep might get £65 per show and a No.3 would start off with £80 per show.

What advice would you give for someone wanting to become a Radio Mic Technician?
Be cheerful. Be chatty. Part of your job is to head trouble off before it escalates into an issue – so you need to find out how people are feeling about things. The best way to get work is to send your CV to No.1's in the West End – find out their name first. You can also get work via hire companies who are often asked to provide staff for shows.

What other roles do you do apart from sound op?

I mix shows too. I also do a lot of events for broadcast – theatre, opera, rock and roll. This varies from NT Live to Take That.

*Zoe is a member of the Assocation of Sound Designers. Interview reproduced with kind permission from the **Association of Sound Designers**.*

Technical Theatre

"You could be demonstrating some kit to a student in need of help, then setting a full symphony orchestra rehearsal, followed by operating a community dance show for 3-16 year olds! The variety just goes on and on."

Theatre Technician

The Theatre Technician is responsible for setting up and preparing sound and light equipment, focusing lights, running technical rehearsals, operating the technical aspects of the production, and then de-rigging.

We asked Stage Jobs Pro member Marita Schroeter the following questions about working as a Technician:

What is the most rewarding aspect of working as a Technician?
For me it is being part of something magical. There is always something undefinable and beautiful that happens when an audience watches a show, something that does not happen in rehearsals, and it stuns everyone watching it. I am proud to say I am part of the reason that this happens.

What are the key skills required to be an effective Technician?
Enthusiasm for the discipline. You have to love what you are doing and you have to want it to be as perfect as it can possibly be. Knowledge about physics you can learn if you don't have it yet, love for the thing you have to feel.

Do you see your role as a natural step on a career ladder, and if so what is the next rung?
Definitely. I am the one and only technician in my little studio venue at the moment. If I master this on my own successfully enough, I can aim higher soon I hope ...

50

How did you work your way into your current role?

I have been head technician in a similar sized venue before, the Operations Manager there was a very experienced technician and he made it into his mission to turn me into the best tech he could. I got my current job as the technical manager of this theatre left. The Council who runs it did want to review the post before re-staffing it permanently, so she had a look on Stage Jobs Pro, found my profile, and asked me if I would be interested in covering the venue in between!

How much do you think networking helps towards landing a job in the industry?

A LOT!!!!!

Do you think you will be working in the industry in the next five years, and if so in what capacity?

I hope so, I hope I can stay a technician and by then I hope to have tried all the aspects and crazy things that sometimes go with this job.

Please describe what a typical day working as a Technician might contain?

In my venue: pre-rig, welcome the company, fit up, focus lights, plot and program board, check sound effects, tech run if possible.

Have you done any additional training courses to further your career?

Yes and no, to be honest, I have done training because I did not have any work at the time, and BECTU had a lot of very cheap courses on offer. It kept me in theatres, helped my skill level and I could network during those courses.

How important is working for free at the beginning of your career?

To me it made all the difference. A head flyman saw me working on an am dram show and knew I would not get a chance at the place where I lived then. He later moved back to his hometown, and when I came to visit him he introduced me to the tech manager and senior tech in the theatre there, and made a point in telling them how good he thought I was. Those people trusted his word and gave me my first paid job ... This was almost seven years ago, and I have not looked back since.

Senior Technician

We asked Stage Jobs Pro member Phil Speck the following questions about working as a Senior Technician:

What is the most rewarding aspect of working as a Senior Technician?
Here at Royal Welsh College of Music and Drama [Phil is a Senior Technician at the Royal Welsh College of Music & Drama in Cardiff], the reward I believe is greater. Completing and running a show under pressure, that many people will enjoy, is certainly rewarding. But, the most satisfying part at RWCMD is seeing students graduate who you've been able to help in the many different aspects of the job. You can't beat it!

What are the key skills required to be an effective Senior Technician?
Concentration, focus, the ability to multi-task, being able to handle pressure and, above all, a desire for the job you do. If you don't have any of these, even the greatest of knowledge won't get you through a production week!

Do you see your role as a natural step on a career ladder, and if so what is the next rung?
Definitely a natural step. Senior Technician bridges the gap to Technical Manager, which is what I aspire to. I still hold interest in lighting design, but would like to remain in Technical Management at University/Conservatoire level. The next step could actually be a step down in salary and responsibility to be a Technical Manager – a bizarre concept, I know. But, moving here to RWCMD five years ago, I went from being in a post as Technical Manager to a job as a Technician. I actually increased my salary, responsibility, quality and volume of work. A step down in title, but ultimately a step up the career ladder.

How did you work your way into your current role?
I arrived at RWCMD as a Technician in 2008, and in 2012 I applied for and was offered the post as Senior Technician. I believe a huge part of gaining promotion was down to dedication, hard work and a willingness to do more.

How much do you think networking helps towards landing a job in the industry?
You really do need to network as much as possible. It's not just about opening doors to future employment. Networking can help with anything such as supplies, hires and, more importantly, emergencies! Whilst you can

network at trade shows like PLASA and The ABTT Theatre Show, simple phone calls or visits to local companies of any type can help you greatly now and in the future.

Do you think you will be working in the industry in the next five years, and if so in what capacity?
Without a doubt. I studied at University from 2000-03 and worked my way through to where I am now since. I love the industry and won't give up on it! But where and in what capacity? I can't be sure. Sometimes you never quite know when an opportunity you can't pass up will come your way ... For now, I love working at RWCMD and don't see myself moving just yet.

Please describe what a typical day working as a Senior Technician might contain?
Here at RWCMD you could be setting up a TV with a DVD player one minute and running a Steinway Series Piano Solo Concert, with one of the best pianists in the world, the next! You could be demonstrating some kit to a student in need of help, then setting a full symphony orchestra rehearsal, followed by operating a community dance show for 3-16 yr olds! The variety just goes on and on. It's one of the things that makes working at RWCMD so enjoyable.

Have you done any additional training courses to further your career?
I've done plenty of training over time. Some of the more notable ones to help try and further my career include: COSHH course, City & Guilds in PAT, and a people management course. That doesn't include things like lighting board training, automated flying and PASMA that improve your day to day operational knowledge. At the moment, I look towards courses that can improve knowledge & understanding such as IOSH and NEBOSH. I believe you should be asking for training that helps move you forward. Not just to be able to do what your job is on paper.

How important is working for free at the beginning of your career?
It certainly won't harm your employability and can give a fantastic impression when applying for paid positions. Often you can generate your own unpaid employment by seeking out professionals and asking to volunteer in order to gain experience, such as asking a lighting designer if you can go and watch them work – I'm sure they wouldn't just let you sit there and observe anyway. There are some incredibly kind and generous professionals out there who will help you. Be very wary of people/companies who are taking advantage though. They are out there, and an unfair advantage is being taken where pay should be forthcoming. If it does happen to you, make sure the people or companies involved are reported.
*Phil's website is **http://philspeck.wix.com/ld***

Technical Manager/Chief Technician

The Technical Manager is in charge of the technical elements of a production, responsible for safety, equipment, budgeting and managing the other members of the crew.

We asked Stage Jobs Pro member Sebastian Barnes the following questions about working as a Technical Manager:

What is the most rewarding aspect of working as a Technical Manager?
Making it happen effectively, and within budget. Encouraging staff to make the most of, and develop their skills.

What are the key skills required to be an effective Technical Manager?
Self initiative, excellent communication skills, empathy, self discipline, diplomacy, effective time and task management, effective people management, current practical theatre skills.

Do you see your role as a natural step on a career ladder, and if so what is the next rung?
Yes, Technical Manager is one natural step on a career ladder. For me the next rung could be Production Manager.

How did you work your way into your current role?
I worked to Technical Manager from casual stage technician, through a variety of technical roles, in several departments. This gave me the wide perspective necessary for a Technical Manager role.

How much do you think networking helps towards landing a job in the industry?
Networking is vital to getting into this industry. I don't agree that this should be the case. It leads to much exclusion by not being in the 'right place and the right time'.

Do you think you will be working in the industry in the next five years, and if so in what capacity?
I intend to remain working in the industry for more than five more years. I expect to develop consultancy and training roles.

Please describe what a typical day working as a Technical Manager might contain?
Phone calls and meetings arranging supplies, people and schedules for upcoming productions. Regular administrative tasks, including budgets, authorising invoices, processing orders and staff time.

Have you done any additional training courses to further your career?
Yes, A1 Skills Assessor training, various management short courses, budgeting, staff appraisal, NVQ Level 4 in Operational Management.

How important is working for free at the beginning of your career?
Working for free is only important if done in an amateur company setting, to improve your experience. Working for free for a professional company is usually damaging to your career and the employer, as it creates an unhealthy, and illegal reliance on unpaid labour.

Production Manager

The Production Manager is concerned with managing with the practical aspects of a production. They must be excellent at planning and problem-solving, able to budget effectively and liaise with the various departments.

We asked Stage Jobs Pro member Jasmine Sandalli the following questions about working as a Production Manager:

What is the most rewarding aspect of working as a Production Manager?
Seeing a production through, right from the initial concept to the press night, and being instrumental in realising the ideas of the creative team. No matter how many shows I've done, there's always a moment during the previews when I look at a set and think 'that was just a modelbox a few weeks ago' and I can't quite work out how that happened. It's a bit magic.

What are the key skills required to be an effective Production Manager?
Different Production Managers work in different ways. In my opinion, you have to be empirical: examine all the possibilities, evaluate what works best, be thorough in your groundwork. Communicate clearly and unambiguously, and be honest: if you're not entirely sure of the answer for

something, don't be afraid to say 'I don't know, but I'll find out'. Plus of course patience, diplomacy, stamina, courage and the ability to survive on vending machine food helps.

Do you see your role as a natural step on a career ladder, and if so what is the next rung?

I've always wanted to be a Production Manager but it took me a while to work out that being a freelancer working on shows alone isn't for me. I want to run my own production department one day; I love being part of a team that makes shows and the challenges that come with it as well as the shows themselves.

How did you work your way into your current role?

I went to Rose Bruford College to study Stage Management, and put myself forward to production manage as many of the student shows as possible, as well as getting involved in as many fringe and unpaid PM jobs outside of college as I could manage. Almost immediately after I left I started at the Lyric Hammersmith as Assistant Production Manager, and ended up spending four years there. I then left the Lyric to do a three month stint as a APM at the National Theatre and I've been here ever since – that was three and a half years ago. I'm currently working on some of the larger technical projects for the NT rather than shows, and freelance as a PM on the side.

How much do you think networking helps towards landing a job in the industry?

Hugely so. It's the worst thing about the job for me because I'm terrible at networking, but the fact remains that you get work through recommendation and word of mouth, or through people knowing you. That's why it pays to do the occasional low-paid or expenses-only job because you never know what the contacts could be worth.

Do you think you will be working in the industry in the next five years, and if so in what capacity?

Definitely, as long as it will still have me! I'd like to think that in five years I'd be on the way to running my own production department but that's probably a little ambitious.

Please describe what a typical day working as a Production Manager might contain?

Always start by checking in on the rehearsal notes and emails to see if there's anything that needs actioning first thing. And that's pretty much the only constant – one of the things I love about this job is the variety of each day. One minute you're arguing with B&Q over a hardware order, next you're learning how to make a person disappear (sometimes useful when you're arguing with B&Q).

Have you done any additional training courses to further your career?
I have done a First Aid course, but mostly taught myself other skills as and when I've needed to learn them. I'm a bit rubbish at making time for training but it's very important, particularly with the speed that technology moves these days.

How important is working for free at the beginning of your career?
As per my Networking answer – particularly if you're studying or have access to financial support so you're not relying on payment from jobs to pay the rent, it's so worth it. You never know where your next job contact is going to come from.

Automation No.1 and No. 2

Automation is the use of non-manually (usually electrically) powered machinery to move stage components. Automation No. 1 is the Head of Automation and is responsible for organising the operation of machinery, maintenance and running the automation department. Automation No. 2 is the Deputy Head of Automation.

We asked Stage Jobs Pro member Nick Page the following questions about working as a Head of Automation:

What is the most rewarding aspect of working as a Head of Automation?
For each performance we want every moving piece to work smoothly and reliably. Being able to make that happen is very rewarding. Knowing that we've worked hard keep the cast and crew safe and so that the audience experiences the show as intended, we can be sure that we have a job well done.

What are the key skills required to be an effective Head of Automation?
Automation, as a field, covers quite a wide variety of skills. When you're responsible for the whole lot, as a Head of Department, it's important that you know your system intimately, and how any one single element can affect everything else, not just within your own equipment but the whole working environment. Above all though, I think some of the most useful skills are being able to keep a calm head and always be prepared. You've also got to genuinely care about what you're doing and why you're doing it.

Do you see your role as a natural step on a career ladder, and if so what is the next rung?

I think once you reach any Head of Department role within the theatre environment, the chances are that your next move will bring you to an altogether different discipline. As you climb that career ladder you'll inevitably find yourself in a less hands on physical role and in a progressively more managerial position. So what's next for a Head of Automation? Perhaps the skills you learn in Automation can set you up for production management, or maybe into something more to do with engineering. Whatever it may be it's likely to be a big step in a different direction.

How did you work your way into your current role?

Good timing! Good knowledge! Lots of experience! I've been involved in technical theatre, one way or another, since I was about eight years old. Over the years I've always been keen on gaining knowledge of as many aspects of the environment as possible. Sadly though, being a jack of all trades ultimately restricts your career progression so I eventually decided I needed to fix myself on a single discipline. I initially thought I wanted to move in to Special Effects (Pyro and the like) but the environment I was in at the time opened my eyes to the prospects of Automation (an area of Technical Theatre I knew nothing about). The timing was perfect – here I was wanting something new to learn and a position opened up to allow me to do so. And it turned out that Automation is pretty close to being a jack of all trades type of job. When I moved to London in 2007 I once again found that timing was in my favour, but this time I also had the knowledge to back me up. So much so in fact that even as a Number 2 and a newbie to the West End, I was asked to program a brand new show. Being able to prove myself at that point is, I think, what set me up to rather rapidly make my way into an HoD role.

How much do you think networking helps towards landing a job in the industry?

I've never been a big networker as such. It would definitely be more useful if I worked more freelance jobs, but up to now I've always followed a path of full time employment and long term contracts.

Do you think you will be working in the industry in the next five years, and if so in what capacity?

Absolutely! Whether I'll still be in the West End, or even as a Head of Automation I don't know for sure. But I certainly can't see myself leaving the industry... ever.

Please describe what a typical day working as a Head of Automation might contain?

So long as everything is in good working order my normal show day can be quite simple. The department comes in to work around two and a half hours prior to show time so that we can carry our Automation Checks. This is where we move every single axis (a controllable moving piece) through their entire range of movement. This ensures mechanical integrity and reliable control over the piece. Depending on the show we may also be required to help out other departments for their checks by moving set into required positions. Once all technical checks, for all departments, are complete, the Stage is usually left in a way so that the Cast can use it for their vocal and physical warm-ups. Once the cast is finished, usually just before the Half Hour Call, we preset everything to the positions they need to be in for the top of the show. At this point the Show Cloth can be dropped in and usually the House will be opened. The show itself will require at least one Operator and depending on how a show is set up other members of the department will have cues to carry out on stage, such as observing moves, checking fixings, setting pieces and so on. It's also useful to have someone available to respond to any issues that may occur during a performance, so it's advisable not to tie your department up in too many tasks. All of these tasks tend to be interchangeable within the department. So as the HoD I'm not just operating at the Control Desk. At the end of the performance we make safe, switch off and go home. We also have a day every week that is specifically set aside for Automation maintenance. On these days we take the opportunity to inspect every element in our system, from the mechanics to the electronics, and if we find anything out of place we make good. We also carry out a preventative maintenance schedule, which aims to prevent the eventuality of discovering major issues.

Have you done any additional training courses to further your career?

There are plenty of opportunities to further my knowledge through training. I've certainly considered several courses, but to be honest my main training has been through real life experience. There are, however, certain things I know I will eventually specifically want to learn, depending on where I take my career over the years.

How important is working for free at the beginning of your career?

This is a difficult question. Generally I would say you should never be taken advantage of, so don't accept work that doesn't pay. That said; the start of my career was all voluntary, and the advantage of voluntary work is that, if you're with others that volunteered, you all want to be there and you all want to learn. It can be a terribly encouraging environment.

Stage Technologies & Automation
STAGE TECHNOLOGIES

STAGE
TECHNOLOGIES

Stage Technologies was founded in 1994 as one of the world's first dedicated theatre engineering specialists and became instrumental in bringing the extensive benefits of automation technology to the live performance industry. This technology takes the form of fixed installation systems in performing arts venues worldwide as well as rental projects for West End musicals, rock 'n' roll touring, and major event spectaculars. Over the years the company has significantly increased its global presence and local expertise. Stage Technologies' design and manufacturing head office is located in London, with permanent support, manufacturing, and project divisions in Suffolk (UK), Macau, Hong Kong, Australia, Las Vegas and Eastern USA. We employ more than 150 automation engineers, manufacturing specialists and support staff worldwide. A combination of global presence and local expertise has enabled our teams to forge strategic relationships with theatre consultants and other industry specialists including general contractors, consultants, architects, audio and lighting outfitters, as well as technical directors.

Stage Technologies has worked closely with Cirque du Soleil® since 2003 on some of their boldest theatrical spectaculars such as Iris and The Beatles LOVE™. Other end users of our equipment and systems include The Royal National Theatre, Liverpool Everyman Theatre, Milton Court at The Guildhall School of Music and Drama, The Royal Opera House, The Royal Shakespeare Company, The Royal Conservatoire of Scotland, Disney, Dragone, the Brussels Opera House, Göteborgs Stadsteater, Princess Cruises, the War Memorial Opera House (home to the San Francisco Opera), Hong Kong Cultural Centre, Sydney Theatre and Perth Performing Arts Centre among many others.

There are several different career streams in stage automation:
- Engineers are required to design the winches and other hardware used to power the movement of props, performers and large scale set pieces such as revolves.
  - Software engineers design the programmes installed in the control desks

used by operators to carry out the actions devised by the creative team. These actions range from flying a performer over the audience, to bringing in a backdrop, or switching scenes by moving a Revolve, to many others.

- Workshop technicians build control panels, put the pieces together and ship the equipment to theatres all around the world.
- The after sales support team is available to help clients 24 hours a day, seven days a week this availability is crucial as more and more venues are installing automation systems. A good support team is able to recommend solutions even for equipment produced by a competing company.
- Automation operators are seated backstage (and sometimes above the stage!), carrying out the plotted axes that move the sets, fly the actors, and many other actions.
- Sales and marketing staff seek out opportunities to get the business brand in front of theatre consultants, contractors and architects who manage large scale automation installations in refurbished venues and new builds.
- The best of all of these professionals combine their training and experience with a love of theatre and performance, and are therefore able to speak the language of the creative teams.

"The best of all of these professionals combine their training and experience with a love of theatre and performance, and are therefore able to speak the language of the creative teams"

Stage Technologies' founders Mark Ager and John Hastie wrote 'Automation in the Entertainment Industry' which is a good starting place to learn about automation. The book is available in print and for Kindle. *Stage Technologies is one of the world's first dedicated theatre automation specialists. You can find out more at **www.stagetech.com**.*

It's a Jungle Out There: Tips & Tricks for Survival in the Freelance World

SIMON LOVELACE, FOUNDER OF CREW CLASS STAGE CREW TRAINING

If you'd have asked me, fifteen years ago, about my life as a freelance technician in the production industry, I would have replied: 'Surely, my job is the best in the world!'

In those days, we could pick and choose the projects on which we wanted to work. We chose how hard we wanted to work, and we could dictate our daily rate of pay! So, for example, one month may be spent working on a corporate roadshow, or a series of conferences. Not exactly inspiring, but an excellent daily rate of pay for sometimes very easy work, and all expenses paid in some lovely hotels!

The next few weeks might have been in theatre production, or on a music tour. Maybe slightly less money, certainly longer hours and definitely not as luxurious, but a great way to earn a living. Then, for a change, one might do a month temping in a corporate HQ in the City. Simply rigging screens and projectors and little PA systems in conference rooms. Good money for minimum effort.

And, because we were regarded as the practitioners of an unknown art, in all cases we were treated with absolute respect by our clients. They knew that we were vital to them, and we were treated, and paid, accordingly. There was always plenty of work to go round. One could take time off whenever one wanted, and pick up another job with ease.

Sounds good, doesn't it? It was.

These days, it's a jungle out there. If you are offered a full-time salaried job with a venue, or an equipment hire, or production, or company, my advice is take it. Even if the money is less than you may like, take it.

Having said that, with perseverance and professionalism, it is still possible to have a rewarding career as a freelance production professional. Here is some advice, tips and tricks.

Skill base

By all means have a specialist skill, be it in sound, lighting, set construction, whatever, but don't limit your options by being too narrowly focussed. There are many opportunities described simply as 'technician'; a role in which you will be expected to know, and be able to do, a bit of everything. Also, it stands to reason that, the wider your skillset, the wider the employment options available to you.

Be realistic in your expectations. Sleeping with the Pro-Tools advanced user manual does not mean you're going straight to the front of house mix position! Similarly, spending hours creating fantasy stadium lightshows in WYSIWYG does not make you a lighting designer! Regardless of your experience in education, or final grade, in the professional world you will be starting at – or very near to – the bottom.

"Sleeping with the Pro-Tools advanced user manual does not mean you're going straight to the front of house mix position!"

Finding work

A subscription to Stage Jobs Pro shouldn't be the only weapon in your arsenal. The search for work is, if anything, a bigger part of your job than actually fulfilling contracts. You should always be looking for new opportunities.

Research is fundamental. Get in touch with all your local venues and establish personal contact with the appropriate managers. Don't just send CVs out into space, go and meet people. Ask to be put on their freelance list. Keep in touch. Don't become a bore, but give them the occasional phone call and ask how things are going. Adopt the same strategy with hire and production companies. This will greatly improve the chances that one day you will get that call back.

Make friends with your peers in the industry, either onsite on projects, online in chat-rooms and forums, or through trade associations. Networking leads to opportunities, either through being approached directly to be part of a team, or through invaluable 'word of mouth' recommendations. The greater amount of people that you are in touch with, the greater potential there is.

Be informed. Keep abreast via the media of all the latest in the industry, in terms of productions and new trends as well as technological developments. Avail yourself of the free training made available by the manufacturers and distributors of technical products. Apart from the obvious benefit to you in terms of finding opportunities, it is also no bad thing to be evidently up to speed in an interview situation or onsite with new colleagues.

Doing the work

In the past, when 'costing' a production, a project manager would decide how many freelancers were needed and include those fees in their quote to the client. This has changed. These days, many hire and production companies are taking on increasing numbers of full-time staff – on a lower pay-scale – and combining their warehouse and/or office duties with work in the field. Not only does this mean fewer freelance opportunities, but it also means that employing a freelancer becomes an expensive 'last resort'. In my recent experience, all the straight-forward jobs appear to be going to the full-timers. If you get a call as a freelancer, the chances are that the project will be challenging.

"If you get a call from a new client for a freelance project, be under no illusions that this is a lucky opportunity, and should be taken seriously"

Most companies already have a pool of established freelancers. If you get a call from a new client for a freelance project, be under no illusions that this is a lucky opportunity, and should be taken seriously.

The usual rules apply:
• Don't be late.
• Carry your own tools and PPE.
• Make sure you are dressed appropriately for the job.

But there are other things to consider:

When accepting a freelance assignment, be absolutely certain that the job requirements fall comfortably within your skillset. As already stated, opportunities are becoming fewer, and the work is getting tougher. In the long run, if you are in any doubt, you would be better off turning down a job rather than accepting it and finding out onsite that you are insufficiently skilled.

Be aware that you are probably joining a team who have worked together on many previous occasions. They will have their own way of doing things. If their methods and practices differ from ones that you have been taught, or experienced onsite in the past, go with the flow. You will impress no one by calling their methods into question, or suggesting that you have a better way!

Your colleagues will be forming an impression of you based not only on your technical ability, but also as a person. Be aware of the social dynamic of the group and work within it. Don't forget, one of your principal objectives is to be offered more work in future. Give the client every reason possible to ask for you again.

Getting paid for the work
When taking on a freelance job, it is vital to have some form of record of your business agreement with the client. Simply making an arrangement over the phone is both unprofessional and risky.

For a medium to long term assignment, such as a tour, you must insist on receiving a formal contract before you proceed. If you have any reservations about what you have been given, seek advice before you sign.

For smaller bookings, ideally your client should give you a Purchase Order. This is a formal document including your clients' business details, the nature, location, time and date of the job you have been hired to do, and the agreed fee. If your employer isn't geared up to provide a Purchase Order, you must insist on an email, or letter, confirming your arrangement.

You will respond to the client with an invoice, which is basically the reverse of a purchase order. I recommend invoicing immediately on completion of any assignment. The sooner you invoice, the sooner you'll be paid. In my experience, if you are working for a regular client, I have found it more effective to send small, regular, invoices, on a job-by-job basis, than it is to group a lot of jobs together and send a large invoice.

Often, people embarking on a freelance career are unsure what to charge for their time and services. Seek advice from colleagues and online. A basic rule of thumb is that corporate jobs pay the highest, with music coming second, and theatre at the bottom.

Your clients will all have their own individual payment terms. Thirty days from receipt of invoice is normal in the corporate world. In theatre it may be at the end of the following week, or an interim payment followed by the balance at the end of the run. It is advisable to establish exactly what the terms are in advance and, again, get a record of them. Do not expect to be paid in cash at the end of the night. That hardly ever happens!

In conclusion, being in business as a freelancer is a challenging career choice. There is support within the industry, and my advice is to take advantage of all of it. Finally, as any freelancer will tell you, you are only ever as good as your last job. Never forget that!

Crew Class is a one day pay-to-attend training course in stagecraft. Supported by the biggest companies in crewing and production, this course not only provides training, but a genuine potential leg-up into the industry. For more information go to www.crewclass.co.uk or email trainme@crewclass.co.uk.

Stage Management

"On the odd occasion that something goes wrong at the last minute, I love being able to fix it and calm everyone down so the show can go on!"

Stage Manager

The role of Stage Manager is highly varied and often highly pressurised as they are in charge of everything on and off stage during performances to ensure the production runs to the highest standard. Stage Managers often progress from being Assistant Stage Managers or Deputy Stage Managers, and can then move on to work as Company Stage Manager or Production Manager.

We asked Stage Jobs Pro member Nicola Ireland the following questions about working as a Stage Manager:

What is the most rewarding aspect of working as a Stage Manager?
The most rewarding part of being a Stage Manager is getting a production from rehearsals onto the stage. The pride and fulfilment that comes with opening a show when you know you have worked really hard to get it there is a great feeling.

What are the key skills required to be an effective Stage Manager?
Being a Stage Manager requires excellent time management, patience, working well under pressure, compromise and communication.

Do you see your role as a natural step on a career ladder, and if so what is the next rung?
I see my role as a Stage Manager as a natural step, up from DSM, and the next step would be Company Stage Manager, however, this is not set in stone. I believe that the more experience you have as an ASM and DSM the better a Stage Manager you are.

How did you work your way into your current role?
Since graduating I have worked as both, ASM (6 years) and DSM (5 years), before deciding to make the move up to Stage Manager. I believe that all experiences make you a better Stage Manager (in the broad sense of the term, ASM, DSM, SM, CSM). You can never know it all – everyday can throw something new at you, no matter how long you have worked in the industry.

How much do you think networking helps towards landing a job in the industry?

I believe that the more companies you work with, speak to or have a relationship with will certainly help with getting the next job. The more companies, producers or Company Managers you can call when you are out of work the better.

Do you think you will be working in the industry in the next five years, and if so in what capacity?

I hope to be working in the industry for my whole career. I want to continue working as a Stage Manager and hope to build up relationships with many more companies to gain more experience.

Please describe what a typical day working as a Stage Manager might contain?

There is not a typical day as a Stage Manager! Rehearsals can throw anything at you, from searching for period props to modern furniture and looking after the company and your SM team. Show running becomes a little more predictable, but it is live theatre, so, you take whatever the day brings and do your job to the best of your ability, while always striving to be better and at the top of your game.

How important is working for free at the beginning of your career?

I would suggest that if you have the passion to work in Stage Management you should gain as much experience as possible after graduating, however, don't feel that you must work for free, and certainly not if you can't afford to.

Assistant Stage Manager

Assistant Stage Managers are mainly responsible for propping and supporting the stage management team during rehearsals and the production.

We asked Stage Jobs Pro member Beth Crock the following questions about working as an Assistant Stage Manager:

What is the most rewarding aspect of working as an Assistant Stage Manager?

The most rewarding part of working as an assistant stage manager is the fact that I truly love what I do. I love the variety that comes with working freelance. No two days are ever the same and I get to meet so many different people, and learn something new every day. I enjoy the challenge of sourcing and organising props and of working with a variety of performers, technicians and creatives.

What are the key skills required to be an effective Assistant Stage Manager?

There are two main components to working as an ASM. Firstly to help source and look after any props and furniture for a production, and secondly to support the stage management team, performers, and creatives throughout the rehearsal and production process. An ASM should have a strong initiative and be motivated to work independently. If you are sent out to find a specific prop, you should know where and how to look for it without constantly having to consult the stage manager or designer. The ability to think on your feet is very important. Productions and situations are constantly changing, so it is good to be able to adapt and come up with solutions to problems as they arise. It is also vital to have excellent interpersonal skills and to be able to work with and communicate effectively with everyone involved in the production. A willingness to be flexible is also essential. There are sometimes unpleasant jobs that must be done that often fall to the ASM to complete. Someone has to do them, so you might as well do it well and do it cheerfully. There are also some really fun elements so you need to be able to take the good with the bad.

Do you see your role as a natural step on a career ladder, and if so what is the next rung?

Personally, I prefer the role of ASM above any other position. For myself, I do not see it as a stepping stone to becoming a DSM or stage manager, but it is an excellent starting place for others considering a career in stage management. I am perfectly capable of working in these roles, and I have done so in the past, yet I still prefer working as an ASM. The next step up the career ladder for me would be to find a permanent position in a regional repertory producing house.

How did you work your way into your current role?

I did a three year BA (Hons) course in Stage Management and Technical Theatre, and I feel it was an excellent preparation for working in the professional theatre world. Part of the training was to get me out and working with professionals. My first proper job came as a direct result of the secondment I competed as part of my degree. Since then, I have been working freelance with very few breaks in employment. I have worked on a variety of productions, including a pantomime that was advertised on Stage Jobs Pro. Nearly every company I have worked for has asked me back to work with them again. All work leads to more work, so it is important to leave a positive impression.

How much do you think networking helps towards landing a job in the industry?

Networking can be very important to getting work in the industry. Several of my jobs have come as a direct result of being put forward by someone I know. In other jobs I have found that I quite often have worked with the same people or for the same companies as the new people I meet. I like to think I have a good working reputation with colleagues and that if I am mentioned, they will speak positively of me, just as I do with people I think highly of myself.

Do you think you will be working in the industry in the next five years, and if so in what capacity?
I very much hope to be working in the industry in five years time. I would like to still be working as an ASM but working for larger companies more consistently and making a bit more money.

Please describe what a typical day working as an Assistant Stage Manager might contain?
No two days working as an ASM will every be the same, but they can be lumped into several categories: propping, assisting in rehearsals and onstage. A day propping can be spent traipsing around trying to find props and furniture for a show. Depending on the design and budget, I will visit a variety of different shops and potentially hire houses. In London I have several 'propping routes' which include areas with a concentration of useful shops, charity, junk, second-hand, discount stores, Army/Navy surplus, etc. A propping day can also be spent researching, looking at a specific period or style for a prop. The internet is also an extremely useful resource for finding objects farther afield such as Ebay or Gumtree, or specialist online shops. Generally most of my days during the rehearsal period will be propping days. Sometimes the DSM will need someone to assist in rehearsals. If the DSM is not there at all, the ASM can cover the book, writing in blocking, prompting and taking notes as a direct cover for the DSM. Quite often if there is a large cast or a complicated props plot, it is very useful as an ASM to be in the rehearsal room setting and running prop and assisting the performers. This can be really useful to get an idea of how the show will run once it moves into the theatre. Onstage the ASM will ensure that all props and furniture are set correctly and will quite often sweep and mop the stage as necessary. During the technical period, the ASM needs to be on hand all the time to help wherever necessary: scene changes, handing props, paging doors, herding performers. This is where they will develop a running plot to use during performances. During showcall the ASM will help to prepare the stage and props for the show and then run any cues they have during the performance and then do any cleaning up afterwards.

Have you done any additional training courses to further your career?
I trained for my career at the Guildhall School of Music and Drama. My training included courses in health and safety, risk assessment, use of

access equipment, manual handling, first aid as well as basic instruction in all areas of backstage. I particularly chose to focus on stage management as well as design realisation and electrics. I feel this was very important in starting my career and providing a good foundation from which to work. Personally I have not done any further training courses, but am considering doing so in order to keep up with changes in the industry due to legislation and advances in technology.

How important is working for free at the beginning of your career?
I very strongly believe that it is wholly UNACCEPTABLE to work for free at the beginning of my career. I spent three years training in a professional environment and was fully able to take on a properly paid position from the day I finished my course. I made the mistake of doing several shows in the London Fringe for very little money, and I now have a reputation within certain circles for being willing to work for nothing. This is NOT an image I want to promote as this is my career, not a hobby. I have to make a living, and there are plenty of companies out there that have been and are willing to pay me a living wage at the beginning of my career. Working for free in stage management encourages low production values and I believe can damage the theatre industry as a whole. More of us need to stand up and insist to be paid a living wage for a job well done. However, working for free as a PART of training can be a very useful experience, but only if you are working alongside a full team of professionals, rather than acting in a role of full responsibility. I had a very useful work experience placement in which I effectively worked as an extra ASM in addition to a full stage management team. I learned so much from the people I was working with and they treated me as another member of the team. There was no pressure on me to deliver as the only ASM, which allowed me to put my full effort into learning as much as I could. The company I worked for was so satisfied with my work experience that the following season they asked me back as a full professional. There is a time and place for working for free, but it should not be part of the professional period of anyone's career.

Deputy Stage Manager / Showcaller

During the rehearsal Deputy Stage Managers tend to compile notes on prompts, cues and blocking. During the show they 'call the show', ie, they give the orders with regard to sound and lighting cues or actors' entrances.

© RICHARD CAMPBELL

We asked Stage Jobs Pro member Carol Pestridge the following questions about working as a Deputy Stage Manager:

What is the most rewarding aspect of working as a Deputy Stage Manager?
Getting the audience reaction after the first night performance. Seeing all of the hard work pay off.

What are the key skills required to be an effective Deputy Stage Manager?
Good communication and people skills, diplomacy, enthusiasm, stamina, a cool head and the ability to multi task.

Do you see your role as a natural step on a career ladder, and if so what is the next rung?
Yes. I have already taken work as a Stage Manager and I would love to do Company Stage Managing in the future.

How did you work your way into your current role?
After finishing my degree in film and theatre studies I did voluntary ASM work and took a few jobs as a Wardrobe Mistress. Once I had this on my CV I got paid work as an ASM and eventually worked my way up to DSM by doing book cover. After my first DSM job I have pretty much got every job from recommendations and word of mouth.

How much do you think networking helps towards landing a job in the industry?
It certainly helps if people know you, as they can recommend you to others if they are in need of a stage manager.

Do you think you will be working in the industry in the next five years, and if so in what capacity?
Yes. Probably still in a form of Stage Management.

Please describe what a typical day working as a Deputy Stage Manager might contain?
Get up and go to the rehearsal space. Grab milk on the way in. Clean the space and put the kettle on. Have a cup of tea. Once the director and actors are in I take notes during rehearsal, prompt and add any cues or blocking to the book. At the end of the rehearsal I go through the schedule with the director. Once I have locked up the rehearsal room I call the ASM on the way home to give any updates. Once I get home I send out the schedule for the next day. Type up and email out the rehearsal notes. Have dinner then crawl into bed.

Have you done any additional training courses to further your career?
No. Well I have done fire warden and health and safety training but I don't think it has furthered my career.

How important is working for free at the beginning of your career?
Well if you can get paid work straight away then great! But it is a very good way of gaining experience and adding to your CV. Yes I think that it is important.

Technical Stage Manager
A Technical Stage Manager position combines the roles of Technician and Stage Manager. This means that they are responsible for the Technician's duties – setting up, operating, and maintaining technical equipment – and for the duties of the Stage Manager, like managing rehearsals, calling the show and looking after cast, props, and paperwork.

We asked Stage Jobs Pro member David Warwick the following questions about working as a Technical Stage Manager:

What is the most rewarding aspect of working as a Technical Stage Manager?
I get the biggest buzz from ensuring that the show runs smoothly for every performance which means that I have to make sure all the technical aspects of the show are working. On the odd occasion that something goes wrong at the last minute, I love being able to fix it and calm everyone down so the show can go on!

What are the key skills required to be an effective Technical Stage Manager?
Obviously it's important to have technical knowledge and I have an

excellent and broad knowledge in lighting, sound, and stage craft. However, I think what's most important are the personal attributes of being organised with super focused attention to detail. You might be technically knowledgeable and proficient at operating equipment but if you can't organise yourself and the work to a high enough standard then you won't do the job well. I am always working to lists and plans so I know that everything has been checked and covered. I work to one simple principle which is that if something should happen to me, it won't matter because I've done the proper preparation so that another technical stage manager should be able to operate the show. This is because I label everything in the prompt copy, each piece of equipment and every cable, and so someone else should be able to pick it up at the last minute should the unthinkable happen.

Do you see your role as a natural step on a career ladder, and if so what is the next rung?
Yes – from the position of Technical Stage Manager, you can become a Technical Manager for a venue or a Production Manager for a show.

How did you work your way into your current role?
By taking every opportunity and working hard. Every production, every job offer, I made sure that I did the best job I could and I became known for my work ethic and the quality of my efforts to ensure that each show was the best it could be. After finishing my training, I started working freelance and doing a lot of touring across the UK and built up a lot of experience that then enabled me to apply for venue based jobs. After my third venue based job, I was head-hunted for my current position because of the reputation I had established.

How much do you think networking helps towards landing a job in the industry?
Yes it can help but won't make any difference if you can't do the job. What I think is more important is to be helpful, have a positive attitude and be excellent at your job. Networking can work both ways: it can get you work but it can also work against you if someone thinks you did not do a good job on a previous production.

Do you think you will be working in the industry in the next five years, and if so in what capacity?
Yes and in a managerial role – either a Production Manager or Technical Manager.

Please describe what a typical day working as a Technical Stage Manager might contain?
I worked as Technical Stage Manager at The Kings Head Theatre and have

toured with a number of Theatre in Education theatre companies. Each day is very different! At The Kings Head Theatre, I would arrive mid-morning to set up for the lunchtime show. I would oversee the lunchtime show and maybe operate if required. Once the lunchtime show had finished, I would clear that away. The rest of the afternoon I would call incoming theatre companies about their technical requirements, check emails and do basic repairs in the theatre. Late afternoon, I would help to set up the evening show and if necessary, operate depending on the show. At certain points of the year, we could have up to five shows (and not all of them being the same show) being performed in the venue on one day so it could be quite a challenge getting them all in and out! When I was on tour with the Theatre in Education theatre companies, my day would start about 6.30am when I drove the van to the pick up point to collect the actors and then go to the school. We aimed to get to the school as early as possible and no later than 8am. With the actors' help, we would set up the stage, props, lights, sound and AV. The show would then be performed and I would operate the lights, sound and AV. Depending on the size of school, we would either perform the show again after lunch or we would pack up, drive to another school, set up and perform again. During the day I would try and phone the schools for the next day's shows to confirm arrangements. I would then drive the actors to the drop off point and then get back to digs or home sometime after 4pm. The last job of the day would be type up the show reports and email them to the theatre company.

Have you done any additional training courses to further your career?
It is necessary to keep up to date with areas such as health and safety and any changes in regulations. I am a member of the ABTT and attend their seminars at their trade shows as well as those run by PLAZA. I am also First Aid trained which needs renewing every three years.

How important is working for free at the beginning of your career?
Before I completed my training, I did work for free on a number of productions and I did this because I liked working with the people on those productions. I worked on them primarily for fun but these productions allowed me to work in different venues and enabled me to gain experience in the technical aspects of theatre and put my newly acquired training into practice. I enjoyed working on these productions but they did not lead directly to any paid work. However, the experience I had gained was invaluable for subsequent job interviews which I have no doubt helped me get those early jobs!

Company Stage Manager

Company Stage Managers combine the roles of Stage Manager and Company Manager. They have a wide variety of responsibilities – supervising the get in, looking after the cast and crew, doing paperwork, managing the technical aspects of the production, and much more

We asked Stage Jobs Pro member Justin Savage about working as a CSM:

What is the most rewarding aspect of working as a Company Stage Manager?
One of the most rewarding aspects of working as a CSM is playing a large part in helping to bring a show to life every night: a well managed company is a happy company, and a happy company makes for a better show. The better the show, the happier the audience.

What are the key skills required to be an effective Company Stage Manager?
Communication. The CSM is the link between the Production Office and the Acting Company, the Actors and Stage Management, the company and the theatre. It is vital to keep all of these parties well informed at all times. Show sense. If you're not getting the biggest kick out of entertaining several hundred people every night, and you're doing it because you like fiddling about with gaffer tape, you shouldn't be doing the job. We put on shows; it's a privilege, enjoy it. Practical ability. Common sense. A calm head. Boundless energy. Diplomacy.

Do you see your role as a natural step on a career ladder, and if so what is the next rung?
The job is enormously satisfying in its own right. However it is also a very useful stepping stone to, amongst other things, producing, general management, casting and production management. As CSM, one gets to see far more of the 'big picture' than more specialised roles within our industry.

How did you work your way into your current role?
I began as an ASM with a tiny dance company. I then worked my way through every aspect of Stage Management, and ran my own production company for several years. However, as a job, CSM was always the position from which I derived the most satisfaction. This is a role to which I have returned, and very happily too.

How much do you think networking helps towards landing a job in the industry?
Networking is vital. This is a big industry, but not so big that one can get lost; the more one stays in touch the better the odds of hearing about that next plum job.

Do you think you will be working in the industry in the next five years, and if so in what capacity?
Yes, I intend to continue in the industry for the next five years at least, either as CSM or in some other role, as yet undefined. You never know what's round the next corner.

Please describe what a typical day working as a Company Stage Manager might contain?
If I'm running a get-in, I'll be at the theatre at 07.30. I then supervise the load-in and fit up. On even the smallest touring show this will consume all of that working day, to be ready to open that night. Once in, and up and running smoothly, a typical touring day might consist of checking with Marketing and Publicity to see if the cast have any radio or TV interviews, working out next week's payroll, scheduling paint and maintenance calls, booking a doctor's appointment for a company member, discussing strategy with the producer and/or the theatre and then preparing to do the same thing all over again at next week's venue. The welfare of the company is paramount, and a conscientious CSM will pay this aspect of the job due diligence. Regular, informal chats with everyone in the group pays dividends in keeping things on an even keel. Theatre is full of personalities; they need to be looked after.

Have you done any additional training courses to further your career?
None whatsoever. Everything I have learned, I have learned on the job.

How important is working for free at the beginning of your career?
That's a tricky one. There's a fine line between gathering useful experience and getting exploited. We all have value; take your space, don't be shy, make sure your efforts are rewarded.

Stage Management as a Career

THIS IS AN ABRIDGED VERSION OF THE CAREER GUIDE WRITTEN, COMPILED AND EDITED BY MEMBERS OF THE STAGE MANAGEMENT ASSOCIATION, REPRODUCED HERE WITH KIND PERMISSION. YOU CAN DOWNLOAD THE FULL GUIDE FREE OF CHARGE AT **WWW.STAGEMANAGEMENTASSOCIATION.CO.UK** © STAGE MANAGEMENT ASSOCIATION

This is essentially a 'people management' job. A Stage Manager must have the temperament and ability to get along with people in both the artistic and technical sides of theatre, and to understand what they do. It is part of the attraction of the work that each new job will introduce new and different challenges. However, the work is never glamorous, often involving long hours and fairly boring, repetitive tasks as well as being physically demanding.

During the initial rehearsal period, the stage management team is responsible for:
- Marking out the set on the floor of the rehearsal room with coloured mark-up tape, based on the designer's ground plan.
- Arranging for basic catering facilities.
- Arranging substitute or rehearsal furniture and props.
- Scheduling rehearsals, and ensuring that all artistes and creative departments are aware of these calls.
- Collecting information about the production e.g. details of sets and costumes, sound and lighting requirements, props, and prop-making and ensuring these are copied to the relevant departments.
- Making sure that the director's wishes are passed on to the appropriate departments.
- Liaising with the Production Manager on costings and production schedules.
- Supervising the gradual introduction of the actual playing furniture and props.
- Making prop and furniture setting and running lists as the production develops.
- Removing the entire remaining physical production including furniture, props and costumes – both rehearsal and playing – from the rehearsal room and into the base or first theatre.

In addition to this, the welfare of the actors is of paramount importance. Making sure that they and the director have the optimum conditions with the best atmosphere and least distractions in which to work is the ultimate goal.

When the show has opened and is running, the stage management is responsible for the management of each evening's performance. This involves setting up the stage and wings with the furniture and props required for the production; checking that all artistes are in the building by their allotted times; giving 'calls' to the actors before and during the show, and other cues to all departments, enabling the changing of scenery, lighting and sound to be co-ordinated. During the run, maintaining and replacing props as necessary.

"When the show has opened and is running, the stage management is responsible for the management of each evening's performance"

In summary, the SM takes an overview to keep the show as the director directed and both the actors and technicians happy.

In smaller scale theatre or on tour, the stage management may also be required to 'roadie'; that is, drive, load and unload trucks, put up the set, and design and/or operate both sound and lighting.

This brief description gives some idea of the variety and responsibility of the job. The acting company must trust their stage management team in a crisis – it must always be the stage management that remain cool, keep their heads and cope with it. In a confrontation situation stage management must calm, soothe and mediate.

Touring or 'One Home'
There is a radical difference between taking a show from venue to venue on tour and a West End or producing theatre show which is static, and the duties are very different for both. With the ever tightening budgets of producing managements, the total team for any but the largest touring shows are usually three – or four at the most – plus wardrobe. This means an ever-expanding multiplicity of duties, encompassing the whole spectrum

of theatre, is needed to cope with the weekly move and set-up of the show.

On tour, the stage management team are expected to arrive at the venue, usually on a Monday morning, put up the set (CSM), organise and set furniture and props and 'dress' the production (DSM, ASM) with the accessories specified by the designer.

The CSM often then has to rig, focus and relight the show working from plans and notes supplied by the Lighting Designer, which is time consuming and can take up most of the day.

The other stage management, working with the resident staff, are also expected to set up and specify areas for extra scenery and furniture storage if necessary, e.g. if used in another act,show cuelight and practical light positions for the resident electrics staff, arrange for the offstage areas to be cleaned and carpeted etc., and sometimes to organise and rehearse key scene and act changes with the show staff, in addition to any prop setting, sound checks and other stage management chores they may have. It can be a very busy day!

> *"It stands to reason that the stage management have to rapidly build up a strong relationship with the resident staff"*

On larger scale touring productions there may be a production carpenter and sometimes also a production electrician (or either one singly) to put the set up and light the show. This relieves some of this burden from the CSM and allows the other jobs to be shared out more proportionally with the rest of the team.

On the largest shows – predominantly musicals – the stage management usually need only to focus their efforts on 'pure' stage management.

It stands to reason that the stage management have to rapidly build up a strong relationship with the resident staff, especially if the show is to open the same night. This sounds daunting, but one must bear in mind that this occurs nearly every Monday in theatres around the country and the resident crew are hardened to it, as you will become. Many teams have a great rapport with the theatre crew and it becomes a social as well as a professional pleasure to work at the venue. Equally, any shortcomings usually only have to be borne for a week – or two – at the most, as another town beckons on the tour.

In the West End, the Production Manager, Designer and at least one Production Carpenter are always present on the fit up to work with the resident Master Carpenter and their staff while lighting is overseen by the Lighting Designer and their production electrician in tandem with the theatre's Chief Electrician and their staff, so most of the carpentry and electrical chores will be handled exclusively by them.

The stage management will, however, need to view the theatre as their home for at least the next few months and so prop table placement, prop and furniture storage and setting will need to be carefully thought out and permanently marked up. All technical requirements such as sound, cameras and monitors for the prompt desk, and communications equipment will be hired in specifically for the venue and so will need to be carefully positioned and tested as they won't have had the 'bedding-in' in that touring affords. There has to be much greater liaison between the theatre staff and the stage management as whatever is decided, be it equipment positions, settings or scene changes will, once set, usually be the standard for the run.

Again, as with touring, an early solid relationship with the theatre staff is helpful and even more important than on tour as you may be there for several months, if not years. While it is important to gently but firmly exhibit and impose your standards and work practices upon the staff, remember that they have been there a lot longer than you and with countless productions and may take time to adjust.

In producing theatres, the fit up would also be undertaken by the resident Master Carpenter or Technical Stage Manager and their staff, and the lighting would be rigged and focussed by the resident electrics crew under the instruction of the Lighting Designer; those and any other technical departments (automation, AV, sound, etc.) would be overseen by the Production Manager at this stage.

The stage management will probably still be busy in the rehearsal room whilst this is going on and will have one or two days at most to set up the backstage areas as required. It is at the technical rehearsal that they will assume responsibility for the show, taking over from the Production Manager.

Runs of shows in such producing theatres are often for about 3-4 weeks, but can be shorter or longer. If the show is a co-production, stage management will have to plan the handover to another team at the end of their run; but most shows will simply end after their run and stage management's duties are to dispose of or return any props and furniture and other equipment which had been borrowed, hired or made specifically for the production, unless it is to be stored for future use. Your relationship with the resident staff will already have been established during the rehearsal period as you will have been, most likely, rehearsing in or near the building where you will ultimately run the show. It is no less important for that, especially as they may know the building much better than you if you are just working freelance on one show, and can be very helpful whilst you learn to find your way around.

Then there are the local authorities to satisfy. You will need to prepare a full risk assessment on the production particularly in respect to safety in all aspects of the show. Particular attention should be taken with naked flame, smoke or mist, special effects, pyrotechnics, firearms, light fittings and even set construction. Good control methods must be in place and observed by everyone.

With unusual sets, extension to the stage into the auditorium, performer flying etc. the local council may send a representative to check all constructions from a Buildings and Safety perspective.

The Production Manager will have all of these areas under their control and with the CSM will take the various agencies for a tour of the production, indicating areas that might be of interest or concern, and indicating the measures that have been taken to deal with any potential problem. They will also supply related paperwork for the production, such as certification for rigging sets and fire retardant timber. These will be needed not only by the authorities, but by the technical managers for the theatre.

The DSM and ASM may be needed to have on hand any special, flame or other effects that the authorities may require to be demonstrated, in order to include them on the licence.

Career Structure
There is often, or for most people, a progression through the roles, starting as ASM, later moving into being a DSM, and later again into SM and/or CSM.

However, as the roles are quite different and require quite different skills and temperaments, most people will find a particular liking or talent for one of the roles, spending years as ASM, for example, because the enjoy propping and prop-making; or the bulk of their career as DSM because they love being in rehearsals and cueing the show; or considerable time as SM/CSM because they are good at, and like, being in charge.

For many – by no means all – stage managers there comes a time, too, when they feel they need to move on from stage management, for a variety of reasons. Often this point occurs around 10 to 15 years into their career. Within the industry, there are many roles they can move into, depending on their individual skills, interests and wishes.

Frequently, stage managers become production managers (building based or freelance) or company managers; they can also become administrators, producers or general managers; they might take up directing; or work for a supplier or manufacturer; or set up their own business, for example as prop maker or buyer. Stage managers also become lighting designers, agents, trade unionists, trainers, teachers, theatre consultants, venue managers and journalists to name just a few recent examples.

"Within the industry, there are many roles stage managers can move into, depending on their individual skills, interests and wishes"

Many at the latter end of their stage management career work extensively in conference/corporate and public events of all kinds (e.g. Queen's Golden Jubilee, Olympic and Commonwealth Games opening ceremonies, large festivals etc), but only very few are able to turn this into a full-time career as there are limited opportunities. Some, but not many, stage managers move into television and film. Most stage managers, unless they leave the industry altogether, prefer to stick with the live arts.

Historically, there has always been about an equal number of men and women working in stage management and the ideal team is usually considered to be one in which both sexes are represented. This balance is about to be restored after recent decades saw a shift towards more women in stage management – the last five to ten years have seen an increase in the numbers of men applying and taking up courses in stage management.

What Do You Do Now?

Go and talk to a stage manager at your nearest producing theatre or if there is a touring company visiting your area, talk to the stage manager about their job and how they gained entry into the profession.

Experience gained through school productions, youth theatre or amateur groups is invaluable. You may even be able to get casual work from time to time at your local professional theatre. In the last instance make an appointment to see the Production/Stage Manager to talk about the possibilities.

Training

Vocational training for stage management is available at many drama schools and these courses are mainly, but not exclusively, at degree level.

Selection is by interview and most courses require GCSE and A level/BTEC qualifications or previous experience in the industry. Although you may not be required to have A-levels or a BTEC (and they don't have to be in 'drama'), they are important and may help the school to decide if you will be able to undertake the study involved. Practical experience, such as with your local theatre, amateur theatre group or on school productions is highly valued by drama schools.

"Vocational training for stage management is available at many drama schools and these courses are mainly, but not exclusively, at degree level"

Funding for courses is extremely limited but you should always check with your Local Education Authority as to what is available from your council. Each individual drama school's admissions officer will also be able to give you funding information. The funding situation for degree courses is the same as for any university degree. Some colleges, universities and drama schools have scholarships or bursaries so contact them directly as these tend to change from year to year.

If you have A-Levels or a BTEC, you may like to take a degree or diploma course in drama or drama related subjects, before going into vocational training at postgraduate level. This would give you a deeper appreciation of the history of the theatre and how it is related to its social, historical and geographical contexts, as well as giving you an introduction to the skills required for working in professional theatre. However, there is virtually no funding at postgraduate level.

While people can and do enter the profession without training, the chances of getting a job are vastly improved if you have trained on a vocational course (particularly one at a college which is a Drama UK accredited School – **www.dramauk.co.uk/drama_uk_accredited_schools** – or a course approved by the SMA for their Graduate status – contact **admin@stagemanagementassociation.co.uk** for advice and up to date information).

Recently, new creative apprenticeships have been introduced by CCSkills, the sector skills council for the creative and cultural industries. Whilst they don't offer a dedicated stage management apprenticeship, it is possible to use the Technical Theatre apprenticeship as a springboard and specialise in stage management further down the road (**www.creative-choices.co.uk/knowledge/creative-apprenticeships**).

A number of theatres also offer local apprenticeship schemes and the on-the-job training can be complemented with short courses from the Association of British Theatre Technicians (ABTT) (**www.abtt.org.uk**) or the Stage Management Association (**www.stagemanagementassociation.co.uk**) and work placements with other employers.

A Career as a Stage Manager

Apart from the specific elements of work in this business, there are other practical and personal requirements. You will need to be a good self-motivator, and will need to manage most of your business affairs yourself. One-off projects and team working can provide a great sense of achievement over short periods of time. You can choose when and for whom you work. You will need to consider the effect of a peripatetic and irregular work pattern on your social and family life. Ill health can mean you cannot earn or get benefits.

Income tax: Ignorance is no defence, you need to be aware of and understand the tax categories of PAYE (Pay as you earn) or UTR. You can be both employed and self-employed in this business. Some employments are classed as PAYE, some freelance patterns of work can qualify for UTR, but – for the time being at least – in most of their contracts stage managers, like actors, will qualify for the dual status of paying Class 1

National Insurance (like an employee, entitling you to sign on in between contracts), but paying tax like a freelance worker (entitling you to offset legitimate business expenses against tax).

Self-employment means you have to register with HMRC (Her Majesty's Revenue and Customs), keep your own records of income and expenses, make your returns by the January 31st that follows the end of each tax year (April 5th), and pay the bill in two instalments as demanded. It mainly means you should not spend all the money you earn! Keep about a third aside for tax and nasty surprises and you might have a little to spare at the end of the year when you have paid your tax. Tax Officers are obliged to help – though some peace of mind can be bought in the form of advice from an accountant.

National Insurance Contributions: Class 1, or 2 and 4, depending on your tax status, can affect your eligibility for benefits. If you have been paying Class 1 NI, you are entitled to apply for jobseeker's allowance; if you pay Class 2 or 4, you cannot do this. Individual offices often do not have the correct information with regard to stage managers' dual tax status, in line with that of actors. Equity is very much involved in this area, and they or the SMA are good sources of advice. Please note that at the time of going to press there are changes planned which are likely to change the arrangements outlined above.

"It is essential for all to be aware of the law, and of the personal responsibility for one's own safety and the potential to affect the safety of others"

Personal Pension / Private Health Insurance / Unemployment Insurance: Decisions made now can affect your future. How much can you afford to spend? You need to take advice from someone you can trust. Equity and BECTU have some schemes with some employers to set up pension contributions during engagements. You will probably need your own scheme as well.

Health and Safety: It is essential for all to be aware of the law, and of the personal responsibility for one's own safety and the potential to affect the safety of others. This is a dangerous industry, we use products in ways they are not normally used, we work in bad light, and there is a lot of adrenaline flowing around when we work. The Health and Safety Executive produces free and priced information on H&S issues and legislation. You should get their leaflet Facts for Freelances in Broadcasting and the Performing Arts. The ABTT and SMA publish regular information about safe practice.

Public Liability Insurance: A grey area. This covers you against injuring a member of the public by your activities. Not legally required, but sometimes needed. Equity and BECTU offer Public Liability Insurance as part of the benefits of membership and the SMA can arrange this and other insurances on preferable terms.

Getting a Job
A full driving licence is invaluable and the importance of trying to obtain one and keeping it 'clean' cannot be overestimated, as the job often entails collecting props or scenery, or driving a fringe company between venues.

The ability to read a musical score enlarges one's job prospects and the SMA training courses are generally regarded as first class.
*Extracts from the SMA Career Guide courtesy of the Stage Management Association. The full guide can be downloaded from **www.stagemanage-mentassociation.co.uk/shop/free-stage-management-career-guide**, along with details of SMA memberships including student membership.*

Costume, Wardrobe, Make Up & Wigs

"When the curtain goes up, or the opening film credits pass, the audience is transported into a different world. The opening visual image you see has been carefully constructed to allow you to quickly understand the world and the character that inhabits it."

Costume Assistant

Costume Assistants work with the Costume Designer to design, develop, and create costumes for the cast.

We asked Stage Jobs Pro member Norma Bonnell the following questions about working as a Costume Assistant:

What is the most rewarding aspect of working as a Costume Assistant?
A costume assistant is the right hand to the designer of the show. I guess the most rewarding aspect of my job would be taking the ideas of the director and working with the designer to make everything happen. Working with a great team of costume persons is also rewarding as it is a team effort to get a production on stage.

What are the key skills required to be an effective Costume Assistant?
A costume assistant has to be very organised. These days computer skills are essential: it is very important to be able to use the programmes available to film and theatre for costume design. The ability to think on one's feet is also vital as there are always many changes in a production, sometimes last minute. The assistant also has to be able to understand a budget, be able to help work within that budget and troubleshoot when things are not quite to spec. This could be something as simple as sorting out a seamstress issue or more complex like finding the right fabric for the lead actor's costume. The old fashioned way of taking notes works very well, lots of times something is mentioned that may be of great importance later on in the production. If a costume build is needed, then understanding how the garment(s) go together helps greatly to create that certain look the designer and director/producer is wanting for that scene.

Do you see your role as a natural step on a career ladder, and if so what is the next rung?
Yes, most definitely. A costume assistant is a full-on position and a lot of

experience in this role would help to take the next step on designing a show. Every designer I have worked with in the past started out as an assistant before jumping in to design a show.

How did you work your way into your current role?
I studied fashion design and fashion arts in college and gradually made my way into the movie industry. I worked in costume shops on many different movies and theatre productions, and each little step helped me to understand the full picture of the role a costume assistant played during a production.

How much do you think networking helps towards landing a job in the industry?
This is so important. Skill is necessary, but it is who you know, or who knows who, that seems to help people land the job in this business. You could be the best in the city, but if no one knows you, a job opportunity can be very difficult to get. Putting yourself out there and telling people what you do really makes a difference.

Do you think you will be working in the industry in the next five years, and if so in what capacity?
Definitely, I will be in this industry for at least the next five years. Hopefully more. I enjoy assisting a designer in the everyday chaos that goes with getting costumes on stage. I might look at designing for a small show in the future but am quite happy doing the job at hand.

Please describe what a typical day working as a Costume Assistant might contain?
Depending on the show, I may have to help with getting the measurements (ie fitting), then going over the idea with the designer. An assistant also has a hand in shopping for wardrobe, fabrics and going to production meetings. Always on the go with last minute changes and final fittings, this is a role that takes full concentration. I find that each designer is different, so it helps to understand where the designer is getting their creative ideas from and work with them as they see things. If the designer is away in a meeting or seeing to an actor/actress, I, as an assistant may have to work with the director or producer personally to help make a scene work.

Have you done any additional training courses to further your career?
Yes. In Canada in order to go on set for a movie, one had to take a set etiquette course. I went further and took a set supervisor course, which involves learning how to lay out each costume for each day of filming and continuity for the film. I also took a course in health and safety: working with chemicals on set and breakdown chemicals on fabrics.

89

How important is working for free at the beginning of your career?
I worked for free here and in Canada on a few shows. It is a great way to get known in this very competitive business. I needed to gain experience on set after taking the extra courses, but the industry in Canada was flat at the time. There were a lot of low budget shows happening and I luckily landed a volunteer job with what turned out to be a Sundance Film Festival winner. This got me more work with the same designer as an assistant later on and definitely got me noticed. Here in London, I knew no one so doing a few hours or days as a volunteer definitely helped. It is something to put on a CV as it shows that hard work doesn't put you off. You never know who knows who in this business and it is a great way to get referrals for paid jobs.

Costume Designer

The Costume Designer designs and conceives costumes for the cast which helps to set the play in a particular period or genre, convey the intended mood of the production and explain more about the characters.

We asked Stage Jobs Pro member Daisy Jane Turner the following questions about working as a Costume Designer:

What is the most rewarding aspect of working as a Costume Designer?
Being able to bring your designs to life. You can spend months in the design process, developing and finalising your ideas to then produce a final design, which is such an exciting journey; the creativity and imagination of this journey is my favourite part of costume design. But it's not until you see your design finalised into a creation worn by the performer that the costume transforms into the character that had previously only been living in your imagination. That is the most rewarding aspect.

What are the key skills required to be an effective Costume Designer?
I believe the key skill would be the ability to adapt within your creative range. You need to be able to push the boundaries and challenge your creativity within theatrical costume for stage, but then have the ability to produce authenticity for stylised costume within film and screen. As a Costume Designer, your role involves liaising with directors, working with actors and being surrounded by a crew of professionals; therefore, it is important to remain professional while maintaining interpersonal skills within the working relationship of your team.

90

Do you see your role as a natural step on a career ladder, and if so what is the next rung?

I see every experience within the film and theatre industry as a step further in my career, however big or small the job. From being a Costume Assistant and learning from experienced professionals, to being Head of Wardrobe and learning on the job, working under the pressure of being your own boss and using your initiative. I continue to develop my knowledge and experience by designing and working for a variety of productions. Every production is completely different to the last, and will only enable you to learn more and grow within your capabilities and confidence in your ability as a designer.

How did you work your way into your current role?

I was very fortunate to have been offered a job as designer and stylist for a short film when I finished University, due to a former colleague recommending me to a managing director when she was unable to take on the job. From then on I have built a good working relationship with this company and its team and have been asked to come back and work on various productions. I have only ever been offered work through being recommended through a contact within the industry. I believe in only ever putting in more than expected within your role. In doing this, you open up more opportunities for yourself.

How much do you think networking helps towards landing a job in the industry?

It certainly helps to have the contacts, and as they say 'it's who you know, not what you know'. But in my case, it's word of mouth that gets me jobs. I don't possess a little black book of contacts in the industry, I just try to be memorable and I do that by going that little bit further and exceeding expectations.

Do you think you will be working in the industry in the next five years, and if so in what capacity?

I don't plan to do anything other than working within the costume industry. In five years I will be designing and creating bespoke costumes tailored to individual clients; I will be building my business of running and directing a bespoke costume house for tailored and couture costume, working with a team of costumiers.

Please describe what a typical day working as a Costume Designer might contain?

As a Costume Designer, the role can not be condensed into a 'typical working day'. The role is diverse and varied with a range of responsibilities and a 'to-do' list that expands through the months from pre-production to post-production; from the initial stages of the design process, to returning costumes to hire houses. As I am still in the early stages of my career, the role of Costume Designer becomes an umbrella of roles and responsibilities that you are expected to fulfil. These responsibilities include the organisation of costumes, sourcing trips to costume houses and styling the actors, as well as working alongside the crew, liaising with directors and making sure your job has been done to the best of your abilities from the beginning of your journey to the end.

Have you done any additional training courses to further your career?
After studying Costume with Performance Design at University, the most beneficial way of furthering myself as a designer is working in the industry. The useful knowledge that you will keep with you is what you take from experience. And that experience can only be gained through jumping in at the deep end and taking risks.

How important is working for free at the beginning of your career?
I have been fortunate enough to have not had to work for free since graduating. Although I know colleagues that have achieved a great deal and gone far in the costume industry by working for free. If you are in the situation that you can work for free, then do – it's only more experience for yourself. Although never decrease your value based on someone else's inability to see your worth. If you have the confidence in your abilities and you know you do your job well, never settle for less than you are worth.

Costume Maker

Costume Makers are responsible for enabling the construction of the costumes – they translate the Costume Designer's ideas and designs into real costumes.

We asked Stage Jobs Pro member Eleanor Moss the following questions about working as a Costume Maker:

What is the most rewarding aspect of working as a Costume Maker?
Getting to see your costume on the stage, on film or at an event and knowing the costume you made enhanced the character making them come alive.

What are the key skills required to be an effective Costume Maker?
Advanced knowledge in the construction methods of costume making, together with excellent finishing skills. The ability to work quickly and efficiently independently, as well as part of a group.

Do you see your role as a natural step on a career ladder, and if so what is the next rung?

Yes as I am currently a freelance maker, I am making the contacts in order to provide myself with continuous work with the companies I am working with. By building up my clientele this will provide me with a steady amount of work. To further my career, I can build on my contacts and get myself fully known within the industry with a good reputation in order to get more work with bigger and better companies. Once I have enough experience as a maker I could also go onto become a wardrobe mistress, cutter or maker within companies.

How did you work your way into your current role?

I studied and gained a BA (Hons) degree in Costume Production at Rose Bruford college and from there I interned at Angels Costumiers to gain more experience within a costume store. I also applied for another internship, where my details were forwarded on to a well known entertainments company to make them several costumes for different events. By displaying my work in a college creative industries fair, I also gained important contacts who then went on to offer me freelance work.

How much do you think networking helps towards landing a job in the industry?

Networking is a crucial part of gaining contacts in order to get more work. All of my paid jobs to date have been gained through networking, meeting people and making vital contacts that have then aided me in getting work. By networking it also enables you to get your name known within the industry and get a reputation for yourself.

Do you think you will be working in the industry in the next five years, and if so in what capacity?

I intend to still be working within the industry for at least the next five years, though due to the flexibility of my skills it also enables me to transfer across to other areas of clothes making, including in fashion and restoration and conservation work.

Please describe what a typical day working as a Costume Maker might contain?

Talking with a designer or company to determine a design for a costume, deciding on a design, or going fabric sampling. Drafting patterns once designs and fabrics have been confirmed. Cutting fabrics, making up the costume.

Have you done any additional training courses to further your career?

A two day beginners shoe making course. Taking on internships and work experience placements in order to gain more experience on the field.

How important is working for free at the beginning of your career?
Very important, it's a great way to gain more experience which is crucial at
the beginning of your career. Again it's another way to get your name
known in the industry and it shows you are keen to work hard, shows
hunger, drive and determination to succeed despite being not paid.

Costume Cutter

The Costume Cutter assists the Costume Maker and Costume Designer
by cutting patterns out of cloth, from which the costumes are then put
together.

**We asked Stage Jobs Pro member Urara Tsuchiya the
following questions about working as a Costume
Cutter:**

**What is the most rewarding aspect of working as a
Costume Cutter?**
When you realise the design and see how design
drawings translate to costumes. Also when you see the
actual show or film with the costumes you made after you
worked on it for a long time. It is really amazing to see them all together.

What are the key skills required to be an effective Costume Cutter?
The ability to communicate well with the Costume Designer, and work out
the most effective way of making it to the vision. Good and fast sewing
skills, and eye for the fitting. Pattern cutting skills are really good to have.

**Do you see your role as a natural step on a career ladder, and if so what
is the next rung?**
I would like to work more as a Costume Designer; it's always good to have
understanding of how things are made if you are on the design side. Also I
like using those skills for my own art works and projects.

How did you work your way into your current role?
I was asked to do it through people I knew.

**How much do you think networking helps towards landing a job in the
industry?**
It's always good if you have worked for someone, even for free, and – if
they liked working with you and the things you made – they can then
recommend you to other people. I think networking really helps. Also it's
assuring for the hiring side if you come recommended.

Do you think you will be working in the industry in the next five years, and if so in what capacity?
I think I will as part time costume maker/costume designer for theatre/film and for art performances, alongside my own art projects.

Please describe what a typical day working as a Costume Cutter might contain?
Measuring actors, making draft for block from the measurements, making toile and doing fittings with actors, going to fabric shops to search materials. Modifying commercial patterns. Dying fabrics, or treating the fabric to make it aged. Cleaning and ironing. Meeting with costume designer/artists to discuss the details of costumes.

Have you done any additional training courses to further your career?
I did a few pattern cutting courses, which is a very useful skill to have. I think corset making courses are a useful thing to do for costumes. I have come from a fine art background, which is helpful if you work with artists to understand what kind of look they want. Most of my skills I just learned it at work.

How important is working for free at the beginning of your career?
I think it's better if you are paid, even in the beginning of your career, even just minimum wage. It's good to work for students/small productions with not much budget for free in the beginning if you think you can benefit in a certain way – learning, gaining experience, for portfolio. But it's always better if you work and paid properly, than you are taken seriously.

Costume Supervisor
The Costume Supervisor is the head of the Costume department and as such they are responsible for managing budgets and deadlines, overseeing their team of Costume Assistants or Designers, and liaising with other departments.

We asked Stage Jobs Pro member Richard Gellar the following questions about working as a Costume Supervisor:

What is the most rewarding aspect of working as a Costume Supervisor?
Realising the designer's designs. Coming in under budget and seeing a successful show, with great reviews.

What are the key skills required to be an effective Costume Supervisor?
Budgets, managing staff, organisational skills, costume cutting, period costume history, excellent contacts.

Do you see your role as a natural step on a career ladder, and if so what is the next rung?
Having worked as a Costumier alongside various teaching and part time admin/management roles, I decided to combine these skills which have allowed me a very successful career. The next step hopefully is costume design or design assistant.

How did you work your way into your current role?
A combination of careers, of which the key one was in costume making, dyeing and breaking down, then working in management part time, having skills in budgets and managing staff. I combined these roles.

How much do you think networking helps towards landing a job in the industry?
For me networking is key: meeting designers and production managers is key to any success costume supervisor. If you're lucky you can become permanent in a production theatre.

Do you think you will be working in the industry in the next five years, and if so in what capacity?
Hopefully and ideally by the next five years hopefully have a few designer credits to my name and Film/TV credits.

Please describe what a typical day working as a Costume Supervisor might contain?
Check and replying to emails, updating the budget, attending fittings, sourcing costumes, touching base with costume makers to ensure deadlines will be met, liaising with production managers and the designer.

Have you done any additional training courses to further your career?
Only personal choice ones, such as tailoring and millinery.

How important is working for free at the beginning of your career?
Only working free for the first couple of credits and then making sure that you get paid for the rest. If you are competent and confident in your profession you should be paid for your skills.

Wardrobe Assistant

Wardrobe Assistants help to develop, maintain and manage the actors' costumes for a production.

We asked Stage Jobs Pro member Madeline Taylor the following questions about working as a Wardrobe Assistant:

What is the most rewarding aspect of working as a Wardrobe Assistant?
The most rewarding is helping pull the show together, working with pretty much everyone, (actors, director, designer, makers) to come up with the best costume for the character and context. It can be a heap of paperwork and admin, but it can also be a lot of fun and a large variety of different small jobs.

What are the key skills required to be an effective Wardrobe Assistant?
Being organised (and the ability to know where your organisational skills will fail, and planning for this to circumvent them). Being able to get along with everyone, and the patience (and ability to hold your tongue) that this sometimes requires. An eye for the small details that make a costume complete.

Do you see your role as a natural step on a career ladder, and if so what is the next rung?
I have moved up, down and sideways on the costuming rungs a few times, but the ability to be a good wardrobe assistant will be a great step in anyone's career. If you are working on a big enough project, after seeing a few of these through (depending on their duration of course) you should feel comfortable to start coordinating small shows in your own right.

How did you work your way into your current role?
I was lucky enough to complete a Wardrobe Traineeship with a professional theatre company, which got me in the door and a year's experience and industry knowledge.

How much do you think networking helps towards landing a job in the industry?
Lots! But please don't do it obviously, and choose your timing wisely! Your best bet may be giving the person who can help you your card and asking them to call you (maybe working for free) if they get swamped. Hopefully this will happen in the next few weeks and you will be able to help them when they are stuck. Thats a really good way to be remembered (as long as you are actually helpful!)

Do you think you will be working in the industry in the next five years, and if so in what capacity?
I am hoping to be working on smaller independent projects with more creative focus, and interspersing this with academic research into costume and society.

Please describe what a typical day working as a Wardrobe Assistant might contain?
Arrive at 8ish, confer with the Head of Wardrobe about tasks for the day, prep for any fittings or meetings of the day, make a heap of phone calls organizing supplies, hires, haberdashery, staff, suppliers, attend a fitting or production meeting and take lots of notes, assist the makers or cutters with any issues they are having, have lunch, head out shopping, hurry back for fitting, have a brief meeting with designer, put stuff away, answer emails.

Have you done any additional training courses to further your career?
Yes, but on the job experience is far more valuable.

How important is working for free at the beginning of your career?
Fairly important as it exposes you to new workrooms, but make sure this is not taken advantage of. You shouldn't work more than one week for free for any company that can afford to pay you, unless you know absolutely nothing (or its for uni/assessment)
*Madeline's website is **www.theloop.com.au/madelinetaylor**.*

Wardrobe Manager
The Wardrobe Manager manages the costume department: overseeing budgets and the other wardrobe staff, and communicating with other departments.

© COLETTE PADOVANI

We asked Stage Jobs Pro member Zoe Baron the following questions about working as a Wardrobe Manager:

What is the most rewarding aspect of working as a Wardrobe Manager?
It ranges from working with great designers to create beautiful costumes, to a small alteration or purchase that will make the actors/artists feel comfortable and confident on stage.

What are the key skills required to be an effective Wardrobe Manager?
A photographic memory! Perhaps not as extreme as that but you do have

to remember a lot of details regarding costume change, rehearsal notes, designer and director comments, orders .... To help you with this, organisation is key – you can never be too organised! You need to be able to communicate well and listen to others, and always try to remain calm – on the surface at least! Above all you have to be able to effectively delegate work, and to always be approachable to your staff. They are wanting to get the job done right and quickly too – if this is a problem then look to yourself before loading the blame on your workers.

Do you see your role as a natural step on a career ladder, and if so what is the next rung?
Wardrobe Manager or Costume Supervisor is in a way the highest you can go with regard to the Wardrobe Department in Theatre. Designing is really a different job entirely, but it is in some respects the next step up. Also there is always work in Film and TV to consider, where the work is different but the skills of a Wardrobe Manager would be valued. This may be considered more of a side step, than a step up but it would still be a valuable experience.

How did you work your way into your current role?
I didn't follow the typical degree route to get into Theatre. I worked voluntarily with local Theatre groups from the age of 17. I attended a Costume degree course at 19 but quit after one year as I was unimpressed with the course and I had found myself a Wardrobe Assistant position. Since then I have gradually worked my way up to Wardrobe Manager and Designer. I would argue that a degree is relatively useless and a waste of money. If you are keen and are willing to work for free for a little while you will learn far more and most importantly you will be making contacts. In the entertainment industry, more than any other I feel, contacts are your most important ally.

How much do you think networking helps towards landing a job in the industry?
Massively. Always take care to network as much as possible. You never know who you might meet and who may have a job for you.

Do you think you will be working in the industry in the next five years, and if so in what capacity?
I'm not sure! Theatre and TV/Film are all consuming jobs – consider it a vocation – and when you start to crave a life outside it you really have to consider which is most important to you. I'm not sure that in five years my job will be the top of my list of priorities, and to be honest it is difficult to do this job well and not make it your priority.

Please describe what a typical day working as a Wardrobe Manager might contain?

Days vary massively, but here is an example of a tech week schedule (not a touring or established production). Generally in work for 9am. Checking of orders, ordering and important emails must be done first. At 10.00am the cast will start coming in. By this time all the dressing rooms should be ready for their arrival, and if this is not the case it is all hands on deck to get things done in time. After 10.00 but before teching begins on stage, go round all the dressing rooms to check that everyone has everything. Go up to the Wardrobe Department and delegate finding/making of the desired items to your staff members. Check all staff are happy with their set tasks and then head down to tech rehearsal. Throughout the day sit with the designer and take notes of desired changes regarding Wardrobe. If there are Dressers working on the production, check they are aware of any changes and on occasion oversee any quick changes that are causing problems. 10.00pm Go home! There are generally some gaps to grab food but it is certainly not unheard of to go entire day living on snatched biscuits and scalding coffee!

Have you done any additional training courses to further your career?

I haven't done any additional training courses but many interest me and I hope to perhaps be able to attend some in future.

How important is working for free at the beginning of your career?

Very important. As I said earlier, I would recommend working for free for a year rather than doing a three year degree. It will leave you with less debt and will be vastly more profitable to you in the future.

Make-up Artist

Make-up Artists use face paint, body paint, prosthetics, and cosmetics to create visual effects and looks to suit the characters.

Wigs Assistant

The Wigs Assistant helps the other members of the wig department to prepare, dress and maintain wigs for performance.

We asked Stage Jobs Pro member Lee Appleton the following questions about working as a Make-up Artist/Wigs Assistant:

What is the most rewarding aspect of working as a Make-up Artist/Wigs Assistant?
Wow it's impossible to pick just one! Being part of a creative process and a bigger team effort.
When the most simple thing is really effective – like shading in exactly the right spot, or an ultra realistic bruise that makes people look twice! Finding solutions and delivering the brief. And then there are the happy accidents along the way! You are constantly developing yourself, your technical skills, the way you handle pressure, mastering something you thought you couldn't do.
The people you meet, the variety of the work. I suppose ultimately it's extremely lucky to get paid doing something you have a passion for.

What are the key skills required to be an effective Make-up Artist/Wigs Assistant?
Aside from technical skills I'd say the absolute key is to be able to work well with people – sounds obvious, but in a team it's vital. Also to be reliable, tactful, discreet, patient, sensitive, thoughtful, persistent, resourceful, efficient, quick-thinking, know how to get the best out of your kit and, when faced with stress or long hours, a positive attitude. A smile goes a long way.

Do you see your role as a natural step on a career ladder, and if so what is the next rung?
Yes and no. I came to make-up relatively late (mid 30's) and I studied Fashion/Editorial so I feel as if I'm always playing catch up in the TV/ Theatrical world. I've had to learn on the job and there is SO much to learn – new techniques, new products, different working practices across the industry. I've worked at both Assistant and Designer level and I'm happy to work at any level – each job is an opportunity to gain experience and and a chance to meet a connection to the next job! I would like to work more with Wigs and Prosthetics and be a permanent Wig/Make-up Technician at a major theatre.

How did you work your way into your current role?
I was working as Hair & Make-up Designer on a TV production and over two seasons I became really good friends with the Costume Department girls. They all worked in theatre as well and I asked them to let me know if any Make-up jobs came up as I'd love to try theatre work. Months later I got a text saying there was an opening and to go for it. I didn't hesitate –

although I knew I didn't have all the technical skills they were looking for, I found a personal recommendation goes a long way.

How much do you think networking helps towards landing a job in the industry?
It's hugely important to network. Always have your business cards on you, but hand them out to the right people. Social networking has really changed the way we can get our work out there and also the access we have to potential employers. I made my own simple website just to have an online portfolio people can reference and I'm really active on Twitter and Instagram BUT don't forget your work and how you work with others will be your biggest selling point – not a cool website! ALL my jobs have come about through word of mouth, chance meetings and working well.

Do you think you will be working in the industry in the next five years, and if so in what capacity?
I hope to be yes, hopefully in a permanent Wigs/Make-up Tech role in a major theatre.

Please describe what a typical day working as a Make-up Artist/Wigs Assistant might contain?
Preparation – Preparation – Preparation!!! Check and address any notes from the previous show. Prep Wigs/pieces and prosthetic pieces. Check make-up/toiletries/laundry supplies. Prep work station, switch on any electricals. Make sure actors are in the chair at their call time. Actors into hair & make-up. Check notes and prep for cues. SHOWTIME! Interval is either a busy make-up time or a chance to grab a cup of tea and clean some brushes! SHOWTIME!

Show comes down and the next phase of work begins. Take off wigs/pieces/ prosthetics. Actors will usually clean their own make-up off unless it requires special remover like facial hair. Clean work station, brushes, towels into laundry. Prep work station for the next show. Set Wigs/pieces/prosthetics for the next show. Write up notes (problems/stock/requests) for next show. Hang up apron and go home!

Have you done any additional training courses to further your career?
No, just learning on the job and if, there's any down time, asking colleagues questions or to show me things I don't know. Also practice, research (I LOVE doing research!) and exploring my own ideas – YouTube is an amazing learning tool.

How important is working for free at the beginning of your career?
While you're studying yes it's a great way to learn about the working

environment, the etiquette, the terminology/language and also to make contacts. Then once you establish yourself do some research into Freelancing/Self Employment/Day rates etc and start to value your time and skills: BE BRAVE AND GET PAID!

Wig Maker

The Wig Maker creates wigs for a performance.

We asked Stage Jobs Pro member Cath Newton the following questions about working as a Wig Maker:

What is the most rewarding aspect of working as a Wig Maker?
I love seeing my wigs on stage, it's so rewarding seeing the artists wearing my wigs when they are in full make-up and costume.

What are the key skills required to be an effective Wig Maker?
You have to be a good communicator and have a keen eye and attention to detail but, above all, patience. It takes time and practice to build your knotting speed up, so patience is key.

Do you see your role as a natural step on a career ladder, and if so what is the next rung?
As a freelance wig maker I use out-knotters as necessary. The next progression would be building my business to employ more knotters. Another option would be working for a large theatre who do in house wig making.

How did you work your way into your current role?
I did a City and Guilds in Wig Making, then started working backstage in theatre doing wigs and make-up. From this I made lots of contacts and my wig making business started.

How much do you think networking helps towards landing a job in the industry?
Networking and word of mouth is extremely important. Lots of jobs, especially wig making, aren't advertised so knowing industry people is vital.

Do you think you will be working in the industry in the next five years, and if so in what capacity?
Yes, I love my work. I also do costume as I like the variety of work, so within the next five years I'll be working in costume for TV and I'd love to make more wigs for film and TV as well as theatre.

Please describe what a typical day working as a Wig Maker might contain?
Typical day would be discussing requirements with designers. Then meeting the artist, doing head wraps and foundation fittings. However most of my time is spent wig knotting, as this is the most time consuming part of the job.

Have you done any additional training courses to further your career?
Yes, I've done further training courses with Wigs Up North. It's important to keep your skills up to date and it's also a way of making new contacts and other people seeing your abilities.

How important is working for free at the beginning of your career?
Very, it's a great way of making contacts. Also it shows industry peers how capable you are, plus what you learn from others can be invaluable.

Wig Supervisor

The Wig Supervisor (also known as the Wig Master/Mistress) manages the wigs department: overseeing budgets and the other wigs assistants, and communicating with other departments.

We asked Stage Jobs Pro member Linzi Bowen the following questions about working as a Wig Mistress:

What is the most rewarding aspect of working as a Wig Mistress?
Managing a fantastic team on a great show. And to be involved in the creative process, with the Designer, on a brand new production.

What are the key skills required to be an effective Wig Mistress?
The key skills required to be an effective Wig Mistress are utilising your professional training and prior experience to confidently manage a team. Following a thorough training period, steadily working up from an Assistant to Deputy Wig Mistress, then enables you to develop the skills required to competently become the Head of Wigs Department.

Do you see your role as a natural step on a career ladder, and if so what is the next rung?

Usually a Wigs Mistress would progress to becoming a Wigs Supervisor then Designer. However, as making wigs is not my primary skill, this is not a career path that I would chose to pursue. For me the next step, having now spent many years working in Theatre, is to establish a career in TV, where I am more likely to be able to utilise my skills in both hair and make-up, rather than just predominantly in wigs.

How did you work your way into your current role?

Initially, I trained as a Hairdresser/Beauty Therapist, working in this field for a year before making the decision to focus instead on becoming involved in Theatre and TV as a Hair/Make-up Artist. I lined up work experience at my local theatres, studied Art and Biology A' Levels then went on to complete a HND course at The London College Of Fashion in Specialist Make-up. After graduating, I was employed as a Wig Assistant by the Royal Shakespeare Company for a 6 month season, enabling me to gain valuable experience, from senior artists, in working with hair, wigs, make-up and special effects before then embarking on a career in the West End. After several years working in London, progressing from Wig Assistant to Deputy, I elected to travel and work overseas in Australia, where I landed my dream job at Sydney Opera House. When I eventually returned to the UK, to resume my career in London, I periodically worked with the RSC, took on some TV work and managed the Wigs Department on several West End Musicals, Plays and Touring Productions. In more recent years, I have worked as a Wigs Tutor, ventured back into a career in TV and spent a season working at Glyndebourne Opera Festival.

How much do you think networking helps towards landing a job in the industry?

I do think that networking helps towards landing a job in the industry, although it is not something that I readily engage in. However, it is a very competitive field, with more and more training schools opening thus more graduates each year competing for the best jobs. Therefore, contacts are vital, especially in the early stages of your career.

Do you think you will be working in the industry in the next five years, and if so in what capacity?

Yes absolutely. Most likely on a freelance basis in Theatre, Opera and TV, both here and overseas, having recently returned from a year in South America establishing contacts there, for future employment. I would also like to pursue more teaching opportunities.

Please describe what a typical day working as a Wig Mistress might contain?

A typical day working as a Wigs Mistress involves managing the department and liaising with the other Department Heads in preparation for the next performance. Additional responsibilities could include providing wigs/make-up for an Understudy performance or publicity shoot, scheduling wig fittings for a cast change, arranging haircuts for the cast and generally overseeing the daily wig maintenance, schedule working hours/holiday and to monitor any stock requirements for the production. Working hours vary depending on the scale of the production and are largely determined by the level of maintenance required of any given day. Typically, on a normal show day the department may start at 1pm and work through until curtain down. On a matinee day, 11am is an average start time, with a 10.30pm finish. The majority of West End productions have a working week Monday through to Saturday, 8 shows per week with 2 matinees. Though in more recent years, a production may include a Sunday performance, rather than a Monday.

Initially, when a production is set up, the Wig Mistress allocates wigs to each member of the team to be responsible for maintaining on a daily basis. At the start of the working day, the wigs are cleaned and assessed to see if they require redressing or resetting. Checks are made for any repairs that may be required. Any wigs that require washing and resetting are done first to allow time for them to dry and take the set/style. The rest of the wigs are then redressed until everything is ready for the next performance. The Wig Mistress traditionally tends to look after the lead actors and will therefore be responsible for preparing them for the show, while the Deputy and Assistant(s) cover the Ensemble members of the acting company. During the half hour call, the actors are prepped for their wigs or alternatively their own hair is styled. Once the show is up and running the team, along with a member of the Wardrobe Department, follow their cue sheet/track notes to cover any changes to the appearance of their designated actors. At the end of the performance, the wigs are all collected up and returned to the department to be prepared for the next day.

Have you done any additional training courses to further your career?

Yes. I try to incorporate additional training courses whenever I'm between jobs. As it's a fair few years since I graduated from LCF, I polish up my skills periodically with short refresher courses. I see this as an essential method of keeping up to date with developments in the industry, therefore ensuring that I am as employable as possible.

How important is working for free at the beginning of your career?

I don't necessarily agree that working for free is important at the beginning of your career, rather you should try to gain as much experience as possible, unpaid or otherwise, before approaching established organisations for employment. For example, there are numerous websites that advertise for crew for short films etc. While these positions are often unpaid or low pay, they can potentially offer a fantastic opportunity to gain valuable experience and develop contacts for future work. With the benefit of work experience, newcomers to the industry can certainly improve their chances of securing employment in their chosen field.

However in the first instance, I firmly believe that choosing the right training school is the most significant priority. Some are more established than others and careful consideration should always be given when selecting the one you wish to attend. If possible, visit the school beforehand and speak with the tutors. Check what courses are offered and what facilities are available. Obviously the financial costs of training must also be factored into the choice and whether that dictates a preference for a short course of a few weeks/months or a longer course with the training offered over one or two years. Each method of study has positive and negative aspects. But as someone who has worked in the industry for a considerable number of years, I can honestly say that the required skills are not learned overnight. A certificate is no match for experience. So wherever you chose, chose wisely.

So You Want To Be A Make-Up Artist
NASMAH

NASMAH

L ife as a professional make-up artist is hard, erratic, challenging, exciting, varied – and extremely competitive!

So You Want To Be A Make-Up Artist?
Many people unfortunately assume that being a make-up artist will lead to a glamorous future. However the hours and working conditions, in most cases, are long and hard – and even the most thorough training cannot ensure a successful career.

Competition for jobs is fierce and there are only so many industry jobs out there. Despite all this, you may wish to find out more.

What Areas To Work In?
There are different areas in the media in which a make-up artist can work: film, television, theatre, editorial, fashion and so on. Some areas are similar and others are quite different and require specific training, though the core skills and elements (like health and safety) are the same.

An Overview Of The Job
The hair and make-up department is responsible for the design, application, continuity and care of hair and make-up during a production. It ensures that actors, performers, presenters, models and others have suitable make-up and hairstyles before they appear in front of the cameras or an audience (be it for television, film, theatre, catwalk or photographic) and that the looks are maintained.

Some productions or types of work have separate hair and make-up departments, but for many jobs you would be expected to have both hair and make-up skills. There are also specialist areas like body painting, wig making, prosthetics, making contact lenses and making teeth.

Key Skills
These are just some of the key skills and attributes you need to be a good make-up artist:

- Make-up skills including corrective, glamour, period and ageing
- Specialised techniques, e.g. making and applying bald caps, applying and dressing facial hair, creating casualty effects (burns, skin diseases, cuts, scars etc), tattoos and body art
- Hair and wig dressing
- Continuity hair cutting
- Good communication and diplomacy skills
- Good organisational and presentation skills
- Ability to work effectively as part of a team as well as having initiative when working unsupervised
- Ability to work under pressure to external and departmental deadlines
- The right attitude and work ethic
- Willingness to work long and often unsocial hours
- Knowledge of the relevant Health and Safety legislation and procedures – and good working practices and hygiene.

"Some productions or types of work have separate hair and make-up departments, but for many jobs you would be expected to have both hair and make-up skills"

Training & Experience
To start down the road of becoming a media make-up artist:
- Completing a good foundation training course in media make-up is important
- Getting good on-the-job experience and training is vital
- Hairdressing is also an important skill for most areas of make-up. Completing an NVQ in hairdressing is advisable

How Do I Find A Course?
There are lots of foundation courses out there. With a little persistence and research you should find the right one for you. The NASMAH website has a 'Find a Course' section for further help and guidance.

Who Runs Make-Up Courses?
As an association we do not endorse or recommend any school or college. Many of our members run their own courses and private schools advertise

courses in most women's and fashion magazines (though these courses are not subsidised). Many Local Authority colleges also run media courses which often include both make-up and hairdressing.

What To Look For In A Course
Make-up artistry and hairdressing are hands-on professions and, therefore, have to be taught in a classroom environment:

- Live models should be used (even if you just practice on each other) for as much of the course as possible.
- Tutors should be readily on hand to offer guidance, assistance and criticism
- Look at what the tutors have done within the industry itself. Many may be qualified to teach, but do they have proper and substantial industry experience?

Doing a course does not guarantee you a career in make-up! Some colleges do not emphasise how hard it often is to get (and keep getting) work, and may even promise you a glittering career if you train with them. NO ONE can guarantee this.

Career Path
Doing a make-up course does not make you a make-up artist! There is a career progression and it takes time to gain the right experience to progress.

After completing a foundation training course, you are a trainee. There is still much for you to learn, not only about hair and make-up but about how a production works, set ettiquette, continuity and so on – things that a course can only teach in theory.

After being a trainee you progress to being an assistant and, after several years of solid experience, you may then be considered a make-up artist.

Being a film or television make-up designer takes many years of experience and NASMAH cannot stress this enough – simply doing a make-up course does not make you a designer!

You never stop learning and developing your skills.
NASMAH is a professional, social and educational organisation who encourage the highest standards in the craft of media hair and make-up, and work hard to promote their members. You can find more information at **www.nasmah.co.uk**

Storytelling with Costume and Make-up

NATALIE BROWN, PROGRAMME DIRECTOR FOR PERFORMANCE AT LONDON COLLEGE OF FASHION

When the curtain goes up, or the opening film credits pass, the audience is transported into a different world. The opening visual image you see has been carefully constructed to allow you to quickly understand the world and the character that inhabits it. You are introduced to the character with subtle clues that indicate who they are, what job they do, how old they are, what social class they are, what their mood is and what their psychological and physical state is. You make assumptions about their personality, emotions and their history within the first scene. All of this information is passed on, seemingly without the audience even noticing that these visual clues have registered.

Costume and make-up designers collaborate with the director, production designer and actors to help to tell the story to an audience. Firstly, the designer will work with the director and production designer to understand the overall vision of the piece. Having a shared understanding of the character's histories and the style of the piece will enable them to create and realise characters that will come to life and are believable, look right and 'fit'. You don't always notice a good costume or make-up design, but you always notice a bad one. Costume and make-up designers are part of the storytelling toolbox, and the story for the designer always begins with character.

The designers will study the script, calculating who is in each scene, what happens and when it happens. They will also make detailed research into the world the character inhabits, the location and time period. The designers will need to know every detail about each character and their story, who says what about each character and what clues the script offers about their personality. The characters will become like best friends, every habit, every detail religiously studied.

Research gathering for a character is one of the most exciting parts of design. When you first read a script you may have some ideas, but like a foggy dream, you can not always see the piece clearly. You need to go out and discover the character, and you can't do this by working with your imagination alone. You need to search, gather and explore.

111

For your primary research, you may need to visit galleries and relevant locations: you may need to draw from objects or paintings looking for colour, textures, and shapes. You could interview people or collect interesting fabrics and textures. Another good source is vintage clothing and fabrics from charity shops or jumble sales. Unpick the clothes to understand how they are created. You could embody the character, live their life, visit the places they would visit, shop where they would shop, eat and drink where they would, observe and photograph people. For secondary research you could look at personal photographs, read firsthand written accounts, seek out pictures of social life and entertainment events, watch documentaries, read historical text books and descriptions in literary publications, look at postcards, newspapers or satirical cartoons from the period. Magazines are a fantastic source for both contemporary and period advertisements and articles. These will give you clues as to what products were available to buy. Portrait paintings will give you clues for colour, style, texture and silhouette as well as hair and make-up of the day. Look at antiques sales catalogues, social event information, posters, archives; what were the available products and dyes? What was happening in politics, science and industry?

"You need to become a people watcher and observer to understand the identity and story clues we all emit"

You need to become a people watcher and observer to understand the identity and story clues we all emit. Next time you are on train, look at the person opposite you. What are they wearing, how do they wear their hair, why do they wear their coat like that? Is that bangle a gift? What does that brown stain on their left elbow come from? Create a story around the person. Who are they, where have they been? How do you know?

Once all of the research is gathered, you can start to inhabit the world of your characters and start to build an image of what they may look like in each scene. What sort of shoes would they wear? What colour would they choose? Why have they chosen that? What have they done before they arrive in the scene?

Actors play a large part in your design process. You are collaborating with them to create a believable person. You may want to restrict their movements to enhance the character, or you may need to add padding to

create a different silhouette. (But it's no good designing a huge brim on a hat if you can't see their face!) Your actor has to feel comfortable and has to leave the dressing room feeling completely at ease, stress free and ready to perform and inhabit the character.

As a costume or make-up designer you have to have oodles of patience. You need to be able to listen carefully and be prepared to negotiate and compromise. The role requires collaboration skills within a team as you will never be working in isolation.

Choose a book or a play, and start to create your own character design using your own investigative research.

The guide was kindly written by Natalie Brown, the Programme Director for Performance at London College of Fashion. London College of Fashion offers performance design degrees in costume, 3D effects and make-up. For more information please go to **www.fashion.arts.ac.uk/courses** *or call on +44 (0)20 7514 7344.*

A Day in The Life: Head of Wigs & Make-up

JO SMEDLEY

I am currently Head of Wigs & Make-up on Dirty Dancing at the Piccadilly Theatre, London. My role is to organise a team of 4 full time and 3 part-time staff to create and maintain the hair and make-up looks on every show for the cast that are performing. The production is set in the 1960's so we work to a period look.

We have around 40 wigs which we set and style for each show. The looks are different for each wig depending on the character. Some artists have more than one wig so we can create different looks or change them into a different character for certain parts of the show.

Wigs are used in theatre to develop an artist into a role. They are designed for quick changes into different characters and to hide microphones during the show. Some artists have their own hair styled and in addition to this we also give them a full aged make-up look to age them into an older role.

A typical day will entail coming into the theatre in the early evening. My team and I will begin to style the wigs to the particular designs. We will have prepared the wigs and hairpieces into rollers the evening before so they can be moulded into the styles required.

35 minutes before the show begins I go to the dressing room of the principal actress playing one of the lead roles. I have 30 minutes to transform her into her character. This time can sometimes be less should they have rehearsals or a note session from the director. It's an added pressure but that's the fun of theatre, it is fast paced and you learn your trade to a high standard and in speedy time.

For this particular character I hide her own hair underneath a stocking and place her microphone into the wig. I attach the wig with a fine lace that is on the front of the wig and this is stuck using surgical glue. I place hair pins in the required places to keep the wig securely placed on. With a show such as Dirty Dancing you have to be 100% sure that a wig or piece is attached correctly, as when a dancer is upside down and spinning there is no room for error.

5 minutes before the beginning of the show I will go down to the stage wings. I check all members of the cast before they go on stage. It's down to

me to keep the show's designs to a high standard, even if it's just checking that the male members have had a shave!

During the course of the show there are many costume changes backstage and the team are in the wings during scene changes to change wigs for different characters.

We have two acts and during the interval I go to the dressing room of my leading lady and check her look, re-style, powder and do whatever it takes to keep her looking the same throughout the show.

During the second act of the show is when I do paperwork: mainly ordering and checking stock levels.

When the show has finished I go and collect the wigs and hairpieces which we then set into rollers ready for the next day. I spray tan cast members one evening a week. Each theatre is different and it's often hard to find extra space so we currently have our spray tan tent underneath the stage in the orchestra pit.

We have 8 shows a week and although we have the same show to get ready every day it can differ so much. Dancers get injured and we have understudies who all have different looks depending on what they look like.

To train for this position I did a degree at the London College of Fashion in Make-up for the Performing Arts. As a graduate I threw myself into the industry and gained lots of work experience, contacting theatres and production companies and going in to see how things worked. I was fortunate enough to get offered a full time position on The Lion King theatrical production and my career started from there.

I worked in many different positions and shows as an assistant and gradually worked my way up. It is a thoroughly enjoyable job and I appreciate loving coming into the theatre for a show.
Jo's website: ***www.joannasmedley.com***

Set, Scenery & Props

"Working as a props supervisor is rewarding because of the variety of work. You're always working on different styles/era of production and with different designers and directors, and there's no set structure to your day."

Scenic Artist

The Scenic Artist paints and decorates all parts of the set, working from a scale model to make the set identical to the Set Designer's plans.

We asked Stage Jobs Pro member Laura O'Connell the following questions about working as a Scenic Artist:

What is the most rewarding aspect of working as a Scenic Artist?
I can't pick just one, but most significant personally is having a constant creative outlet. I feel very lucky to be earning a living doing something I love. The diversity of the work, the problems to solve, and the interesting people you work alongside mean the job is constantly stimulating. And the curtain going up on opening night is still a buzz.

What are the key skills required to be an effective Scenic Artist?
Artistic skill: excellent painting and drawing ability, and adaptability of technique and style. Communication: understanding a designer's language and being able to understand and interpret their ideas effectively; liaising with other departments; the ability to get along with different people with different ways of working and to work as an efficient member of a team when necessary. A 'good eye': an understanding of art, design and architecture and their histories. Stamina: it can be a physically demanding (and sometimes physically precarious) job. Days can be long, weekends and holidays can be lost, but the payoff is unexpected days off. Seeing everyday as a school day: observing your surroundings, buildings, trees (you paint a lot of trees), how light hits objects, etc. You never stop learning from others in this job: everyone you work with will have done at least one thing you haven't. The best piece of practical advice I was ever given was from David Perry who told me to always use a bigger brush than you think you're going to need. Experimentation: there are many ways of producing certain effects but that doesn't mean you won't find another. Problem solving: making things bigger; making things fit; making things stick; making things

convincing; making things shine; making things match ... And decent maths skills help. Good tea making: don't be afraid to offer to make a brew. You'll get asked back.

Do you see your role as a natural step on a career ladder, and if so what is the next rung?
I don't see where I am as a 'step'. My work is so varied that it is still satisfying after fifteen years.

How did you work your way into your current role?
I graduated Uni with a BA in Theatre Design and an MA in Scenography. I used contacts I'd made through work experience during my studies to get bits of work helping out on small shows until I started getting regular work with a large scenic company, at first doing everything from cleaning buckets, sewing, gluing, mixing paint until, eventually, painting. Meeting other freelance scenics and showing skill and willing led to other jobs elsewhere, including work for themed attraction companies working on theme parks and visitor attractions. I then got some work with the Belgrade Theatre in Coventry and loved being part of a producing house. The then Deputy Scenic Artist moved on and I applied for, and was given, the job until I progressed to Head of Scenic Art. I left to live and work (painting copies and murals for a bar) in South America for a while and when I returned to the UK I decided to go freelance. Since then I have worked all over for theatres, scenic companies, museums, theme parks, bands, private homes, a bit of kids' TV, one film and a Turkish aquarium. For the last four years I have also been designing sets and costumes.

How much do you think networking helps towards landing a job in the industry?
It's vital. It doesn't come naturally to a lot of artists, but it must be done. Back it up with skill and hard work and you shouldn't have a problem finding work. Contact theatres and (more so these days) scenic studios/set building companies with a CV or website link, and follow this up – but don't nag. There's a fine line between persistence and pestering.

Do you think you will be working in the industry in the next five years, and if so in what capacity?
Absolutely. I can't imagine not doing it. (Funding willing and providing the printers don't take over.) I'd like my plan for my own scenic studio to come to fruition within the next five years.

Please describe what a typical day working as a Scenic Artist might contain?
Anything from painting a wooden door to look like a different type of wood, to being up a fully extended cherry picker with a spray gun. A typical day

at the start of a set build though may involve: a production meeting to discuss the design, studying the model in order to asses time allocation and materials needed, ordering paint and producing samples. Then comes pinning cloths, mixing colours and textures, scaling things up and drawing out, priming and basing. Next could be graining, marbling, a 12m wide tropical island scene, thousands (literally) of bricks, trompe l'oeil, crumbling plaster, rust, glittering, intricate detailing or actually throwing paint. And that's the joy of the job.

Have you done any additional training courses to further your career?
There's no substitute for experience. I've had to do things like obtaining a scissor lift ticket, first aid etc, but nothing other than that. There are some great scenic art courses around that didn't exist when I was studying and it's fantastic that the art is valued enough for them to exist now. But, I do think it's vital to remember that no course will teach you everything and that you will continue learning, every day, whether through trial and error or from learning from the experience of others.

How important is working for free at the beginning of your career?
I don't agree with it in principle. Graduates accrue more than enough debt these days without having to give their time and skill for no financial gain. If you feel it's your only route to gain experience/exposure then my advice would be to first question the likelihood of it leading to further employment. Question why the employer is not offering pay; if they are a small theatre company lacking decent funding then there's some justification, but if they're a decent sized scenic company wanting a trial then make sure you know exactly how much of your time is required for free before you start. In my opinion, it's better to wash buckets in a paintshop for a week, learning from the other scenics and getting paid than it is to paint a cloth for nothing.

Set Designer
Set Designers develop and design a scale model or scale drawings of the set for a production.

We asked Stage Jobs Pro member Bek Palmer the following questions about working as a Set Designer:

What is the most rewarding aspect of working as a Set Designer?
It is a hugely creative job and has the benefit of always being a collaboration with other inspiring people. It is also fantastic to see your ideas become reality and seeing other people inhabit your creations and bringing new ideas, doing something unexpected, with what you have given them.

What are the key skills required to be an effective Set Designer?
Communication, through many mediums: conversations, drawings, models.

Do you see your role as a natural step on a career ladder, and if so what is the next rung?
Yes, it has taken a long time to make the step up to this from fringe theatre. I would like the next step to be productions where there are proper departments to work with to realise my designs.

How did you work your way into your current role?
I studied Theatre Design at degree level and then worked in youth theatre and community theatre, designing alongside working as a propmaker and wardrobe mistress to support myself. I then went back to college to retrain at postgrad level as I didn't feel my traditional design skills were at the same level as other people at my stage in their career. I then began in London designing for fringe theatre and assisting established designers. Through contacts made during this period I got involved with larger theatre companies as an assistant and then designer.

How much do you think networking helps towards landing a job in the industry?
I feel it is essential. Other than one design job which I got through the traditional interview process, all jobs have come through people I have met on other jobs or met whilst networking.

Do you think you will be working in the industry in the next five years, and if so in what capacity?
I hope to still be working as a designer but more established.

Please describe what a typical day working as a Set Designer might contain?
It is hugely varied. It could be researching a particular period or another artist's work, making 1:25 scale furniture, drawing ideas for characters, making a puppet, filming something for projections ... every day seems to be different which is one of the great parts of the job.

Have you done any additional training courses to further your career?
Well, I did the Postgraduate Diploma in Theatre Design at RWCMD five years after my degree. I also did a short course in puppetry and object manipulation as that is my specialist area of interest. I regularly take part in drawing courses to improve my skills there.

How important is working for free at the beginning of your career?
I have found it really useful in some cases, and it has led to paid work. This

is not always the case. It is only useful to do free work as long as you are gaining experience or making contacts. Some jobs feel like they do neither and are just taking advantage of free labour, in which case it's best not to continue with them for too long as they are preventing you from doing something more beneficial.

Carpenter

Carpenters work with wood to create stage components, props, and set.

We asked Stage Jobs Pro member Frankie Tolmie the following questions about working as a Carpenter:

What is the most rewarding aspect of working as a Carpenter?
Seeing a concept turn into a drawing and then seeing that drawing come to life by the work of your own hands. Once you see that piece of set/scenery up on the stage you feel very proud of what you have achieved.

What are the key skills required to be an effective Carpenter?
You need training or a good detailed background in woodwork, a hands-on attitude and good communication skills. If you get a chance to crew backstage you will also find this a great advantage in understanding what is involved and expected of a Scenic/Production Carpenter.

Do you see your role as a natural step on a career ladder, and if so what is the next rung?
Yes, I enjoy my job as a Scenic Carpenter as I get a lot out of it and feel it is something at which I excel. At the moment I am happy getting stuck in, whether it be building the set or going out as a Production Carpenter and fitting them up. I guess the next step would be either a Chargehand in a scenery workshop or as a Master Carpenter in a theatre.

How did you work your way into your current role?
I was crewing on stage in two of my local venues as a casual whilst undertaking an apprenticeship in construction site carpentry after I gained my NVQ level 1-2. I continued working on construction sites and working in theatre casually until I decided I'd like to progress to working in theatre full time, so I applied and got a trial building for a London- based set company and have never looked back.

How much do you think networking helps towards landing a job in the industry?

I think networking is very important in this industry. Networking can be the difference between a really successful career or just a mediocre one. The more people you meet and impress with your skills and work ethic, the more work you are likely to be offered.

Do you think you will be working in the industry in the next five years, and if so in what capacity?

Yes, I think I will still be in a similar position building sets, and occasionally going out as a Production Chippy. But if the opportunity arises and I feel it's right, I may be on the next step of the ladder as a Deputy/Master Carpenter or Chargehand in a workshop – only time will tell.

Please describe what a typical day working as a Carpenter might contain?

Production meetings discussing the building or fitting-up or a show. Workshop time actually getting your hands to do what they do best and show off your skills in producing a piece of set/scenery/props you will be proud of. You could also be overseeing and instructing on the load in and fit-up of a set/show in a venue.

Have you done any additional training courses to further your career?

I did a rigging course. I have found it useful to understand the components and different types of rigging when it comes to working with, and producing, bits of scenery which will be in the flown.

How important is working for free at the beginning of your career?

Working for free can be useful if you are gaining the knowledge and experience and not being used as cheap/free labour.

Set Builder

The Set Builder uses the designs of the Set Designer to set components.

We asked Stage Jobs Pro member Nathan James the following questions about working as a Set Builder:

What is the most rewarding aspect of working as a Set Builder?
The different challenges that arise from different designs. They allow you to be creative with your materials and mean no job is same.

What are the key skills required to be an effective Set Builder?
Adaptability. Understanding the context of a design or what you're making, and the limitations of the materials you're using. Good teamwork and enthusiasm. Good workshop practice and health and safety.

Do you see your role as a natural step on a career ladder, and if so what is the next rung?
I don't think this career is very linear, but with greater understanding and experience comes bigger, more ambitious builds.

How did you work your way into your current role?
I searched for jobs, contacted a set building company and slowly built up a client base that kept me busy in a freelance capacity.

How much do you think networking helps towards landing a job in the industry?
Networking is very important but one of the hardest things to do for someone new to the industry. I think actually meeting people is the key. A face is a lot harder to forget than an email. If possible arrange a visit with a potential employer to show your CV/portfolio rather than send a standard email.

Do you think you will be working in the industry in the next five years, and if so in what capacity?
I'm certain I will be working in the industry in five years due to my love for the job and not wanting to do anything else.

Please describe what a typical day working as a Set Builder might contain?
A typical working day really depends on the build. It can be creating a cutting list, pre-fitting scenery together, making something from scratch,

working out a problem, or doing the finishing touches. Every day is different and something unexpected often comes up.

Have you done any additional training courses to further your career?
I did a BTEC in performing arts/production and then went on to do the scenic arts degree at Rose Bruford before starting out as a freelance set builder.

How important is working for free at the beginning of your career?
I don't think people have to work for free to enter this career. When considering any job you weigh up the pros and cons. A pro could be that this potentially leads to other work, in which case – if there is a high chance and you can afford it – it may be worth your while. At the same time don't sell yourself short. Often people have paid to get skills for the arts. Try not to give those skills out too freely.

Prop Maker

Prop Makers create the props – the objects seen and used in a production.

We asked Stage Jobs Pro member Chiok Li the following questions about working as a Prop Maker:

What is the most rewarding aspect of working as a Prop Maker?
Working on some of the most interesting and detailed aspects of a film shoot. Good props make a story seem possible and great props make it come to life. Anything that is handled is a prop and most of the time they will be generic everyday items. But every so often you'll get the opportunity to design and make something that no one will have ever seen before, and that is the greatest reward.

What are the key skills required to be an effective Prop Maker?
A diverse mix of fabrication skills and an awareness of techniques are required to work out how a design on paper can be made into a 3D object. So you should learn the basics of wood, metal, fibreglass, sculpting, casting, material knowledge, painting etc. Experience will come when you can look at a drawing and identify what materials and processes can be used to create it. Being good with a hot glue gun always helps.

Do you see your role as a natural step on a career ladder, and if so what is the next rung?
A prop maker post can be seen as the goal: it is the stage where a person will be hands-on and responsible for the build. Like an artist, it is your hand that shapes the creation and it will always be your work. There are further roles available (prop master, standby props or property warehouse manager), but you always want to be the person making the things.

How did you work your way into your current role?
I came into the role sideways from a degree in mechanical engineering. Using the engineering skills I had and learning new skills in my own time, I created a variety of props and models to demonstrate my skills and compiled a portfolio which I show to employers as an example of my abilities. I always enjoyed making things and watching films so it was nice that there is a job which combines the two.

How much do you think networking helps towards landing a job in the industry?
Pretty much essential. If you work freelance for yourself, you need to be on people's radar to have work offered to you. Employers will only advertise crew positions if they don't already have the right person in mind. So it should be your aim to be the right person for their job and show how you alone can benefit the production. It always helps to be in the front of people's minds when they think a prop needs making. Having business cards and a website will always help. The other option is to work for a props production company. Most employees are still freelance, but work on the projects acquired by the company who generally have more power in gaining contracts and so work is more constant. The downside is that you won't always get individual credit and see the final product to the end.

Do you think you will be working in the industry in the next five years, and if so in what capacity?

I hope to always be making things in some capacity and with greater experience comes bigger and more impressive jobs. Working freelance has the benefits of freedom but no assurance of constant work, so the other goal would be to become a production manager for a props warehouse where you would be responsible for other prop makers but still create things from time to time, with the safety of a salary.

Please describe what a typical day working as a Prop Maker might contain?

Liaise with the clients regarding their opinions and decisions for the designs and how the manufacturing process is progressing. Constant communication is required to ensure that everyone is happy with the finished product so that you deliver the specified item. Generally you'll be working in a studio or workshop and continuing with the fabrication according to the plan. Plan out the work so you spend the day moulding or sculpting or painting and then leaving things at the end of the day to dry or harden so you can return the next day and continue working on it.

Have you done any additional training courses to further your career?

A lot of the work provides its own experience and training, and working with other prop makers is a great opportunity to pick up new skills. There are courses and degree programmes which will teach these skills in a credited environment but as long as you can demonstrate the same skills in your own way, only the results matter.

How important is working for free at the beginning of your career?

If you are working freelance for yourself, very important. Props are an often neglected aspect of a production and expected to be created with minimum hassle. As long as your expenses are covered, the experience of dealing with clients and their specifications is the experience to take from the project. However if an unpaid work experience programme extends further than three months, then you are being taken advantage of. Signing on with a production company is a good way to gain experience and get paid.

Props Supervisor

The Props Supervisor is in charge of the props team, responsible for supervising the development, creation, purchase, rental and use of props.

We asked Stage Jobs Pro member Celia Strange the following questions about working as a Props Supervisor:

What is the most rewarding aspect of working as a Props Supervisor?
The variety of work. You're always working on different styles/era of production and with different designers and directors, and there's no set structure to your day.

What are the key skills required to be an effective Props Supervisor?
There are a wide range of skills needed for the role due to the variety of the job, however, these are a good starting point: an understanding of art history and periods of design; attention to detail; budget management; good bartering skills; the ability to visualise and realise a drawing/design into a 3D object; understanding how props are used on stage and ensuring that they are fit for purpose; artistic and technical skills, including painting and finishing skills; maths! Whether it's managing budgets, mixing the right proportions of catalyst to resin, working out a compound angle whilst cutting a piece of wood, calculating the proportion of shrinkage whilst dying fabric or allowing enough spare fabric for a seam allowance whilst making curtains, maths is an important part of the job. And finally, good communication skills and the ability to work well under pressure and to strict deadlines.

How did you work your way into your current role?
I've worked my way up to being a Props Supervisor. I started as a freelance Prop Maker, then worked as Deputy Head of a Props Department and now work as Props Buyer and Supervisor. Each progression is important as it helps you to build the experience required to work as a Props Supervisor.

How much do you think networking helps towards landing a job in the industry?
Being good at communicating and being approachable is invaluable. The industry is a very tight network and therefore networking can be a good way to increase your contacts.

Do you think you will be working in the industry in the next five years, and if so in what capacity?
I've currently been working in theatre for twelve years. The work is hard, hours are long and the wage is not great, but I love it! I would have thought I'll still be working as a Props Supervisor/Buyer in five years time.

Please describe what a typical day working as a Props Supervisor might contain?
There is no such thing as a typical day! However within a week I would be out props buying, attending design/production meetings, talking to/meeting with prop makers and maintaining the budgets/accounts.

How important is working for free at the beginning of your career?
I didn't work for free as such at the start of my career. However I did have an appreciation that I was slower than my colleagues and therefore put in an extra couple of hours here and there that I didn't timesheet for to stay on top of the work. I also did as many work placements as I could when I was studying, generally in my half terms, which gave me a lot of valuable experience that was relevant on my CV.
Celia's website is **www.straingeprops.co.uk**.

Video/Projection Designer

Video and Projection Designers create films which are then used in theatre productions to set the scene, create a special effect or enhance the storytelling process.

We asked Stage Jobs Pro member Victor Craven the following questions about working as a Projection Designer:

What is the most rewarding aspect of working as a Projection Designer?
I love being part of the design team and using modern technology to add another dimension to the theatrical experience. I am very insistent that the projection design is used to add to the overall theatrical experience of a production. If it's not theatrical, it should not be used. It's all too easy to throw projections onto a production. It's important to remember that I am part of a team creating a piece of theatre and not a film! It's incredibly rewarding to watch a show that I have worked on when the projections are an integrated part of the overall theatrical design.

What are the key skills required to be an effective Projection Designer?
There are the obvious technical skills required such as graphic design, motion graphic design, animation creation and programming skills to design the computer systems to run the projections during performance. An understanding of the overall process of staging a production is key, as is the ability to work with the production team to service the vision of the director. Also, the willingness to cut the work you have produced if it does not work with the final production even if you may have spent many hours producing it! Seeing a lot of theatre is also important. It amazes me how often you find people that are passionate about making theatre but haven't actually seen that much!

Do you see your role as a natural step on a career ladder, and if so what is the next rung?
My work is heavily reliant on technology which is continually improving with costs coming down and the creative possibilities expanding. I see these increasing technical opportunities as my career progression. It's almost impossible to imagine where these advances will take my work.

How did you work your way into your current role?
I have been hugely passionate about theatre since seeing the National Theatre's production of Alan Ayckbourn's A Small Family Business in the late 80s. I have also been lucky enough to grow up in an exciting era of computer development and was the proud owner of a Sinclair ZX81 at the tender age of nine! Both of these passions have continued throughout my life with the huge advances in technology enabling me to teach myself video editing, graphic design and animation. After many years of creating work in my spare time, I managed to convince a large European bank that I was the ideal candidate to set up and run an in-house video production and animation department. After two years, I left the bank to set up my own company with the aim of using my skills to create work in the arts. To start with, I worked with world class orchestras creating and performing animations for live concerts. I was then asked by the Shunt collective to curate an evening of my orchestral animation work at their exciting multi-disciplinary arts space in the vaults under London Bridge. This led to my first theatrical commission to produce animations for a production of Frankenstein at the same venue, which in turn has led to a number of theatrical productions. I am so happy that my childhood passions of theatre and technology have come together in my projection design career.

How much do you think networking helps towards landing a job in the industry?
It is essential! Making theatre is very high risk. There are so many factors in any production that have the potential to bring down an entire show.

75 years
OF CONTEMPORARY
THEATRE TRAINING
1936 – 2011

BIRMINGHAM
SCHOOL OF ACTING

BIRMINGHAM CITY
University

BA (Hons) Stage Management

Do you want a course that gives you practical stage management experience from day one? Do you want to learn and be involved in all production processes, from preparation to props, rehearsal to the run itself? Our course will give you just that, as well as a six-week placement at an external, professional theatre to further enhance your employability.

Open Days held throughout the year.

www.bcu.ac.uk/bsa

drama uk
Accredited

ual: university
of the arts
london
london college
of fashion

London College of Fashion

BA (Hons) Costume For Performance
BA (Hons) Hair, Make-up and Prosthetics for Performance
BA (Hons) 3D Effects for Performance and Fashion

London College of Fashion's excellent workshops, teaching by industry practitioners and work placement opportunities will help you to succeed in roles such as 3D Effects, Costume, Hair, Make-Up and Prosthetics.

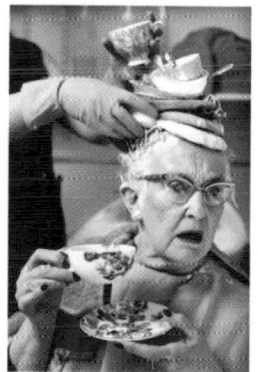

For further information visit:
www.arts.ac.uk/fashion/courses

LCF Course Enquiries
T: +44 (0)207 514 7344 / 7973
E: hello@fashion.arts.ac.uk

Image credits (clockwise from top left):
Aleksandra Kurcharska, Francesca Jordan, Eleanor Gibson, Ruth Kelly.

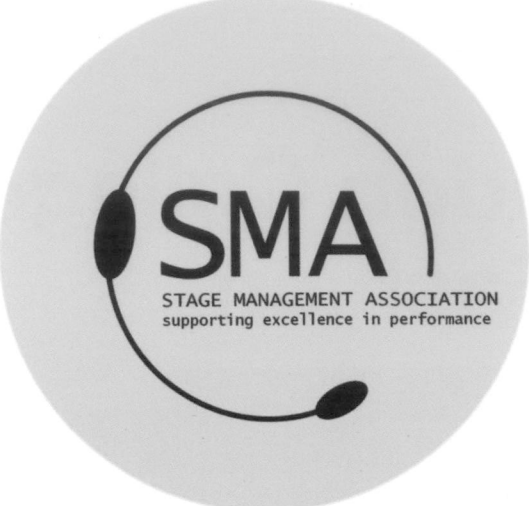

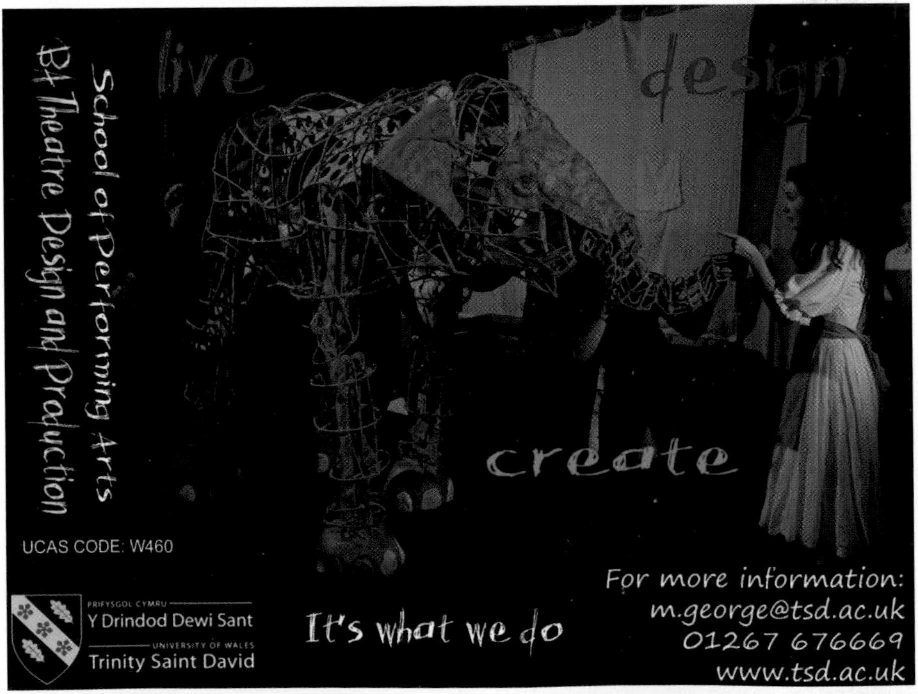
live
design
School of Performing Arts
BA Theatre Design and Production
create
UCAS CODE: W460
PRIFYSGOL CYMRU
Y Drindod Dewi Sant
UNIVERSITY OF WALES
Trinity Saint David
It's what we do
For more information:
m.george@tsd.ac.uk
01267 676669
www.tsd.ac.uk

There is a lot of trust involved. Directors, designers, producers etc all have to feel that if they engage you on a project you will be a good member of the team. Networking is not just about getting your first job. It's something that never stops. It could be the actor with a small part that you never speak to that is friends with someone important that could lead to your next high profile job. It's a fairly small world within the industry and the networks you build up will soon start to pay dividends.

Do you think you will be working in the industry in the next five years, and if so in what capacity?
I very much hope so! It's really hard to imagine where new technology will take us in just one year, so who can say where things will lead us in five years! My work will continue to evolve artistically with the new opportunities this technology offers.

Please describe what a typical day working as a Projection Designer might contain?
There are a number of stages involved with creating projection design for a theatrical production so a typical day will vary quite considerably. A large percentage of time on any project is dedicated to the design and animation of the individual projection elements. Then we move into the rehearsal process which typically involves working with the director and designer to workshop ideas for the projection designs used in the show. Ideas will often change considerably at this stage. I love this phase of the process. Then there is the tech week where all the elements are brought together using software to integrate the projection designs with the set, lighting, actors etc. This again can create new ideas and require changes to be made. The tech week is often a very intense period normally accompanied by lots of coffee and late nights!

Have you done any additional training courses to further your career?
No.

How important is working for free at the beginning of your career?
This is always a tricky one! There is so much competition and so little money in the theatre world that often this is the only way of getting a foot in the door. It's important to make sure you maximise this type of opportunity. Gain people's trust. Talk to as many people as you can. Work hard. Be part of the team. It can be as simple as being the person that someone remembers and recommends in a future meeting that can lead to that next job – and hopefully to one that is paid. It's really important to know your worth, to know when it's the right time to say no to unpaid work. Free work should be a stepping stone to gain the industry's confidence in you, not a way of life. *Victor's website is **www.10to1productions.com**.*

We asked Stage Jobs Pro member Cate Blanchard the following questions about working as a Video Designer:

What is the most rewarding aspect of working as a Video Designer?
Unlike most other strands of theatre practice, video design is widely unexplored. You make your own rules with a small team creating beautiful results!

What are the key skills required to be an effective Video Designer?
I came into video design from a set design background, so understanding the stage and the platform this creates for actors, to me, is essential. I think it's a rare skill to know when and when not to introduce a digitised image onstage; its light levels, movement and size could completely overpower that scene in the production and ruin it for the audience. A basic understanding of all stage elements is essential including direction, lighting actors and strong feelings on design aesthetic. The curiosity to produce your own content and films and the willingness to lead a team.

Do you see your role as a natural step on a career ladder, and if so what is the next rung?
I moved into video design by total chance at university, realising my interests were different to that of the other designers. My study of content creation has allowed me to teach video editing for a leading computer firm, and this year I'm also working with students at The Royal Central School of Speech and Drama advising them on their use of video in projects, so it really has gone full circle! My main goal now is becoming a leading university lecturer in my field. I wish desperately someone had been there to guide me in my training. Also, I've got a few music videos, and an exciting charity project with Autism West Midlands planned. The real thrill is never knowing where video design could take you!

How did you work your way into your current role?
I asked to take the Video Design role on a public production whilst studying. I just thrust all my knowledge and took over the theatre with TVs and cameras and thankfully the stunt paid off, people loved it and saw what a powerful and clever tool in theatre it is.

How much do you think networking helps towards landing a job in the industry?
It's essential, particularly in my line of work. Word of mouth and recommendation from other theatre practitioners is how I have attained most of my high profile jobs. Start this in your training!

Do you think you will be working in the industry in the next five years, and if so in what capacity?

Yes. People that really enjoy theatre can't really do anything else. With my current aspirations I hope to maintain my current position educating others as I find it very rewarding.

Please describe what a typical day working as a Video Designer might contain?

After meeting with the director, I'd head back to my studio to begin story-boarding. I never could quite leave my set design background behind so in the very early stages I do a lot of drawing and model box experimentation. There's a fantastic little tool on the market called a mini projector that allows me to simulate the use of video onstage much in the same way a set designer would demonstrate the set pieces. The afternoon would be spent out and about in London with a camera. Filming for me ranges from high profile cameras to my smartphone and anything that I see that could be useful goes on the harddrive! The most exciting place I've filmed content to date has been the Underwater Stage at Pinewood Film Studios, where we filmed British Olympic athletes for a theatre production in an old Victorian swimming pool! Footage acquired, it's then back for the studio for small bits of editing, then looking at equipment to use and how video will be operated during the show – I prefer to select my own team or program myself. I entered the world of video via research so I like to set aside time in the evening to learn something I didn't previously know. Just a force of habit now!

Have you done any additional training courses to further your career?

I've gained a certification in video editing program Final Cut, but the rest of my knowledge I'd say is self study and learning on the job.

How important is working for free at the beginning of your career?

I was lucky enough not to work for free due to the surge in video-based roles as I left university, but I think the most important thing is to assess the job you will be doing, the time commitment and the experience gained. I feel in the industry it's important to have a sense of self: I definitely lower my fee to work with a charity, or somewhere where people will benefit from seeing or interacting with my work. We are all doing this to make people happy and create magic.

Directing, Choreographing, Producing & Writing

"You start with a cast that know nothing, uncostumed on a blank stage. Come opening night everything is rehearsed and in place."

Director's Assistant

The Director's Assistant works with the Director to achieve their artistic vision, taking care of administrative duties, giving notes and assisting in rehearsals.

We asked Stage Jobs Pro member Hannah Drake the following questions about working as a Director's Assistant.

What is the most rewarding aspect of working as a Director's Assistant?
Probably the pastoral aspects of being a confidante to not only the director and actors, but other departments too. Being able to work with other creative people towards a common goal, and seeing the goal come to fruition.

What are the key skills required to be an effective Director's Assistant?
Discretion, patience, organisation and empathy are key, plus a positive and helpful attitude and the stamina to watch rehearsals for hours (without necessarily saying anything) and give insightful notes. But beyond that, the ability to understand fully what the director wants to achieve, and to help them do that – whether that involves research, running warm-ups, or staying quiet at the back of the rehearsal room and giving feedback at the end of the day. The most important thing is to leave your own ego as a director behind and support the production.

Do you see your role as a natural step on a career ladder, and if so what is the next rung?
Assisting offers an invaluable experience to inform your own methodology as a Director, which is my main career path. I do see it as a way of progressing my career by working with new people and companies, learning from far more experienced people and having the chance to work in theatres that are often difficult to become established in. These are the kind of relationships that can only be created over time, but are so invaluable in getting work made. However, I don't see Assisting as a step

that can be completely left behind – rather, something that I return to over time, and as new opportunities arise. There are also degrees to which you can progress as an Assistant, moving on to Associate or Resident Director on the longer West End runs, for example. But, as with most creative careers, there is no real A to Z path in Directing or Assisting.

How did you work your way into your current role?
I trained at an accredited drama school after directing a number of productions at university. At drama school I made the contacts that have led to the work I have done so far. It was while I was at drama school that I learned how to be an Assistant Director, and was fortunate to work on a variety of genres and sizes of shows. A highlight of my time there was assisting Andrew Hilton at Shakespeare at the Tobacco Factory. I have since assisted on the fringe and at the Bolton Octagon, while developing and directing my own small and mid-scale productions in the South West.

How much do you think networking helps towards landing a job in the industry?
There's no substitute – this is a people-based industry and so much matters about who you know. Not just in terms of getting a job, but also in sourcing set/props, meeting actors and writers, as well as building an audience. And while many jobs are listed on sites like Stage Jobs Pro, many are also found by word-of-mouth and recommendation, so the more people you know the greater the chance of being in the right place at the right time when that new job comes up.

Do you think you will be working in the industry in the next five years, and if so in what capacity?
Yes – it is my aim to become an associate artist to a large regional theatre.

Please describe what a typical day working as a Director's Assistant might contain?
A typical day, during a rehearsal period, might include: – pre-rehearsal briefing with the Director – running a warm up with the company (or taking part in one) – observing and noting rehearsals – running a parallel rehearsal or running lines with actors (on request from the director you might be tasked with staging or choreographing a particular scene depending on your skill set) – attending production meetings, props parades etc – doing additional research in the rehearsal room e.g. internet/computers/resources already brought in, or doing visits to local libraries or museums – liaising with the marketing department to provide information for the programme – debriefing with the director at the end of the day. Increasingly through the production period the emphasis will shift to observing and noting the show until its performance run, when you are often left to take care of the show in the director's absence.

Have you done any additional training courses to further your career?
Yes, I completed an MA in Drama Directing, and have attended a variety of
masterclasses with companies whose approaches I admire.

How important is working for free at the beginning of your career?
It is, sadly, the nature of the beast. Assisting and Directing is a skill that
has to be proven in a way that stage management (for example) doesn't.
You are judged entirely on the quality and type of work you produce, and
until you have a number of reputable credits to your name people won't
take you seriously.

Director

Directors are responsible for bringing a play from the page to the
stage: directing the actors, managing the crew, and developing a
creative vision for the play.

© DAVID PRICE

We asked Stage Jobs Pro member Andrew Hobbs the
following questions about working as a Director:

**What is the most rewarding aspect of working as a
Director?**
When you sit down to watch the first night and see how
well a show has come together. Directing isn't for those
who want to be in the spotlight or get the credit for a
great production – that's for the performers! A good
script doesn't automatically translate into a good performance, so the
director's job is to act as an effective bridge between the two, and the
rewards are in taking quiet satisfaction in your work and thinking 'I did
that!' when the crowd give a standing ovation at the end of the show.

What are the key skills required to be an effective Director?
Other than the obvious like a good knowledge of stage composition, the
ability to view the production as a whole and an in-depth understanding of
the individual parts that go into making it, the most important one for me is
people skills. To take an example, you'll get a situation where you've been
trying to get an actor to do something a certain way for an hour and they're
just not getting it, and then suddenly they'll turn round and suggest
exactly what you've been trying to explain as if it was their idea. If you're
the sort of person who can't resist saying 'I told you so' then directing isn't
for you. Instead you need to be able to say 'that's a great idea why didn't I
think of that?' and move on.

Do you see your role as a natural step on a career ladder, and if so what is the next rung?

I'm passionate about being involved in the creative process for exciting and original theatre, be it as director, writer or producer. I suppose the ultimate would be for me to have my own theatre to run where I could programme what I like, with enough funding to ease the commercial pressure of having to sell a large volume of tickets. Maybe one day!

How did you work your way into your current role?

I initially trained in directing, theatre administration, sound design and acting at university. I then went off to do a postgraduate year at drama school and went into acting. From there I became involved in producing and directing, and discovered over time that life backstage was more appealing to me than pursuing a career on it. Having my own theatre company, which I've now had going for 8 years, has given me the freedom to develop all these aspects of my career and get more and more of my writing on the stage.

How much do you think networking helps towards landing a job in the industry?

Love it or hate it, it is probably one of the most important aspects of the industry. From every level right from the tiniest pub theatre to the biggest West End venue, people naturally look to work with people they know, or people they have worked with before who have done a good job, purely for the sake of convenience and reduced risk. So put simply, the more people you know the more work you'll get.

Do you think you will be working in the industry in the next five years, and if so in what capacity?

Definitely. I'll keep my theatre companies Facsimile Productions and British Touring Shakespeare going and also continue to work as a freelance director and writer.

Please describe what a typical day working as a Director might contain?

I'll take that to mean a day of rehearsals. I'd start off by looking through the scenes that are on the schedule that day to gather my thoughts together about them. I try and come into the rehearsal room with a fairly open mind so that I can incorporate the actors' ideas, but at the same time you need to have a clear structure of where you want it go in your head, so it's important to get a balance between. I'd then start the scene rehearsal with a read through of the text, then sit down for a discussion about how the actors see their characters in the scene before getting it up on its feet and making it work. You've then got the slightly more hectic days like tech rehearsals and opening nights, when it's just about keeping a cool head under pressure and making sure you're on top of everything and in control.

Have you done any additional training courses to further your career?
Not since I left drama school. I think there's a certain amount of theory that you can learn, and then like anything else, it's just about doing it as much as possible and learning on the job. I don't think anyone ever gets to the point where they've got nothing further to learn in their chosen field, but you definitely get better with every job that you do.

How important is working for free at the beginning of your career?
Unless you're very lucky it's pretty much essential. Like any industry, people are chosen on the basis of their experience more than anything else, so you need to get those credits on your CV, and given the general lack of money around the theatre industry at the moment, most of the projects you'll have an opportunity to work on at any one time aren't going to have much funding behind them, so it'll either be low pay or none whatsoever. There are three reasons why you should take a job which are if it pays well, furthers your career or you'll enjoy doing it. As long as at least two of those are the case then go for it!
You can find out more information about Andrew and his theatre companies, Facsimile Productions and British Touring Shakespeare here:
www.facsimileproductions.co.uk
www.facebook.com/facsimileproductions
www.twitter.com/BTSFacsimile

Composer
Composers write music for performances, ranging from songs for musicals to background music for plays.

We asked Stage Jobs Pro member Ben Osborn the following questions about working as a Composer:

What is the most rewarding aspect of working as a Composer?
Getting to work with incredible musicians, directors, designers, actors, and artists as part of an ensemble.

What are the key skills required to be an effective Composer?
The ability to turn a concept into a piece of music: the main thing you need to do this is to have no ego (that is, no sense that the music is 'yours'; you need to understand its purpose instead, and be objective about whether it works). You need to be open-minded to every sound and contribution, and very hard-working even when you don't feel inspired, as there are a lot of deadlines.

Do you see your role as a natural step on a career ladder, and if so what is the next rung?
I'm still trying to find a way to make it cost-effective. I think that is the next step.

How did you work your way into your current role?
Student theatre gave me lots of opportunities to compose.

How much do you think networking helps towards landing a job in the industry?
A great deal.

Do you think you will be working in the industry in the next five years, and if so in what capacity?
Hopefully as a composer, writer, and songwriter.

Please describe what a typical day working as a Composer might contain?
Going through an ever-growing list of ideas. Conversing with the director, and listening to the kind of music that's inspiring them. Reading carefully through a script and listening to the tunes that start happening in your head, then going to a piano to play them. Recording them, trying them out on different instruments, arranging them for an ensemble. It differs, but there's a lot to do.

Have you done any additional training courses to further your career?
No.

How important is working for free at the beginning of your career?
I'm at the beginning of my career now, and I'm working about half-and-half free/paid. If I didn't work for free, I wouldn't get a lot of work. I'm getting a day job, and I imagine I'll need to have one for a while yet.

Musical Director

The Musical Director leads the cast and musicians in the musical aspects of a performance, working with the cast to learn and perfect the music, and directing them in their vocal performance.

We asked Stage Jobs Pro member Gareth Weedon the following questions about working as a Musical Director:

What is the most rewarding aspect of working as a Musical Director?
I've been lucky enough to say that I have worked with some incredibly talented singers and musicians. Couple that with working alongside musical supervisors, sound designers and directors who share your vision and aim, and you have the reward. Being able to then share that each day with your audience is the ultimate satisfaction.

What are the key skills required to be an effective Musical Director?
Primarily to facilitate the intricacies of the musical score each day, consistently. To keep the show fresh for the audience, making it consistent for the supervising management and exciting and fulfilling for all performers. As a manager yourself: being able to enthuse, encourage and empower the people on stage and in the pit to perform to their best.

Do you see your role as a natural step on a career ladder, and if so what is the next rung?
Frequently-working musical directors (and usually those who are experienced in man-management as much as musicianship) progress to working as musical supervisors if they wish to 'progress from MDing'. The role is similar in nature but usually more creative in the initial stages, then consultative and more hands-off once production is running.

How did you work your way into your current role?
In my youth I worked as a rehearsal pianist for local and regional productions. From there I went on to MD some regional pantomimes before embarking on my first national tour as assistant musical director and moving up.

How much do you think networking helps towards landing a job in the industry?
Being consistently good at what you do is what helps you move on. Being seen and heard to be doing so is what ultimately helps gain work amongst industry professionals. Word of mouth plays an important part. If that means 'networking' then yes, but empty networking or cold-calling rarely has any lasting effect.

Do you think you will be working in the industry in the next five years, and if so in what capacity?

I would hope to still be working in five years. Ideally as a creative musical supervisor, yet conducting a musical that excites me. I would also like to have written some arrangements for a show and be able to hear them regularly performed.

Please describe what a typical day working as a Musical Director might contain?

The day on an established, up-and-running show would normally begin with collating any notes from the previous evening's performance to give to the cast. These would be given after the vocal warm up which is normally the first call of the day (assuming there are no rehearsals, auditions, or other business to attend to).

Have you done any additional training courses to further your career?

Conducting lessons, observing other MDs, listening to other arrangers' work, concert-going and recording your own work are all ways to train yourself further for the role.

How important is working for free at the beginning of your career?

I think it depends from person to person. Getting your foot on the ladder involves a different route for everyone. Working for free is often a way to gain superb experience; that can either be at the beginning of or many years into one's career. You never know who among the people you're working with now will become the next big player in the field. It's competitive and exciting working amidst talent, wherever it is.

Choreographer

Choreographers develop, design, and direct movement in a production.

We asked Stage Jobs Pro member Jess Fairfield the following questions about working as a Choreographer:

What is the most rewarding aspect of working as a Choreographer?

Seeing the finished product. You start with a cast that know nothing, uncostumed on a blank stage. Come opening night everything is rehearsed and in place. As a choreographer you have played a big role in that show coming together and it is a wonderful feeling.

139

What are the key skills required to be an effective Choreographer?
- Strong dance skills and ability – Even stronger ability to be able to convey to the cast what you want them to do – Organisation and time management – Leadership – Imagination – Flexibility and the ability to work as a team – Being a hard worker that doesn't mind long hours

Do you see your role as a natural step on a career ladder, and if so what is the next rung?
It can be seen as a step onward from Dance Captain and Assistant Choreographer, but I do think of it as a career in itself. You could go onto direct, but this requires additional skills.

How did you work your way into your current role?
Having trained in Musical Theatre and performed for a number of years, choreography is always where I wanted my career to settle so it was natural progression for me. I made myself a showreel and contacted companies. I got my first job by someone contacting me through my website – lucky break I guess.

How much do you think networking helps towards landing a job?
It is a very important part of the industry especially in the backstage roles as a lot of work comes from personal recommendation etc.

Do you think you will be working in the industry in the next five years, and if so in what capacity?
I hope so! As a choreographer and dance teacher which is what I do now.

Please describe what a typical day working as a Choreographer might contain?
Taking rehearsals: choreographing new pieces and polishing others that have been created earlier in the rehearsal process. Taking notes on runs of the show, production meetings, scheduling the rehearsal period, late night rehearsals, blocking on stage, tech runs, dress runs, changing and tweaking the work ... so much can happen in one day!

Have you done any additional training courses to further your career?
I haven't but there are courses for Choreography out there.

How important is working for free at the beginning of your career?
I think it is beneficial to get experience and credits on your CV, learn from others in the industry and also get some footage for showreel purposes. I think it depends on an individual's circumstances as to whether they are able to do this or not though.

*Jess' website is **www.jessfairfield.co.uk***

Producer

The Producer oversees many aspects of the production and may be responsible for marketing, budgeting, attending rehearsals, meeting with the production team and problem solving.

© ALEXANDER PARSONAGE

Stage Jobs Pro member Flavia Fraser-Cannon is a Producer. We asked her the following questions about her career:

What is the most rewarding aspect of working as a Producer?
Standing outside the theatre when the show comes down and seeing an audience fired up about it. The buzz of a satisfied and engaged audience is thrilling.

What are the key skills required to be an effective Producer?
Time management, a strong sense of responsibility, determination, trust, empathy, strength, good judgement and a head for figures (or a good spreadsheet/calculator).

Do you see your role as a natural step on a career ladder, and if so what is the next rung?
The next rung for me I think would be moving towards becoming an executive director. Slightly different skill set, but still people and money management. You can of course be a producer for life though, and plenty of people do. It's such a varied career that there's plenty to keep you on your toes!

How did you work your way into your current role?
I have had experience in almost all areas of theatre from front of house, duty management and box office to stage management, acting, helping with costumes, teching and even directing. I think the better you can understand the various roles the better you can manage all the aspects of a production, talk on a level with people etc.

How much do you think networking helps towards landing a job in the industry?
A great deal, as with all industries. You will move forward quicker if people see you around, get to know you personally and find you personable. People are always more inclined to work with someone they know. Plus if people see you around you are keeping yourself fresh in their minds when they are looking for someone.

Do you think you will be working in the industry in the next five years, and if so in what capacity?
Same capacity, moving more into touring rather than being rooted in London and the Edinburgh festival. Longer runs are more financially sustainable and regional venues have a more producer-friendly guarantees model.

Please describe what a typical day working as a Producer might contain?
EVERYTHING! But really, sifting through the morning emails, making a list of things that need to be addressed from contracts to distributing schedules, liaising with marketing, press, tech etc, keeping an eye on the budgets and cash flow, paying invoices and sending invoices out. And then getting on with all those things! Then probably seeing a show in the evening.

Have you done any additional training courses to further your career?
Stage One are great for starting out commercial producers. They run a short course once a year and offer various schemes for work placements, bursaries and investment in start-out projects. Otherwise, I believe there are some MA courses now, though I don't know a great deal about them though if I'm honest. Just go out and get some experience, intern with a bigger producer and start producing small projects to begin with and build up.

How important is working for free at the beginning of your career?
If I put all the time I worked for free back to back I'd probably spent about 2 years at it! But it was spread out over a few years and I would get paid stuff in between. The industry as it stands needs people to do work placements to survive and continuing arts cuts will not help this issue. Interning does also offer the fantastic opportunity to learn from observation – you can avoid making a few nasty little starting out mistakes by doing this. I still help friends out here and there for free even now, as a goodwill gesture. You never know when you might need to ask for a favour back.
Flavia is the in-house producer at Theatre503: ***www.theatre503.com***

Writer

The Writer creates theatrical pieces for stage.

We asked Stage Jobs Pro member Maria Athini the following questions about working as a Writer:

What is the most rewarding aspect of working as a Writer?
The moment of absolute happiness, when your story becomes alive on stage for the first time and you watch it silently, whispering the lines that you wrote like a prayer.

What are the key skills required to be an effective Writer?
Read literature and poetry to build your writing skills with quality. Live a life full of experiences so that you will have the courage to be true and expose yourself.

How did you work your way into your current role?
I collaborated with talented directors, they showed me the way to write good scripts.

How much do you think networking helps towards landing a job?
Networking helps in every aspect of your professional life. You have to find the best collaborators and build strong relations with them to optimise the result of your work.

Do you think you will be working in the industry in the next five years, and if so in what capacity?
I hope to see my plays on stage for the rest of my life.

Please describe what a typical day working as a Writer might contain?
Long walks, listening to music, reading, feeling lonely, doubting everything. Writing. That's a typical day in my life.

Have you done any additional training courses to further your career?
I have attended screenwriting workshops and masterclasses by professional writers and directors. Any training course can help a lot when you work on a project.

How important is working for free at the beginning of your career?
A writer most of the time works for free, in the sense that when you start writing you never know if your play will be interesting at the end. If you are lucky you will get hired to write and get paid in advance but this is very rare and cannot be a rule.

How Do I Write A Directing Proposal?

ANDREW LORETTO, CO-DIRECTOR, CHOL THEATRE, HUDDERSFIELD. REPRODUCED IN ITS ENTIRETY WITH KIND PERMISSION FROM GET INTO THEATRE

getintotheatre

There is no set format to writing a directing proposal as it will reflect your personal flair, passions and interests as a director, as well as the particular requirements of that project.

However, I would suggest that you should always try and get the following basics into any proposal (I'll call the project a 'show' for now – but of course, it could be a play, an event etc.):

1. The title of the show
2. What the show is about
3. Why you want to make the show – why here? Why now?
4. Who you want to make the show with
5. How you envisage making the show
6. Who the show is for (ie. who is the audience?)
7. Your background as a director
8. Your full contact details (you'll be amazed how many people forget this...)

And then, if required and/or useful...

9. Timescale
10. Suggested budget
11. Marketing suggestions
12. CVs of yourself and key artistic personnel, script extracts, photos, images, DVDs, CDs as appropriate
13. A stamped address envelope if you want the material returned when finished with

Depending on the circumstances, you can write as short or long a pitch as required. But generally speaking, you want to be able to get the main info across in a concise fashion in two pages – a bit like writing a CV or job application.

You can always offer more detail to supplement the initial 'hook' page or pages.

The other thing about a directing pitch is that your creativity and passion should come across on the page – but still with clarity. If you wish, run the pitch past someone who knows nothing about the project to see if it makes sense to them before you send it to theatre companies.

The other thing is, yes it is a sales document, but it needs to be an honest sales document. Please don't pitch a project that you know you can't deliver or is not within your skill set. Be honest about your strengths and play to those.

Good luck!
Get Into Theatre hopes to open your eyes to the huge variety of careers in the industry – and the different ways to get there. You can find out more at **www.getintotheatre.org**.

"In a directing pitch your creativity and passion should come across on the page – but still with clarity"

How Do I Get My Play Read?

ANDREW LORETTO, CO-DIRECTOR, CHOL THEATRE, HUDDERSFIELD. REPRODUCED IN ITS ENTIRETY WITH KIND PERMISSION FROM GET INTO THEATRE

getintotheatre

The people who you need to target are literary managers and directors of new writing. If they like the work, and see your potential, then you'll hopefully get your foot on the development and commissioning ladder.

Don't send out work in a blanket fashion. Which theatres you should send your work to depends on the type of plays you have written. Check out the new writing venues and organisations local to your region in the first instance. Look at their websites first to see if they commission the type of work you are writing.

Policy
Most producing theatres have their new writing and submissions policy on the website. Look at the mix of work they develop and stage. For example, some companies are interested in plays for young people, others not. Some venues have a preference for more naturalistic, linear narrative forms, and others will steer away from narrative, preferring to use words in a more experimental fashion. And some companies don't develop traditional playwrights as such but take a very broad view of writing eg the writer as performance poet or MC.

Companies
There are many venues and companies interested in new writing. There are also new writing agencies and support structures around the UK – such as Script Yorkshire. These are of course just some of the key new writing venues and producers. There are many smaller companies and fringe-based organisations offering opportunities for new writing to be developed and staged.

Festivals
There are also some excellent new writing festivals around with open submissions policies such as High Tide and 24:7. Again, check out websites, find out about their policies for new writing.

146

Listings
Read The List, Time Out magazine – whatever listings guide is local to your area – see where work is being staged and then go and see it if you're interested.

Put yourself on free mail and email newsletter lists – including Artsnews nd Artsjobs (sign up via Arts Council England main website). A really useful resource for screen/radio new writing is the BBC Writersroom website.

Agent
In terms of getting an agent as a writer, that tends to happen once you've had a play staged or promoted by a reasonably high-profile theatre company or as part of a festival. If your work has been seen by the agent and they like it enough, they might take you on.

If and when you have any work staged – either fully or as part of a 'work in progress' type of event – do your utmost to get people along to see it. As with approaching the venues, choose the agent carefully according to the type of work (and level of writer) they are interested in representing.

Have a look at who their other clients are – that usually gives you a clue as to what kind of work they're into.

"If and when you have any work staged do your utmost to get people along to see it"

Groups
Writers' groups are useful if they operate at a level that challenges and stimulates you creatively. If you feel you are going over old ground, then it can actually be counter-productive. If you're checking out a writers' group, do a little research into who's leading it, who else is currently in the group, and what kind of work they're doing at the moment. You might be able to take part in one or two sessions on a trial basis. One thing I would always caution against is paying money up front for a whole series of writers' sessions – especially when the larger theatres offer free and low-cost training options.

Good luck!
Get Into Theatre hopes to open your eyes to the huge variety of careers in the industry – and the different ways to get there. You can find out more at **www.getintotheatre.com**.

The Persistent Playwright

DIANNE CUTLACK, WITH ADDITIONAL CONTENT BY THOMAS WILLSHIRE

⁼PERSISTENTPLAYWRIGHT

I call myself 'The Persistent Playwright' for a reason. It sums up how I feel about the basic insanity of what I am doing: creating new works for the stage in a risk-averse age when a tidal wave of tried-and-tested plays, some going back centuries, could be used to entertain a paying audience instead of one of mine.

Perseverance is the key.

Another absolute necessity is getting plays into production. All good writers are natural writers who have been committing their stories to paper since they could first grasp a crayon.

Settled into the groove of playwriting, writers can produce a pile of scripts from here to the Moon, yet if those plays are not boosted into a public realm the playwright languishes unseen and unsung.

Factor in ever-diminishing grants for the arts and relatively few theatres commissioning new work, and where does that leave the playwright? Having to be more resourceful and flexible than ever before.
Bearing this in mind, here are the thoughts and experiences of two London-based playwrights, myself and Thomas Willshire. We hope the following advice will help you at the start of your playwriting career.

Use your experience
Despite the proliferation of playwriting courses and programmes, playwrights are not churned off a production line ready-made, and everyone's background is different. Tom's introduction to playwriting was a young writers' group at the Birmingham Rep called Birmingham Rep Transmissions. My first scripts were written for broadcast while I worked as a college intern at radio station CKFM in Toronto. Tom progressed to the Birmingham School of Speech and Drama where he combined his writing with acting. "I was always doing both," says Tom. "I was either in drama

school learning about acting or I was rehearsing a play I had written."
Tom's career as a playwright, which later included a young writer's
programme at the Royal Court Theatre, was a natural progression. Mine
was an extension to a career in book publishing.

There is no single route for a playwright to take, or magical 'perfect age' for
a playwright to be. Writing is about life experience. Use everything you
have – education, background, past jobs – to inform your writing and
advance your writing career.

Seize every opportunity

Never say no, and don't be shy – send your scripts to everyone. "I would
recommend Ideas Tap, the London Comedy Writers, short story competi-
tions, the High Tide Festival," says Tom. "A lot of theatre companies do
Scratch Nights, 10 or 15 minute plays. You write something and they'll
perform it for you."

"There is no single route for a playwright to take, or magical 'perfect age' for a playwright to be. Writing is about life experience"

This 'anything goes' mentality applies to play venues as well as the plays
themselves. Theatre companies without large budgets perform in libraries,
pubs, warehouses, theatre foyers and many other public spaces. I set
myself up as a producer to use a Grade I listed country house, and
benefitted greatly from the experience. A heritage property provides
atmosphere, history, a novel and rewarding venue for the actors, and ready-
made sets (the rooms) which require no dressing and look glorious when
fully lit. Be experimental – find your own perfect environment.

Be adaptable

"Don't write an hour-long play and limit yourself to that," says Tom. "Think
of it as a story and look for ways and opportunities where that story can be
told. Chop it to smithereens (if necessary) and get it out there. Think: I've
got this idea, this story, and I can tell you this story in a screenplay, a radio
play, a stage play."

© Nick Smith

'The Last Great Lady' by Dianne Cutlack

Create a community

Most writing takes place in solitude, but the staging of a play is a collaborative social process. All writers need the support of generous and like-minded people to get their plays on the stage. "If I were talking to a young writer who wanted to start producing plays," says Tom, "I would say do it as a team, don't try to do it on your own. Think about your friends." Utilise their different talents and skills. "And while you're getting the play on, you're meeting people, you're making connections, you're meeting new actors." This social interaction is vitally important, as is the use of social networking sites. Like them or loathe them, Facebook and Twitter are a cheap and reliable way of publicising your plays and communicating with other creative people.

Have patience and common sense

Naturally all playwrights dream of the Big One: the play that runs for eternity in a decent theatre with a good reputation (and plenty of positive critical feedback). The reality, for the majority of us, is very different. Reputations are built slowly. Rejections are commonplace (like fishermen, all writers have tales of The One That Got Away). Tom says: "Pick yourself up and think: I've still got plenty of plays in me and plenty of time. As a new writer, take any interest as confirmation that you're doing the right thing."

Rejected scripts are a huge, crushing disappointment, but they are an inevitable aspect of a writing career and they mustn't overwhelm you. I've been sent enough rejection letters to wallpaper my bathroom. They make me more determined than ever to succeed.

Show some humility

You're not changing the world, you're writing a play. "People get too caught up in the romantic notion of a writer," says Tom. (I call it the Hemingway Syndrome.) "It's irrelevant how I write, it's relevant what I write. Tell stories, entertain people, don't preach at them. If there is a message to be had, the audience will pick up on it. Don't be dull." Or too worthy. Respect your audience, don't hammer them over the head with an 'issue' for two never-ending hours, and remember that they can think for themselves.

Treat your actors with even more respect, and focus on their feedback in read-throughs and early rehearsals. Remember that they are your first audience. If they don't understand something about the play or their characters, the audience won't either. Don't be precious – change the script for them.

Remember what you're up against
It takes a lot to persuade people to leave their PlayStations and Game of Thrones box sets for a night at the theatre. As Tom puts it: "There are regional theatres closing left, right and centre because a whole generation of people who had King Lear hammered into them at a young age are so turned off by the whole thing, the moment you say 'play' they think boredom. Play equals tedium. This is what people fear." The challenge that playwrights face is finding new ways to keep theatre, one of the oldest forms of entertainment, fresh and exciting. We've got to hook audiences in new ways and keep them coming back for more. Each new generation must learn the power of words.

So why do we do it?
Make no mistake, getting your original play into a production is an exhausting, rewarding and terrifying experience. Why do we keep trying? "I like showing off," says Tom. "I like people laughing at my jokes and I like having my ego massaged. I love the unexpected laugh, the unexpected gasp, the moment when the audience have their expectation confounded." As for myself, it's the sense of achievement when months of effort culminate in that opening performance. Listening to fine actors delivering my lines is one of the most profound pleasures I've ever experienced. I've created something unique, and it makes all the effort worthwhile.
*Dianne's website is **www.thepersistentplaywright.co.uk** and Thomas' is **www.thomaswillshire.wix.com/thomaswillshire***

Administration, Marketing & Front of House

"There's no such thing as a typical day!"

Working in Theatre Management, Administration and Marketing can provide an exciting and varied career path. If you work in a receiving theatre there will be a constant stream of incoming and outgoing productions, the logistics of which require an immense amount of planning and a very particular skillset. If you work for a producing theatre you'll get to experience the full circle of theatre production – from development and marketing through to the final production.

We've listed the most common roles when working in this environment, with some interesting case studies from Stage Jobs Pro members who are working in this area of theatre and great guest content.

Theatre Administration & Management

"If you perfect your skills to become a good Company Manager then the world is your oyster."

Administrator

Administrators are responsible for general day-to-day administrative tasks (such as paperwork, dealing with emails, answering the telephone, organising meetings and events, and managing diaries) to help the company or production run smoothly.

We asked Stage Jobs Pro member Anna O'Dell the following questions about working as an Administrator:

What is the most rewarding aspect of working as an Administrator?
Seeing something you've been working on coming together, such as a festival or programme of events.

What are the key skills required to be an effective Administrator?
Organisation, time management, clear communication, rolling with the punches.

Do you see your role as a natural step on a career ladder, and if so what is the next rung?

I suppose the next step would be something similar in a bigger venue with different challenges, a scaled-up programme and more responsibility. I'd like to learn more about the development of a venue, and the programming side of things. Camden People's Theatre [where Anna works] is a great place to see a lot of this happening.

How did you work your way into your current role?

I started working Front of House at CPT, then did an internship in the office in the lead up to Sprint 2013 (our flagship festival which happens every year). I was then offered the administration and marketing role.

How much do you think networking helps towards landing a job in the industry?

It's always good to know people, but I don't 'network' as such. You meet a lot of people working in a venue and it's nice putting the links together. For interviews I think it makes you looks plugged in if you can talk easily about artists you've seen, work you like etc.

Please describe what a typical day working as an Administrator might contain?

I don't have a typical day as such, they're always different. When it's a quieter period it's keeping things ticking over, catching up on admin-y bits like paperwork and filing, box office returns and paying invoices, sorting out the theatre and making sure our equipment is still in tact. In the lead up to busy periods, there's lots of emailing about shows, ticketing, updating the website, artists requirements etc. I also do the marketing so there's lots of that too. We're in the process of getting a new website and ticketing system, so I've been doing a lot of work on that.

How important is working for free at the beginning of your career?

I did a lot of voluntary placements before I started at CPT, and I wouldn't have got this job without them. They're a great way to dip your toe in the water, and see what you like and what you don't. I learnt an awful lot from my voluntary positions, but I was lucky with mine. I think it depends how much you're willing to commit to it, you've got to enjoy it if you're willing to work for free.

*Anna works at Camden People's Theatre: **www.cptheatre.co.uk***

General Manager

The General Manager oversees the day-to-day running and future development of a company.

We asked Stage Jobs Pro member Michael Poynor the following questions about working as a General Manager:

What is the most rewarding aspect of working as a General Manager?
The satisfaction of achieving the smooth running and administration of the enterprise. Ensuring that your 'team' is capable, efficient and effective at their individual jobs.

What are the key skills required to be an effective General Manager?
A General Manager needs to have a wide range of skills, and will have, probably, worked in quite a few Support and Admin departments. Key skills are people and team management, planning skills and ability to use planning tools such as Artifax, Microsoft Project Planner and complex spreadsheets. Some GMs will have considerable input to the financial running of the enterprise and in this case budgets and budget control programmes, including Risk Assessment and Risk Management, will be necessary. In some enterprises the GM may even be the senior financial employee, in which case familiarity with accounting programmes will be necessary. The latter will apply to smaller enterprises, as any large company/building will have a dedicated finance team – some with a financial director, who may, or may not, report to the GM.

It would be very useful to have had some business study training: a decent MBA would undoubtedly help. The Open University provides a very good one that can be fitted around your work schedule. It would also be useful to have some practical knowledge/appreciation of all other departments e.g. performance, construction (sets/wardrobe/props etc), building management, technical stage systems, box office systems, front of house management, catering, marketing and legal (contracts/licenses/building controls etc) are major areas of complex enterprises.

Do you see your role as a natural step on a career ladder, and if so what is the next rung?
Depending on the nature of what your enterprise sees as the function of the GM. In many enterprises the name General Manager has been supplanted, or combined with, the role of Chief Executive, or Administrative Director or

Administrator. If the enterprise carries both then the next step would be to CEO or Admin Director. Increasingly, in the performing arts sector, companies are being run by Administrators rather than Artistic Directors. Some enterprises have ADs and CEOs working in tandem, but many have a CEO as the senior position – this has evolved as finance has become the lynch-pin to survival in what many perceive to be an increasingly underfunded sector. International companies such as the RSC and National Theatre still have very high profile ADs but they work in tandem with their Admin Directors. Some enterprises have even ceased employment of an AD and employed a CEO only e.g. Lyric Theatre, Belfast. Of course, a non producing house will be run entirely by an Administrative Director who is, in effect a General Manager.

How did you work your way into your current role?
I started in industry with Trust House Hotels, as a Trainee Executive combined with Economics and Law at Westminster College. Upon graduating I became Chief Purchasing Officer for three companies in the group. At 27 I went to LAMDA and did the Technical and Stage Management course then went into rep as a Stage Manager, lighting designer and actor. Over the years directing became the main interest, so I was AD at various reps and companies and ended up in Northern Ireland, where I married and settled. I still direct, but was CEO of the Millennium Forum in Derry during its building and opening phases, then General Manager for Belfast Festival at Queen's, then Head of Culture and Arts at Queen's University. Now I'm AD and CEO of the Ulster Theatre Company so I can indulge my love of planning and management with the need to be creative (writing and directing). In a way, I've gone back to the old school Artistic Director who managed the enterprise as well as directing productions.

How much do you think networking helps towards landing a job in the industry?
Everyone will tell you a different story. Larger organisations have a pretty fixed methodology for short-listing and interviewing candidates. If you tick the right boxes you will be seen – if not, not. Then, it's up to you in an interview scenario. In smaller companies, networking and peer influence does have an effect.

Do you think you will be working in the industry in the next five years, and if so in what capacity?
Yes. As a Director, Writer and Administrator.

Please describe what a typical day working as a General Manager might contain?
If there was a typical day, I'd probably have given it up ages ago! It's the sheer variety and continuous change (and change management) that makes

the job interesting. Yes, there's always e-mails, reports, applications etc to do – and they are repetitive – but each day brings its own challenges. The smaller the enterprise, the wider the range and the bigger the enterprise, then the bigger the fish you are chasing!

Have you done any additional training courses to further your career?
Yes, MBA; Risk Assessment Course; Fundraising Strategy for the Arts; Project Management Courses.

How important is working for free at the beginning of your career?
I never did that ... but was probably lucky.

Theatre/Venue Manager

The role of Theatre/Venue Manager encompasses a huge variety of obligations and may be responsible for human resources management, customer services, health and safety, financial management and company development.

We asked Stage Jobs Pro member Mel Dixon the following questions about about working as a Theatre/Venue Manager:

What is the most rewarding aspect of working as a Theatre / Venue Manager?
Being happy that everything and everyone is running smoothly.

What are the key skills required to be an effective Theatre / Venue Manager?
The ability to prioritise and multi-task. The ability to work under extreme pressure and stay calm. Flexibility – you need to switch priorities at a moments notice. The ability to balance budgets, utilise every bit of knowledge, every scrap of information to its best advantage. The ability to spot and maximise on any potential. The ability to understand, organise and adhere to legislative requirements. The ability to manage staff. The ability to manage budgets. The ability to negotiate, project manage, schedule and write concise reports. The ability to adapt in any and all directions.

Do you see your role as a natural step on a career ladder, and if so what is the next rung?
As I would like to freelance and only do short interim cover, I have to answer no. My target is to obtain work in any theatre-based role while I develop my own projects. I prefer breezing in and out to full-time

employment, doing lots of different things and resolving problems in a wide variety of roles. I enjoy alternating between leading and following and dislike being in either position for any great length of time.

How did you work your way into your current role?
I finished my last contract and started looking for freelance opportunities.

How much do you think networking helps towards landing a job in the industry?
Totally indispensable.

Do you think you will be working in the industry in the next five years, and if so in what capacity?
Yes – I'd be miserable if I wasn't. Workshop practitioner (freelance), emergency managerial cover (short interim cover), casual/freelance technician (lighting) and stage crew/ds, freelance LD project co-ordinator/manager, writer and possibly producer or director

Please describe what a typical day working as a Theatre / Venue Manager might contain?
There's no such thing as a typical day! However... You could be dealing with: hire enquiries, contracts, licensing, invoicing, staffing, maintenance, interviews, budgeting, credit control reports and analysis, marketing, company/board meetings, repairs, facilities, development of facilities, staff training and development, H&S inspections, fire risk assessments, licensing agreements, PRS, insurance and CRBs, co-ordinating logistics for festivals or events, greeting or assisting with a get in, rolling up your sleeves to help cafe/FOH/technical or any other staff who are up against it. The list is endless ...

Have you done any additional training courses to further your career?
Not really. I'd like to have but either I've been too busy working or I haven't had the money to spare. I learn on the job mainly.

How important is working for free at the beginning of your career?
A good idea generally – and volunteering throughout your career can give you experience that might not otherwise be available when you need it.

Company Manager

The Company Manager oversees the management of the production, performing day-to-day administrative tasks such as dealing with legal and contractual work, and looking after cast and crew.

We asked Stage Jobs Pro member Bernard Davies the following questions about working as a Company Manager:

What is the most rewarding aspect of working as a Company Manager?
All my Company Management experience has been in opera, however, I believe all of the following would apply to any Company Management role. So some of the rewarding aspects are: you get to meet the most wonderful, fascinating and beguiling characters; supporting, and at times guiding, them while they perform their trade; being a facilitator between the myriad of departments/sections involved in the rehearsal and performance process; solving puzzles whether it be sourcing something or getting an understudy from miles away to keep the curtain up!

What are the key skills required to be an effective Company Manager?
Now this one is an interesting one. When I am asked what I do, I simply say that I am diplomatic headmaster/nanny. So based on the above, I would say that you have to be able to listen, have an inclination towards wanting to solve problems, be organised, be firm/stern when you have to be whilst still being approachable, gentle and supportive in times of need. Negotiating and diplomatic skills are also good to hone as every performer/situation is different. Great sense of humor for yourself! Being a bit scary at times is what some of the artists I have dealt with might say too!

Do you see your role as a natural step on a career ladder, and if so what is the next rung?
If you perfect your skills to become a good Company Manager then the world is your oyster as all the skills required can be turned to any other form of administration. There is no reason why you can not become the General Manager of a theatrical organisation, a producer or working with an artists' agency.

How did you work your way into your current role?
After holding the role of Head of Company Management and Planning at Glyndebourne Opera for eighteen years, three years ago I decided to

embark on the life of freelancer. It was a decision I did not take lightly, but I wanted to work with more companies, which I am currently doing. It makes for even more variety and far less office politics.

How much do you think networking helps towards landing a job in the industry?
Networking is something that I am not great at, however, if you go down the route of freelance work then it would be essential. I have managed to secure several contracts from talking to people who have passed my details on to other parties. Not only does it allow you get your name out and about it allows you to meet some very interesting characters.

Do you think you will be working in the industry in the next five years, and if so in what capacity?
I hope to be still be working in the industry in the next five years, but then again, you never know what is around the corner! Life is about learning/experiencing, so if something interesting comes up which isn't related to the industry – why not?

Please describe what a typical day working as a Company Manager might contain?
The wonderful thing about working in Company Management is you can never really know what a typical day will hold. The nature of the job means you are reacting to the now – implementing changes to rehearsals or dealing with potential cast problems, whether being someone is ill or they need you to find them a bike hire place or advise them on travel plans. The constants would be compiling and publishing the weekly/daily rehearsal schedules and, depending on the company, you could also be making the arrangements for the payroll or at least providing information for the payroll.

Have you done any additional training courses to further your career?
I have not done any training courses to further my career as everything I have learnt has been while on the job. I am not that old, but back in my day there were no courses. Today however you can study for an Arts Management degree etc. However, what these courses do not provide is experience in dealing with situations that are different each time and learning how to deal with temperamental egos. This can only be learnt by first hand experience. Yes you will crash and burn at times, however, from the ashes you will know instinctively what to do next time.

How important is working for free at the beginning of your career?
This is a difficult one. I began my 'career' working for someone outside my usual working hours so you could say that was free. I wanted to do that so

I could learn. I was not interested in earning more because knowing the business was more important. In today's world I would say the same as long as you are going to be guaranteed to learn and not just make the coffee or do the photocopying.

Tour Manager

Tour Managers are responsible for the practical aspects of touring – controlling finances, booking accommodation, preparing schedules, looking after cast and crew and communicating with theatres.

We asked Stage Jobs Pro member Dave Taylor the following questions about working as a Tour Manager:

What is the most rewarding aspect of working as a Tour Manager?
Although considered a 'behind the scenes' part of the theatre world, there is nothing more rewarding than receiving feedback and letters from pupils and teaching staff saying how moved they were by a production, and to thank you for that initial phone call or visit to organise the event. Never forget where and how that first contact was made as it is where your future audiences will come from.

What are the key skills required to be an effective Tour Manager?
Decision making, and executing those decisions on time and within budget is key. Being organised so if any tough decisions come about you're ready with possible answers. And don't just see your role as 'line managing' a team on the road – sometimes you need to be that person they turn to when touring and being away from home, family and friends takes its toll.

Do you see your role as a natural step on a career ladder, and if so what is the next rung?
Currently I am managing a theatre in education tour, which is great in itself, but I also wrote and directed this piece. The three elements definitely work well together and is a great way to progress. However I strongly believe that a step on the ladder doesn't always have to be up to the next rung. Taking a step down or back is equally as rewarding and sometimes needed in order to see the ladder in its entirety, to make sure that you plan and actually want to climb in the first place.

How did you work your way into your current role?
I started out as an actor (still do bits). Drama college in both UK and the States really helped get different perspectives of theatre and performance.

Gaining a BA then my MA helped massively in that I always have something to fall back on – but there is nothing like 'doing' to get the juices flowing. I was also a Resident Actor at 'Theatr Genedlaethol Cymru' (Welsh Speaking National Theatre of Wales) for two years. Working with some of the best Tour Managers and Stage Managers really taught me how not to 'manage' actors, and how to get them to see things from your perspective.

How much do you think networking helps towards landing a job in the industry?

I've never been a fan of the word 'networking' – it has way too many angles and a terrible reputation for itself. Meet people and get to know them, but most importantly let them get to know you as a person first and then impress them with what you can do.

Do you think you will be working in the industry in the next five years, and if so in what capacity?

In the next five years?!! Forever more like!!! Doing whatever comes my way – sweeping stages or washing costumes. I'm not one to turn down a role just because it doesn't mean being in the limelight.

Please describe what a typical day working as a Tour Manager might contain?

Up at 6:45. Go for a run to clear my head and get ready to contact schools and organisations regarding possible shows in the future. I like to have organised and booked a tour a term in advance. I would contact the team on the road pre-event to see if they've arrived and go through any possible tight spots, then I would be collating feedback forms I have received and organising meetings or tele-conference calls (I'm based in Wales as this is where the touring is) for the company I work for in London. Scripting after lunch, and on Tuesdays and Thursdays arrange lesson plans for a drama club I run for a local theatre.

Have you done any additional training courses to further your career?

On this current tour, the topic is Food Hygiene and Food Safety so I have now been on three courses to get my NVQ Level 2 ,3 and 4 – so I guess level 5 & 6 could always follow and I become an Environmental Health Officer!!

How important is working for free at the beginning of your career?

Hate to say it but 'there is no such thing as free.' There is always some payment, okay, it might not be money but a thank you from a co-worker or a pupil that you had in one of your workshops should sometimes be taken as your payment!

Artistic Director

It's the Artistic Director's remit to shape the ethos of a theatre company or venue and decide what they're going to commission, produce or schedule.

© POLLY CLARE BOON

We asked Stage Jobs Pro member Alexandra Rutter the following questions about working as an Artistic Director:

What is the most rewarding aspect of working as an Artistic Director?
It is twofold for me. Firstly, I love helping artists develop and learn – and learning from them in turn. There are endless possibilities in a rehearsal room and the energy and atmosphere this inspires is magic; there is nothing like it. I love seeing raw work and channeling it. The second thing is the sheer power of seeing a fragment of your imagination breathed into life onstage. There is nothing more thrilling than that moment.

What are the key skills required to be an effective Artistic Director?
Leadership and determination: you need to be in control, take responsibility, make clear decisions and always have the overall goal in mind, but most importantly people need to trust you. You must be a rock people can rely on. Understanding, collaboration and communication: I believe a piece of performance is only as good and as strong as the sum of its parts. You need to work out what makes people tick in order to understand how to get the very best out of each and every person. Taking the time to communicate is crucial. Patience and ability to self-critique: you have to be able to stick things out when they aren't working and be self-critical to understand where the weaknesses or failings are in order to be able to fix them.

Do you see your role as a natural step on a career ladder, and if so what is the next rung?
At the moment and for the foreseeable future, my career is my company: Whole Hog Theatre. I tried to work up a career ladder, but couldn't even get on it as I didn't have enough 'professional experience.' But how do you get professional experience? Well, if you can't get on that ladder you have but one option: make your own ladder! This is why Whole Hog Theatre exists, to be a ladder for those without 'professional experience' but with a hell of a lot of talent who only need a platform. However, that is not to say my path cannot change and that I am not open to this. I think the nature of the industry is cut-throat: if an idea isn't working, understand this, learn from it and move on!

How did you work your way into your current role?

I didn't work my way in but chose a different road: I created my own role and my own work independently. If doors seem closed and opportunities scarce, make your own! This won't work for everyone and it is a very hard road, but there is more than one way to skin a cat.

How much do you think networking helps towards landing a job in the industry?

A lot – I wish I had time to do it more! It is crucial to most careers in the industry. However, I think if you want to be a director or creative leader of some kind then I think at the end of the day it will be your work, and not who you have connected with that matters. It can only get you so far if you don't have the skills to back it up.

Do you think you will be working in the industry in the next five years, and if so in what capacity?

I very much intend to be yes and in the role I am in (Artistic and Executive Director at Whole Hog Theatre) now, but the progression will be that we will be much stronger and better supported – there is always a lot of development work to be done as we are a young company. If I achieve this and we get the support we need I will still be here in five years time. I hear it takes ten years to be where you want to be in the industry so I don't imagine anything will move fast!

Please describe what a typical day working as an Artistic Director might contain?

There is no typical day because I direct a company and direct theatre productions, so it depends on the immediate needs of the company. You have to be imminently flexible, but essentially I, and the people I work with, do everything that the company needs doing and have to prioritise depending on the opportunities that come up and whether a production is running. One of the hardest things in this kinds of multi-role position is having very little 'daily routine' – you do what needs to be done and that changes day to day.

Have you done any additional training courses to further your career?

I try and get to workshops in quiet periods, but essentially no! This doesn't mean I don't think it is important though. It is due to the nature of my role: I have to be on the ground running the company and/or a production at all times and that leaves little time to get experience elsewhere. This is why the people you work with are so important: they bring different skills and expertise to a process so you learn by working with different people. By having an open company at Whole Hog Theatre I learn a lot from the casts, designers and production teams I work with, and because these people

163

change I am always learning from new people, new ideas. It never stagnates.

How important is working for free at the beginning of your career?
Sadly, in many cases sadly I think it is essential. There are other ways in of course – I know a lot of people who end up in very successful paid theatre jobs, but it isn't the job they wanted. I tried to get a job in the industry myself, it didn't happen, so I made a decision. I felt that if I was serious about being a director nothing was more important than finding a way to learn as a director by plying my craft. I do not encourage not paying people, but I also don't think the 'volunteer' label should be as dirty a word as it is. The problem is that it is assumed that there is a fat cat somewhere making money whilst others work for free, but this is not always the case. I think the fact that people come back to projects and companies, even for little to no pay, proves not only that there is sometimes no choice but to work for free – but the fact that some people want to come back instead of taking paid work proves there can be value in volunteer work that isn't monetary. I don't think people should be exploited and that is all that really matters. The principle of dismissing volunteer work comes from the right place and is the right principle, but I think in reality, in some circumstances, there can be real value there.
Alexandra's website is **www.wholehogtheatre.com**.

Marketing, Education & Fundraising

"I love standing at the back of a cheering crowd, being sidestage at a packed venue or watching an inspiring moment unfold in a studio and knowing I made it happen."

Press & Marketing Manager

The Press & Marketing Manager plans, develops, and runs marketing campaigns to advertise a production or venue.

We asked Stage Jobs Pro member Della Edwards the following questions about working as a Press & Marketing Manager:

What is the most rewarding aspect of working as a Press & Marketing Manager?
The variety of communication tasks within the role. From managing social media, to writing press releases, organising media interviews or writing direct mail letters there are so many different and interesting activities that the job is never boring!

What are the key skills required to be an effective Press & Marketing Manager?
To be able to multi-task and function effectively, at times under pressure, is vital. Sometimes when a production is due to open and a busy press night is ahead, it is still necessary to focus on another production that hasn't even opened as the marketing plan is ongoing. Being able to drop something you're currently working on as an important press story has broken or an actor needs escorting to a radio interview, whilst emailing journalists about a forthcoming show is typical of the juggling required on an everyday basis. It is important to be flexible, creative, autonomous and manage work priorities independently, but not lose sight of the whole production team of which you play an important part.

Do you see your role as a natural step on a career ladder, and if so what is the next rung?
Now I am freelancing in PR I don't see my current role as a direct intention to progress my career. If I do decide to go back working in-house full time I know that I could always come back into freelancing which offers such diversity and variety.

How did you work your way into your current role?
I worked in the marketing departments for a variety of leading provincial theatres before undertaking PR for a leading Arts Centre in London. I now undertake freelance PR contracts for productions and personal PR for actors requiring publicity. Certainly before becoming a PR Manager I acquired as much experience as possible working on a wide variety of Marketing/PR campaigns for a diverse array of productions. I found that progress is sometimes measured not from climbing vertically but by gathering the broadest experience across the board as possible in Arts Marketing and PR roles.

How much do you think networking helps towards landing a job?
Quite important, obviously contacts are valuable. Equally useful is knowing where to look for vacancies, ie, what publications and websites where jobs are advertised. It is also a good idea to contact venues directly to see what vacancies they might have coming up.

Do you think you will be working in the industry in the next five years, and if so in what capacity?
I would always hope to continue working within arts and entertainments as I love it and have much experience within the marketplace. As it can sometimes be a specialist field I think it is important we re-use our knowledge, and working in the arts is important, especially in times of recession, to ensure culture continues to be available to all and experts will therefore always be in demand.

Please describe what a typical day working as a Press & Marketing Manager might contain?
First thing on a Monday morning a marketing meeting with the team, perhaps contacting journalists about interviewing an actor in a forthcoming production, finishing writing a press release or emailing a direct mail letter as well as keeping tabs on Twitter and Facebook feeds.

Have you done any additional training courses to further your career?
I have undertaken communication courses including press release writing as well as how to make press releases stand out from the competition and win the journalists' interest to write about it in their publication.

How important is working for free at the beginning of your career?
For me vital. I undertook 6 months voluntary work at a provincial theatre in the south east after I graduated, shadowing the Marketing and Press Manager. I got a firsthand insight into the rudiments of the job and the pressure of just how demanding the workload can be. This showed my interest and dedication to succeed in a competitive field.
*Della's website is **www.centrestagepr.com***

Education Officer

Education Officers and their departments develop special projects that engage schools, teachers, local communities, families or specific groups beyond the stage.

We asked Stage Jobs Pro member Sarah Cant the following questions about working as an Education Officer:

What is the most rewarding aspect of working as an Education Officer?
It is an incredibly varied job and gives you the opportunity to work with a range of different people.

What are the key skills required to be an effective Education Officer?
Communication, people skills, being able to relate to lots of different people – from company directors to young children. In essence it is an administrative role, so they need to be organised with good time management/IT skills and understand finance and budgets.

Do you see your role as a natural step on a career ladder, and if so what is the next rung?
To Education Manager/Head of Department, or as a step onto producing your own work.

How did you work your way into your current role?
I undertook a work placement as part of my degree in the Education department at Glyndebourne, which led into employment as Education Assistant and then progressed to other roles within the department.

How much do you think networking helps towards landing a job in the industry?
It is very important to make a good impression with everyone you meet. It is a small industry and people talk!

Do you think you will be working in the industry in the next five years, and if so in what capacity?
Yes, I have most recently been working with young people in professional shows as Children's Administrator and chaperone, also developing my own theatre company creating work for families. In five years I would like to have gained further funding to be able to spend more time producing work for families with an education programme surrounding the productions.

Please describe what a typical day working as an Education Officer might contain?

There is no such thing as a typical day. One day will be office based answering the phone, processing invoices and photocopying, the next will be supervising a workshop in a school or working backstage on a performance for hundreds of people.

Have you done any additional training courses to further your career?

I have undertaken various administrative training courses and chaperone training. It is important to keep up to date with current educational practices so that the work you are doing is relevant.

How important is working for free at the beginning of your career?

It is important to get as much experience as possible whilst you are studying / training. I worked during college holidays in the Box Office and Front of House at my local theatre gaining experience of working within the industry, then undertook a three month placement as part of my degree.

Fundraiser

The Fundraiser is responsible for raising money for the theatre or theatre company. They identify sources of funding, create fundraising strategies and complete funding applications.

We asked Stage Jobs Pro member Phyllis Martin the following questions about working as a Fundraiser:

What is the most rewarding aspect of working as a Fundraiser?

The most rewarding part of being a Fundraiser is seeing the projects you have worked on come to life. It can be a very long time from initial concept and beginning fundraising to seeing a result, but there is nothing like it. I love standing at the back of a cheering crowd, being sidestage at a packed venue or watching an inspiring moment unfold in a studio and knowing I made it happen. Opening grant offer letters is pretty good too – but they are rarer than rejection ones so opening the post is a double edged sword! There is also a thrill to hearing about an artist or a project, and realising that it has the magic combination of being inspiring, feasible and fundable.

What are the key skills required to be an effective Fundraiser?

Imagination – I have to be able to picture the end result clearly in my mind long before it exists. A vivid imagination also helps me stay excited and motivated about an idea through the long planning process. Patience – it can take years for the conditions to be right. The first version of an idea is not always the one that gets funded but no creative planning time is wasted time. Projects can reform many times before they reach the right structure. It also depends on getting the right partners, the right political landscape or the right shift of taste. Storytelling – every person in a creative and production team has their area of expertise about how long things take, how much they cost, what their outcomes are and why those outcomes are important. You don't have to be able to do everything they do, but you have to be able to write about it in the right way to the right audience. Psychology & Storytelling – you have make people believe in the project and those can range from a distinguished Board of Trustees to a community council or a group of young people. You have to tell a compelling and convincing story to get them onside. You have to understand what funders want, what their concerns will be and what language they will relate to and understand. I specialise in Trust & Foundations grant writing so have to do this in written form, but Individual Giving Fundraisers need to be able to do it in person. Opportunism – support can come in many forms and from many routes. You have to be open to partnerships from anywhere and always be thinking about how your projects might fit a fund's objectives. Pragmatism – you have to be able to tell when a budget line is realistic, and what a funder will be willing to support. You have to be able to assess what parts of a project are essential and which can be scaled back or cut entirely if need be. You will have a much smoother ride if you can articulate these views to the project team. Diplomacy – no one wants to be the first person to put money on the table, so you have to find as many supporters and partners as you can – especially in this landscape of cuts and instability. You need to convince venues, programmers, promoters and funders that your project can deliver and get one of them to put their name to it. Then others will follow. Tenacity – you have to take rejection on the chin, get feedback, keep trying and be willing to change your mind. Practically you have to be good with numbers, have rock solid office and IT skills and be an articulate writer.

Do you see your role as a natural step on a career ladder, and if so what is the next rung?
Being a Fundraiser gives you an insight into every area of a project, because you have to know about how it works and why it is important to be able to budget for it, describe it and timescale it. You are at a crossroads that can lead in a number of different roles if you are willing to learn the technical skills that go with them. I trained in sound, lighting and stage management to progress into more hands-on roles. I think a natural progression for the Fundraiser with a practical temperament is into production management, where you need to have the big picture and a

solid grasp of the resources needed by each area. There is also a good route into press, marketing and PR, since a lot of the job is talking about and selling projects, and into producing.

How did you work your way into your current role?
I studied English Literature and Art History and was the arts editor for my student paper, which meant I got good at writing, analysis, discussion and persuasion – sometimes with very little concrete to go on. I was active in the circus community as a student and knew a lot of performers and young companies. I wrote my first applications for friends who ran a fire and circus performance group and taught myself how to do it. I helped lots of people edit and wrote applications for small funds for 4 or 5 years before I started writing them for my own projects. I worked in admin roles for arts organisations and learned about how projects got delivered, while writing at least one application a month. I transferred to corporate events for a few years and wrote a lot of sponsorship pitches and proposals. All of it fed into my fundraising skills and two years ago I joined a small company and started writing myself into applications for their projects.

How much do you think networking helps towards landing a job in the industry?
Networking is vital to getting work in all industries, but particularly ours. The Fundraiser has the unique element of being able to raise their own wages. That's how many people I know started out – either straight up volunteering, working on commission or having a paid role within a project once it is up and running. Networking is also important to build the relationships you will have to draw on to be a successful fundraiser.

Do you think you will be working in the industry in the next five years, and if so in what capacity?
I imagine so! Bringing things into being is very addictive. In five years I'd hope to be in a strategic role as an Executive Director, Producer or head of a fundraising team.

Please describe what a typical day working as a Fundraiser might contain?
It will be different depending on where in the cycle you are. I usually separate grant writing, reporting and evaluation into different times as they are quite different mind-sets. I am also very hands-on with financial management for the projects as it gives me an overall view. I might spend the morning making payments, printing and coding invoices and updating the budget ready for when I need to write an interim report. I'll be chasing attendance figures and audience demographic information from people involved in the delivery of projects for final reports. I'll check my calendar of

funding deadlines and usually have two or three that I am working on at any one time. For each application there'll be some research needing done, a lot of which is online. Some is factual – getting up to date costs or distances. Some is wider policy research – finding and reading studies that back up the claims I want to make for the project outcomes. I'd usually be speaking to and emailing project partners to discuss proposals or secure agreements. I'll be checking in on marketing materials and press to make sure all supporters have the right logos and credits. If we have a recently successful grant I'll be checking what we said we would do, looking for match funding and feeding information to the team members about what they can spend and when. I'll also make and monitor a cashflow to make sure there is always money in the bank. When a project is complete I'll do a lot of checking the results against the original funding applications. Many Fundraisers would not be so hands-on with delivery, but it's a good way to get better at the job by seeing every aspect of the project. It's a lot of spreadsheets, emails and calls to keep all the information at your fingertips.

Have you done any additional training courses to further your career?
I've not attended any courses but usually a new perspective is useful and it's always heartening to meet other people in the same field. I get a lot of people to read over applications and ask other fundraisers for suggestions and help. If you are starting out I'm sure workshops and short courses would give you valuable knowledge.

How important is working for free at the beginning of your career?
It was how I started, and is a viable route in. It's also good to try a few places to find the right workplace for you. Fundraising is most successful when you have an ongoing, committed relationship to an artist, company or group, so that you can really get to know the work. Being a volunteer allows you to do that. If you can secure an entry level position as a Fundraiser, or as an Administrator then you can certainly learn on the job. There is never enough money – so an offer to help source funds will always be welcome!

Learning & Participation

Hannah Griffiths, Learning & Participation Manager at the Royal Opera House

ROYAL
OPERA
HOUSE

My current role is Learning & Participation Manager for Opera at the Royal Opera House (ROH). There's a whole range of terms you might hear to describe my line of work: education and community, access, outreach, creative learning or bespoke names for specific organisations' programmes, such as ENO Baylis, named after Lilian Baylis who founded English National Opera. At the heart of all this work is the desire to create opportunities for a wide range of people to discover and explore our artforms, in ways that go beyond simply buying a ticket and attending a performance.

People tend to assume that my work involves children and schools. That's a small part of a much bigger picture. At ROH, we devise and lead a huge range of projects, including developing children and young people with raw potential, work with families, schools and universities, engaging with communities, professional development for teachers and artists, commissioning with specific audiences or performers in mind, devising new work... Last season, I led on many projects, from creating an installation with a composer, sound engineer and various participants, to training teachers to devise original operas with their students, to running a sleepover at ROH!

My route into this work was fairly meandering: I did a BA in Italian and an MA in European Thought before I even clocked that arts organisations were busy forging new links between audiences, artforms and artists in inspiring ways through the work of their education departments. I'd done a year-long performing arts course with English National Opera after university and they asked me to get involved in a new series of family days, as an assistant workshop leader. Working on those was my lightbulb moment.

In Great Britain, there are two main sets of roles in Learning & Participation. Firstly, there are artists – singers, actors, directors, designers, conductors – who work in education and community settings. These might be artists who are engaged on a full-time basis within an arts organisation (such as members of the Orchestra of the Royal Opera House) and get involved in

L&P projects as part of their work. Often, artists delivering L&P projects are people with busy portfolio careers; they are engaged by a number of different arts organisations to bring their skills to specific L&P projects.

The other main career path in L&P is in arts administration and management. This is where I come in. I create projects, based on my knowledge of opera and ROH, then bring them to life. I love the initial phase of a new project: exploring the artistic identity and programme of ROH, dreaming up innovative ways of engaging people in our world, forging relationships with teams of artists (and often partner organisations) to collaborate in making it happen. That's then combined with the more practical aspects of a project: scheduling, managing a budget, contracting people, sourcing resources, working with colleagues to raise money, considering what press and communications we want around the work.

The L&P team at ROH is huge: there are 21 people dedicated full-time to managing and delivering our L&P programme. When I first started out at Spitalfields Music, there were ten people in the entire organisation, with three of us working on a year-round programme engaging schools and communities in Tower Hamlets. The organisation has since grown, but for me at that time, it offered a fantastic way of getting involved in everything and enabled me to understand the workings of an arts organisation at large.

"At the heart of all this work is the desire to create opportunities for a wide range of people to discover and explore our artforms, in ways that go beyond simply buying a ticket and attending a performance"

When people ask me what a typical day at ROH involves, it's tough to answer. It's a cliché but true, that every single day is different. For that reason, I'm taking an average day in November as an example! I started the day at the Roundhouse in Camden, to discuss a Royal Opera/Roundhouse co-production and how we'll work together to put Learning & Participation at the heart of our partnership. I spoke on the phone to a colleague who was in Manchester. He was there with a composer, delivering a 'taster' workshop for one of our teacher training programmes as part of a music exposition. I dashed back to ROH, where we were holding our first 'Big Sing Friday' event. Around 120 people had come to ROH in their lunch hour to learn a duet from Don Giovanni with ROH music staff and singers. There's no official performance or end-point: it's about people finding out more about what we do by taking part. I then spoke on the phone to colleagues at some other national arts organisations, hatching a plot for a new, national programme of work. I caught up with a colleague in finance, to go through my expenditure for October and re-forecast my budgets. Finally, I zipped over to Commercial Street to take part in a workshop with Streetwise Opera, who use music to help homeless people make positive changes in their lives. We're collaborating with Streetwise in 2014, so I'm keen to get to know the organisation and their participants better.

What skills do you need to work as an arts administrator or manager in L&P? Firstly, and most importantly, you need to be passionate about the arts. You'll be working long hours on fairly low pay. If you're crazy about your artform, you probably won't mind. Secondly, you need to want other people to have the opportunity to discover the arts. It's no coincidence that my colleagues in L&P are all pretty generous-spirited. Following that, you need to be highly organised, able to juggle many tasks and conversations at any one time, able to anticipate problems but also solve problems you hadn't foreseen on the hoof. You also need to be able to engage with and get on with a huge range of people, from MPs and wealthy donors, to participants who are engaging in your work in the midst of extremely turbulent lives. The work is demanding, but hugely satisfying – I work with amazing people and have a lot of fun. While I don't want to sound boastful, I believe I have the best job in the world.

*The Royal Opera, under the direction of Antonio Pappano, is one of the world's leading opera companies. Based in the iconic Covent Garden theatre, it is renowned for its outstanding performances of both traditional opera as well as commissioning new works by today's leading opera composers such as Harrison Birtwistle, Mark-Anthony Turnage and Thomas Ades: **www.roh.org.uk***

Front of House & Box Office

"Working in this role opens doors to all sorts of career paths in lots of different types of venues."

Front of House Manager

The Front of House Manager manages customer service at a venue, making sure that the theatre systems and Front of House staff are working to a high standard and that the audience's experience is the best it can possible be.

We asked Stage Job Pro member Cathy Scott the following questions about working as a Front of House Manager:

What is the most rewarding aspect of working as a FOH Manager?
It's hard to pick. My top two would be helping to develop a team and seeing them learn skills and gain confidence in a role. The other would be the moments when you get a second to look into the auditorium and see everyone enjoying the finale, followed by a standing ovation and huge round of applause. It's a great feeling knowing everyone has played their part in making the evening a great experience for the audience.

What are the key skills required to be an effective FOH Manager?
Very quick thinking and quick to adapt to changing situations, the ability to stay calm under pressure, organisational skills and excellent time keeping are a must and, whilst maintaining all these skills, excellent customer service needs to be delivered on top of that. Being friendly, approachable and the ability to put yourself in other people's shoes will help with teamwork and customer service aspects of the role.

Do you see your role as a natural step on a career ladder, and if so what is the next rung?
Within my current theatre I am based in the Operations department and there is certainly opportunity for promotion. The next natural steps would be towards Assistant Operational Manager and Operational Manager positions, but working in this role opens doors to all sorts of career paths in lots of different types of venues.

How did you work your way into your current role?
Having gained bar experience whilst studying I was lucky enough to land a casual bar job after being turned down for a permanent position. As soon as another permanent position came up I applied and was successful. The job was a multi-skilling role where we worked on the bar, cafe, ushering, hosting, ticket office and stage door. While in this position I went from 25 hours to 39 hours and when our staff structure changed I became a member of the stage door team. I then became half stage door attendant and half duty manager and then became a full-time duty manager.

How much do you think networking helps towards landing a job in the industry?
The theatre world is a very small world! The more people you know, the better, and the more opportunities could come your way.

Do you think you will be working in the industry in the next five years, and if so in what capacity?
Most definitely. I couldn't imagine doing anything else. I like to be kept busy, so I'd like to work my way into bigger venues – perhaps more music-based concert halls.

Please describe what a typical day working as a FOH Manager might contain?
I work a mix of show shifts and office shifts. My day to day duties that I manage during my office time include the management of stage door, management of merchandise and programme sales, first aid, foyer music and riders as well as lots of other more general tasks. During show shifts we will gather all the info we need from the company, brief the ushering team and accept the house from the Company Stage Manager, once the audience are seated I will hand the house back over to the Stage team for the show to get started. During the shift I'll attend to any customer queries and oversee the running of all FOH areas. Banking, payroll and show reports will also need to be completed and once the building is clear of customers I will lock up. We also hold conferences, graduations, open days and rehearsals at the venue which means we get a good variety of different shows and events to manage.

Have you done any additional training courses to further your career?
I completed my BA and MA degrees in arts-related subjects which has been a help. More specific to the role though, I have a first aid certificate, SIA license and personal license as well as completing general training like manual handling, COSHH, fire marshalling, etc.

How important is working for free at the beginning of your career?
Very important. When we look at applications it all comes down to
experience and a well-written application. If someone has volunteered as
an usher that experience is invaluable. As well as looking good on your CV
it also helps you develop so you can feel confident in your role and
potentially progress quicker.

Box Office Manager

The Box Office Manager is responsible for managing the box office:
they oversee the box office staff, analyse ticket sales, write sales
reports, help develop sales strategies and attend staff meetings.

**We asked Stage Jobs Pro member Billy Partridge the following questions
about working as a Box Office Manager:**

What is the most rewarding aspect of working as a Box Office Manager?
We're in the entertainment industry, so seeing the audiences coming in to
have fun and then leaving with smiles on their faces and chatting about
what they just experienced, or humming a song from the show. That's the
satisfaction you get. Plus any direct feedback that comes through about the
service they've received from your team tells you you're doing a good job
and inspiring others to do so also. We all need a little more fun in our lives.

What are the key skills required to be an effective Box Office Manager?
Lead by example and be well organised. Try to strike the correct balance
between the best for the customer and the best for the business. In the end
happy customers will make a happy business. Invest in your staff and
encourage them to feel empowered in their role.

**Do you see your role as a natural step on a career ladder, and if so what
is the next rung?**
I have worked in theatre and the arts for more than 10 years, in various
positions but I'm currently looking into taking a side-step to another
customer-focused industry, doing research and putting together a business
plan. Before I set off on that though, I'd like to do some travelling. Of course
if an amazing job in ticketing came my way it would be difficult to refuse!

How did you work your way into your current role?
A friend suggested I might like to do some casual work in a Box Office of an
arts venue that had not long been open. After a couple of weeks a full time
position opened up and I worked my way through the company until I was
the Deputy Box Office Manager. A couple of years in between working in

the corporate and hospitality departments of the venue broadened my experience and I left to take up the position of Ticketing Manager on two consecutive international arts festivals with an audience of 250,000 bi-annually. Following that I managed my own Box Office at a new venue, and saw it through the opening and the first 18 months.

How much do you think networking helps towards landing a job in the industry?
I think it's good to get to know others working in the industry in your area, and further afield, to share best practice and bounce ideas off as well as keeping in the know about job opportunities. Online networking can be tricky without first being introduced, but I have found that online forums are a good way to strike up a conversation and make introductions.

Do you think you will be working in the industry in the next five years, and if so in what capacity?
I do have a five-year plan to open and run a Bed & Breakfast with a small evening-only restaurant. It's small steps at the moment but I feel the experience I've gained so far in customer service, management and hospitality has set me up to succeed in running my own business. If it's not possible I'd like to be a freelance ticketing adviser, something I've dipped my toe into and enjoyed.

Please describe what a typical day working as a Box Office Manager might contain?
Once your staff are in position and have everything they need to sell and welcome guests it's usually time to get the morning's sales reports and banking done. As sales are now 24hrs a day with the majority of bookings made online we need to account for all sales made in the previous day. Many systems now support automated reports but there are always some that have to be done manually. There may be events to add to the booking system or website, offers that need setting up for shows that aren't doing so well and information to share out about current shows, ticket allocations to festivals or ticket agents have to be checked and accounted for. Any customer service emails or letters need to be responded to. A day is not complete without a meeting or two, usually with the Marketing or Front Of House team, plus regular staff meetings, either as a team or 1-2-1 for full-time assistants. We'll usually be working on some administration or marketing projects so I'd check in with the team to see where they're up to. A couple of hours before the show it's time to get things ready for guest arrival: printing tickets, checking guest lists and releasing those last few tickets that were being held. We may be selling merchandise so the stock must be counted in and sold through the booking system for accounting purposes. I like to let my staff take the lead when welcoming guests, but

always be on hand if there are any problems or I can see it starting to get busy. Close communication with the Front Of House Manager in the few minutes before the show starts is crucial to ensure everything starts on time. Once all the tickets are collected its time to cash up and close down and leave the Box Office tidy for the next day.

Have you done any additional training courses to further your career?
I've not had time! I'd love to do some further relevant training and perhaps get some qualifications to add to my experience working in the industry. I did recently complete WorldHost training which I found interesting and a good catch-all when you're trying to set a standard for a team.

How important is working for free at the beginning of your career?
I'm lucky to have not had to work for free at the start of my career. Volunteering does give you the opportunity to show a potential employer your abilities and give you the chance to see if you like the company. I do think that the arts relies heavily on volunteers and it's great to see that so many people will give up their time to assisting with life-enhancing experiences.

Chapter 2
Training

When and How to Choose Your Course

ROBIN TOWNLEY, ASSOCIATE EXECUTIVE OFFICER AT THE ASSOCIATION OF BRITISH THEATRE TECHNICIANS

The purpose of this section is to help you decide when and how it would be best for you to choose a course or apprenticeship. Choosing a suitable way to provide you with some of the tools you will need to pursue a career behind the scenes is always a very important decision. You will always be in a position whereby you will be investing a great deal in the process. You will be committing to invest your time, your energy and your money, not only to pay for tuition and examination or assessment fees, but also in living and travel expenses. You will want to be confident that your investment is worthwhile and that it will achieve the goals you have set yourself. To help you do this you must always think about what it is that you really need to do next to prepare you for work or allow you to progress in your career. When you have identified exactly what you need to do to reach your goal you must analyse carefully the next step, or steps, you need to take to get there.

To undertake any job you need to be competent at the tasks that job requires. Competence is the ability to undertake responsibilities and to perform tasks to a recognised standard on a regular basis. Competence is always a combination of three fundamental ingredients:

1. Skill,
2. Knowledge and
3. Experience.

When thinking about how to choose the best way to prepare yourself for any kind of job it is always sensible to consider not only how you will gain the necessary knowledge you will need for the work, but also how you will gain the skills you will need and how and where you will find opportunities to develop the necessary experience that you will require.

Very often you will decide that in order to most effectively gain the skills and knowledge you need next you must first gain some related experience.

When thinking about how to prepare for a career and how to go about choosing a course or apprenticeship it is always a good idea to identify what you need in terms of skill, knowledge and experience. You can do this by talking to people who already work in the industry, potential employers who may or may not run apprenticeship schemes or to advisors and teaching staff involved in running related training and courses of education. It is also very helpful to speak to organisations which represent the interests of the different backstage careers: Association of British Theatre Technicians; Association of Lighting Designers; Association of Sound Designers; Stage Management Association; etc.

When choosing a course or apprenticeship remember that not all courses are designed to achieve the same thing and that different types of course will be more appropriate for your own needs at different points in your education and career.

"You must always think about what it is that you really need to do next to prepare you for work or allow you to progress in your career"

In order to understand exactly what a course or apprenticeship is designed to provide it is always best to talk to employers, advisors or teaching staff involved in delivering the course itself. However, it is useful to think about four general types of courses when you start your discussions:

1. Educational Courses with a vocational context
2. Vocational Courses
3. Educational Courses in Preparation for a Vocational Career
4. Career Development Courses

There are now also apprenticeships available in a number of areas, known as frameworks, which relate to working backstage or front of house. These frameworks are:

1. Community Arts
2. Cultural and Heritage Venue Operation
3. Costume and Wardrobe

4. Live Events and Promotion
5. Music Business
6. Technical Theatre

Information on apprenticeships in these frameworks can be found on the National Apprenticeship Service website under 'Arts, Media and Publishing'.

Educational Courses with a vocational context.

This type of course is designed to continue the delivery of a general educational syllabus but using the context of a particular industry or career to provide a basis for learning. These courses are a very useful way of continuing general education while beginning to gain foundation knowledge in a particular career area.

Vocational Courses

These courses are specifically designed to provide students with the knowledge they require for a particular job. They also provide opportunities for skills to be obtained and for participants to begin to gain the experience they require to gain competence in their chosen career. These courses are often a very good way of obtaining sufficient competence to commence professional work in a particular job.

Educational Course in Preparation for a Vocational Career

This type of course is very often a higher education course leading to a degree in a particular vocational subject. The course will develop academic skills as well as providing for the acquisition of vocational knowledge and perhaps some skills and experience.

Career Development Courses

These courses very often provide specific training in particular equipment or techniques. They may be short courses and they are often designed to be taken as part of on-going career development.

Apprenticeships

By becoming an apprentice you gain immediate access to employment in your chosen career. Your employer will pay you the Apprentice National Minimum Wage and if you are over 19 the full National Minimum Wage for your age group once you have completed the first year of your apprenticeship. You will be given the opportunities to gain skill and knowledge both in the workplace and by attending courses which may be at a local college or delivered by industry trainers. Some Technical Theatre apprenticeships use industry training provided by the Association of British Theatre Technicians, BECTU, the media and entertainment union, and other industry trainers and you will undertake the training elements of your apprenticeship with employed and freelance technicians from other parts of the industry, not just with other apprentices.

The great advantage of following an apprenticeship is that you are in the perfect place to develop your experience at the same rate as you acquire new skills and knowledge. As you are in the working environment you will have the opportunity to put into practice the skill and knowledge you gain and apply it in varying conditions over a significant period of time.

As a general point all courses tend to include good opportunities to achieve new knowledge. Some, but not all, provide opportunities for developing and practising new skills both mental and physical. The hardest element for a course to provide is experience whereas apprenticeships are very good at providing this.

"Working behind the scenes is very interesting and challenging and can provide a huge amount of satisfaction"

It is also worth remembering that it is very often the case that it is much easier to absorb new knowledge and indeed gain much more benefit from a knowledge based course if you have had some experience beforehand. It is certainly true that you will find studying on a course related to working backstage much more beneficial and interesting if you have already had the opportunity to become familiar with the working environment behind the scenes.

Working behind the scenes is very interesting and challenging and can provide a huge amount of satisfaction. However, it is never possible to predict what knowledge, skills or experience will be useful in solving the next problem with which you will be presented. In planning a training path towards working backstage it is always worth continuing a broad education as long as possible while pursuing opportunities to gain experience in the working environment whenever you can. Such experience can be gained through the support of performances at school, college and university. There are many local, community, amateur and professional companies who will give interested volunteers the opportunity to gain experience working on the presentation and support of performance. There are opportunities for part-time employment in many theatres and venues through which experience can be gained while still pursuing general education.

Of the four types of course discussed above the first three very often represent the last opportunity within your working career by which you are able to continue learning and pursue the acquisition of knowledge on a full-time basis. After the completion of these courses the fact that you will wish to start working in the industry means that you will have to pursue further learning at the same time as being employed. Such courses very often provide you with the biggest single component of your professional knowledge and will be the basis on which you found your career.

Apprenticeships allow you to enter the world of work and still have a proportion of your working day dedicated to learning new skills and knowledge. For the rest of the time you are developing your experience which is an immensely valuable asset.

In conclusion here is a brief checklist which you will find helpful when con-sideringwhen and how to choose a course or apprenticeship:

1. Seek to pursue a broad education when it is available while gaining experience behind the scenes wherever and whenever possible.
2. Always identify what your learning requirements are and what the balance is between skill, knowledge and experience.
3. Remember that some prior experience is very useful in making the most of opportunities to gain further knowledge and skills.
4. Identify your learning aims and make sure you understand what steps you need to take to achieve them.
5. Always discuss your needs and the content and strengths of courses or apprenticeships with the appropriate advisors before making any decisions.
6. Remember that you will continue to gain new skills, knowledge and experience throughout your career and that this can be one of the most rewarding aspects of your working experience.The ABTT campaigns to provide education at all levels in the technical subjects connected with the theatre and theatrical presentation. They also contribute to appropriate regulation, guidance and training for the theatre industry.

*You can find out more about The ABTT at **www.abtt.org.uk**.*

Training: Your Checklist

Training at a reputable drama school is perhaps the best route into a career backstage. Not only does it afford you a thorough grounding in your chosen area and an opportunity to hone your craft with like-minded people who share your drive and passion whilst demonstrating your ongoing commitment to your area of interest, it also gives you credibility in the eyes of employers.

Q. How do I choose a course?

There are lots of other factors you should take into consideration when choosing your school. Your checklist:

- Start by looking at the institution itself: is it a university or college dedicated to drama, media or stagecraft?
- How long has it been established and how long has it been offering a backstage course?
- What facilities do they offer?
- Who would be teaching you – do the teachers have the necessary experience to teach you what you need to know to succeed?
- Check out the institution's past record by researching the alumni – what do past students go on to do?
- Location is important – you may be spending up to three years there, so you have to like the place! If you'd have to move away from home remember to factor in living costs: university digs, food, bills etc all add up on top of tuition fees.
- How much are the course fees? Remember that financial help and support is out there in the form of Student Loans and scholarships.
- Course selection is pivotal – do you want a broad cross-section of disciplines or to focus on a specialism from the start? The school's website will give you a good idea of the course content, but you can always contact them directly should you have further questions – they'll be happy to help with your enquiries.

You might also want to consult Drama UK, who are the national body championing quality drama training in the UK. In addition to the guide below, do check out their website – they've also got a great section on funding your training.

About Drama UK

Drama UK provides a unique link between the theatre, media and broadcast industries and drama training providers in the UK.

The organisation gives a united, public voice to this sector; encourages the industry and training providers to continue to work together; offers help and advice to drama students of all ages; and awards a quality kite mark to the very best drama training available.

Drama UK's mission is three-fold:

1. **Advocacy** – to lobby the Government and key influencers so that they understand the importance and value of high quality drama training to the UK's economy and society.
2. **Advice** – to provide anyone interested in drama and the careers related to it with a route map to the training and opportunities available whatever their age or ambitions.
3. **Assurance** – to ensure that drama training in the UK is of the highest standard through a rigorous programme of quality assurance.

Drama UK Quality Assurance
Drama UK delivers the Quality Assurance role originally undertaken by the National Council for Drama Training (NCDT).

The main quality mark it awards is Accreditation. Accreditation is only awarded to vocational conservatoire training and has been an industry recognised quality mark since 1976. Drama UK recently modified the Accreditation System and now quality assures drama schools rather than individual courses. All vocational courses which can fulfil 'The Hallmarks of Conservatoire Training' at an Accredited School now come under the Accreditation umbrella. Full details can be found on the Drama UK website.

Drama UK Accreditation exists to give students confidence that the training they choose is accepted by the drama profession as being relevant to the purposes of their employment. It also gives the profession confidence that the people they employ who have completed this training have the skills and attributes required for the continuing health of the industry.

Accreditation is monitored regularly by top members of the broadcasting, theatre and media profession.

Drama UK is constantly reviewing its quality assurance function. For the latest information on Accreditation and for details of other quality marks including Recognition, please visit the Drama UK website.
Drama UK was formed in 2012 following the merger of the Conference of Drama Schools (CDS) and the National Council for Drama Training (NCDT).
www.dramauk.co.uk info@dramauk.co.uk

"Drama UK Accreditation exists to give students confidence that the training they choose is accepted by the drama profession as being relevant to the purposes of their employment"

What are Creative Apprenticeships?

ROBERT WEST, PROGRAMMES DIRECTOR AT CREATIVE AND CULTURAL SKILLS

An apprenticeship is a great way to break into theatre. Targeted at people over 16 years old who are non-graduates and not in full-time education, apprenticeships provide an alternative route into creative industries, including theatre. Apprentices get on-the-job training, whilst studying for a qualification and earning a fair wage for their work.

As employees, apprentices work alongside experienced staff to gain job-specific skills. At the same time, apprentices receive training to work towards nationally recognised qualifications, and there are now various Apprenticeship qualification pathways to follow relating to the theatre industry, such as: Live Events and Promotion, Technical Theatre, Costume & Wardrobe, and Venue Operations. Apprenticeships available in other areas of the arts include Design, Community Arts, Jewellery, Silversmithing and Allied Trades, and Music Business.

There are three levels of Apprenticeship available: Intermediate Level Apprenticeships, Advanced Level Apprenticeships, and Higher Apprenticeships, and an Apprentice can work their way through these levels. Apprentices are employed for the length of time it takes to complete all the qualifications within the Apprenticeship, and each level usually lasts somewhere between nine and eighteen months.

For a theatre, apprenticeships offer the opportunity to develop their workforce for the future, teaching good practice, values and beliefs from the moment the apprentice joins the organisation. In turn, an apprentice can help businesses gain a better appreciation of a younger and more local audience. We've been told by almost 80% of employers across the creative industries about the value that apprentices bring to their business, and arts organisations are increasingly recognising the benefits of offering these opportunities.

That's why over the next 1,000 days, we're aiming to put a further 6,500 young people into employment, through apprenticeships or paid

190

internships. Further information about our apprenticeship programme, including case studies and opportunities, can be found at **www.creative-employment.co.uk**.

All Apprenticeship vacancies can be found on the National Apprenticeship website **www.apprenticeships.org.uk**.

Creative & Cultural Skills is a charity that gives young people opportunities to work and learn in the creative industries.   Find out more at **www.ccskills.org.uk**

"For a theatre, apprenticeships offer the opportunity to develop their workforce for the future, teaching good practice, values and beliefs from the moment the apprentice joins the organisation"

Getting into Technical Theatre Training

ANDY FRANKS, DIRECTOR OF PRODUCTION AT MOUNTVIEW ACADEMY OF THEATRE ARTS

MOUNTVIEW
ACADEMY OF THEATRE ARTS

Getting into technical theatre can be daunting. There are many places you could apply to that offer production skills training. Some deliver training in one specific area (for example stage management, design or lighting), or a few, like Mountview, offer a general all-round timetable of subjects in the first year, then specialise as you progress through the course. Some are run by large universities, some by smaller, specialist, independent drama schools. Then you have the choice of either two-year foundation degree courses or three-year BA (Hons) degree courses. So where to start?

This guide will hopefully help answer some of these questions and give you advice for preparing for and making the best of your interview. Of course I can't speak on behalf of all colleges who run theatre production courses, so this is a guide to what we at Mountview are looking for in an ideal candidate. There will be however similarities, so I hope you find this useful.

Choosing the right course is difficult: all courses will require dedication, commitment and drive to complete. Research is key to making this decision. Do the legwork, look at all of your options and speak to current students on the course – often there is a social network link you can use. Look at the alumni, see who has trained there and what they have gone on to do. Talk directly to the course provider, what do they offer, and if you can, go and see the work they produce. Most will have public performances, exhibitions and events you can go to.

At Mountview, we believe that thorough training in theatre production arts is vital to provide the industry with imaginative, professional production and stage managers, lighting, sound and digital creatives and set, prop and theatre designers. Mountview offers three distinct theatre production arts courses of study: a two-year Foundation (FdA), a three-year BA (Hons) and a one-year Postgraduate Diploma. Mountview offers technical students the finest tuition from a full-time staff who have a wide set of skills and experience in theatre, live performance, events, TV and film as well as freelance staff who split their time between tuition and professional practice. We have a strong reputation for the employability of our production students. The detail of training and professional attitude that our graduates possess have led them to work in many areas of the industry.

Application for courses is through UCAS, although you can also apply directly to Mountview. We hold interviews throughout the year, mostly at our production department in Wood Green in North London. The interview process normally takes about four hours and includes a tour of the department and the chance to meet and talk to current students.

Students tell us that one of the most worrying things about the interview process is a concern that they don't have an impressive enough CV or portfolio. Don't worry – you are about to start a course that will give you a huge range of skills and experience. What we are looking for at interview are candidates who have some experience, are keen to learn more and have a real interest in production for theatre and similar industries.

The Interview
The interview itself will last about 20 minutes, and this is your chance to tell us about your achievements, skills and abilities. Unlike a job interview the interviews are informal. The panel want to know about you, they want to see if you are able to take the level of study you are applying for. Most of all they want to see that you have a desire to work in the industry. Be open about your ambitions. Tell us where you are heading and what drives you. You should bring along a portfolio of examples of your work or a CV which outlines your experience to date, but remember that, from the interviewer's point of view, having too much work to look at can make it as hard to see the potential of the candidate as too little work.

"Training will require commitment, organisational skills, dedication, the ability to concentrate over long periods of time and – above all – the ability to communicate at all levels"

Training will require commitment, organisational skills, dedication, the ability to concentrate over long periods of time and – above all – the ability to communicate at all levels. When you have been trained you will have improved all these skills but the interviewers will be looking to see your potential.

Remember this is also your time to interview us and makes sure this is the right college for you. Think of questions about the teaching and learning on the course, what opportunities will we give you, how will we help you get that dream job. This makes the interview a two-way process, so come with a plan to get a real sense of what is on offer.

Your Portfolio

If you are bringing a portfolio keep it simple: think about each page and ask yourself the question 'why am I using this picture, programme or drawing? Will this item generate a discussion, does it really show what I can do or have done?' Make sure the portfolio is clearly labelled and avoid large amounts of written work (remember a picture speaks a thousand words). A variety of work is good if you have it.

Practice presenting your portfolio to family and friends. Get them to ask you questions about the work so you can feel confident in answering. Make sure you are clear about your involvement in each piece of work.

"It is getting harder for students to get practical theatre experience, but remember experience comes in many forms. This could be working in a local shop, voluntary work, even doing a paper round"

If you bring a digital portfolio make sure you have rehearsed opening the file, playing the media and that you have enough battery life left. If you are bringing physical examples of your work (such as props, a model box or masks) make sure they are easy to carry and unpack at the interview. The panel will not have time to read lots of information so if you are bringing prompt copies just bring some example pages rather than the full script.

References from past employers or directors/stage managers/designers you have worked with are great, but bring copies to leave with the panel.
If you do not have much work to show you could make something for the interview. For example, find a play that interests you and have a go at

sketching your design ideas for the show or generate a props list etc. Being able to generate your own work is a key fundamental of the course and would show the panel that you are able to push yourself.

Experience
It is getting harder for students to get practical theatre experience, but remember experience comes in many forms. This could be working in a local shop, voluntary work, even doing a paper round. Joining a local drama group or taking part in extracurricular activities at school will prove a great advantage. Mountview prides itself on enabling students to discover new skills and career opportunities that they may not have had exposure to on their previous courses. If you are lucky enough to come from a school or college that has its own theatre you will probably have more experience than someone whose school only has a hall. Don't worry about this. We are looking for a student who is hungry to learn, someone who is open to the many opportunities the course will present to them. Read, watch and learn. Read plays as this is the starting point for most of our work. Go to see productions, and visit galleries and other cultural events happening nearby. Look at today's creative practitioners and see their journey and how you can follow in their footsteps.

Remember: our industry is wide ranging and the skills you will acquire from the course will enable you to work in many of those industries. Be open about your ambitions. Tell us where you are heading, what drives you, why you have this ambition and how you plan to achieve it.

Good luck. In my opinion this is the best industry in the world. You will have the opportunity to work on amazing projects with dynamic and creative people. I wish you every success as you start your own journey. *Mountview is one of the UK's leading drama schools, with a long-standing and international reputation for providing the highest quality training to actors, musical theatre performers, directors and theatre technicians:* ***www.mountview.org.uk***

Why Study Technical Theatre in Scotland?
ROYAL CONSERVATOIRE OF SCOTLAND

Royal Conservatoire
of Scotland

Scotland has a rich cultural heritage with a thriving performing arts industry.

With countless performance venues and a programme of international arts festivals held annually, Scotland is a creative centre for the performing arts.

Performances are created in Scotland and tour the world, such as the National Theatre of Scotland's Blackwatch; it really is a launchpad for truly international productions.

Scotland is home to a diverse creative community who produce theatre works from classical drama and opera to cutting edge performance art and as a result there are a range of Technical Theatre employment opportunities and study options from short courses to degree level training.

Training opportunities
There are technical theatre training opportunities at degree level in both Edinburgh and Glasgow. Queen Margaret University in Edinburgh offers a BA (Hons) in Costume Design and Construction and in Glasgow the Royal Conservatoire of Scotland (RCS) offers two undergraduate degrees in production arts: BA Production Arts and Design (including set and costume design, prop making, scenic art, costume construction and set construction) and BA Production Technology and Management (including production lighting and lighting design, sound technology, stage management and stage technology).

The Conservatoire is Scotland's only conservatoire and as a result students benefit from invaluable industry contacts. It has established working relationships with companies such as the National Theatre of Scotland, Scottish Opera, Disney Cruise Lines and Stage Technologies and organisations such as the Association of British Theatre Technicians (ABTT), the Professional Lighting and Sound Association (PLASA).

The Conservatoire also offers a range of specialist short courses in technical theatre which allows access to purpose-built facilities and experienced teaching staff who teach on its undergraduate degrees.

Several colleges in Scotland offer post school qualifications in technical theatre such as the Higher National Certificate and the Higher National Diploma. These courses cover a breadth of subject areas ranging from stage management, set construction, props for production, lighting, sound and costume. These colleges are represented by and can be contacted through the Scottish Drama Training Network (STDN).

Why study in Scotland?
A diverse, energetic, friendly, and vibrant nation, Scotland is the perfect location for any student of the arts. So, here's what you need to know – there is a wealth of urban landscapes to explore in Scotland's cities, from Inverness in the heart of the Highlands to the Granite City, Aberdeen, in the east. In the central belt, Glasgow and Edinburgh offer an abundance of arts venues, clubs, restaurants, museums and galleries and, wherever you choose to study, you won't be far from breath-taking scenery. There are excellent transport links with the rest of the UK and Europe, via train, rail and air…

"Performances are created in Scotland and tour the world, such as the National Theatre of Scotland's Blackwatch; it really is a launchpad for truly international productions"

Help and advice
If you're already based in Scotland, there are several organisations which can help you decide whether a career in technical theatre is for you. The Federation of Scottish Theatre (FST) runs a comprehensive programme of training throughout the year covering various topics including communication and management, health and safety and practical technical skills. It also hosts a Winter School at Pitlochry Festival Theatre: 3 days of technical theatre and production skill focused training, professional development, demonstrations and networking.

Training

The Scottish Drama Training Network (SDTN) also exists to help you make the right decision. It facilitates networking and development opportunities in further and higher education all across Scotland. It also runs a technical theatre roadshow bringing colleges and prospective students together and showcasing the opportunities available to study in Scotland, in which you have the chance to tour facilities, attend talks and take part in technical demonstrations led by education and industry experts. SDTN also runs workshops and masterclasses catering to individual staff and student needs.

FST works in partnership with SDTN and Creative and Cultural Skills on the Creative Production and Technical Skills (CPTS) Project which funds a bursary to encourage employers to engage with recent graduates and young professionals. In addition the project works with industry leaders to create training and development opportunities, ensuring that professionals working in technical theatre and production get the best learning experiences possible.
*Keep an eye on both websites for further information: **www.sdtn.org** / **www.scottishtheatres.com***

Theatre & Film

CHRIS HUNT, COURSE LEADER: CREATIVE ARTS FOR THEATRE & FILM AT THE UNIVERSITY FOR THE CREATIVE ARTS

UCA

university for the
creative arts

'Theatre that feels like an art installation. Film that feels like theatre. An evening at the British Museum that could be a night at The Proms and a play that's essentially a film. The single art discipline is starting to feel passé. The art forms are merging like never before – no more so than in the theatre.' [1]

Blurring of the boundaries between the roles of the designer, the scenic artist, the propmaker, the concept artist – in fact all roles that go toward making theatre and film. As arts journalist Miriam Gillinson notes on the National Theatre blog, *'The recession has a role to play in this theatrical trend. Artists can no longer afford to rely on just one specialist talent..... [and] are stretching themselves as far as possible and picking up new skills along the way. These new skills are increasingly finding their way onto stage.'* [2]

Where previously traditional stagecraft roles had been more clearly defined, artists and makers working in cross-disciplinary ways behind the scenes are now integral to productions large and small. Universities are recognising this – there exist courses that are offering a wide spectrum of disciplines that cover various areas of the industry, equipping graduates with the skills and knowledge needed to work in a range of roles and careers.

Look for courses that allow you to work between different disciplines. For example, at UCA , BA (Hons) Creative Arts for Theatre & Film develops students' skills across a broad range of disciplines – students undertake modules in which they design and make for theatre and performance, employing the research and design processes of the designer, and the fabrication skills of the costume, set and propmaker – often in live professional projects.

An example is their recent production of 'Entres les Actes', based on Virginia Woolf's last novel and performed at the Comedie de Picardie in Amiens in Northern France. The play is a professional production, currently touring France and planned to arrive in the UK in 2015. The students worked with theatre designer Fiona Watt in designing the set and costumes, and subsequently fabricated them with professional prop makers, set builders and scenic artists, including seven days working at the Royal Opera House Production Park.

Universities can also offer other opportunities for different kinds of cross-disciplinary collaboration. Students on UCA's Creative Arts for Theatre & Film course take advantage of the opportunity to work closely with those from the School of Film & Media. The students work together on an annual project in which they collaborate to design and make sets for TV productions. This project is devised and developed at the Maidstone Studios, where UCA's Television Production course is housed. Collaborative projects such as this one allow a different kind of cross-disciplinary sharing of knowledge and skills between students.

This practice of working across disciplines is what enables students to thrive in a changing world – combining intellectual abilities with technical and practical skill to respond to the fast-moving theatre and film industry. *The University for the Creative Arts has campuses in Canterbury, Epsom, Farnham, Maidstone and Rochester and is one of Europe's largest specialist Universities of art, design, architecture, media and communication. For more information see **www.ucreative.ac.uk/ba-theatre-film***

[1,2] The Great Merge: The Advance of Cross-Disciplinary Art' by Miriam Gillinson http://theshedtheatre.tumblr.com/post/56979785729/the-great-merge-the-advance-of-cross-disciplinary-art

What Do You Do With a BA in Theatre?

BRODERICK CHOW, LECTURER IN THEATRE AT BRUNEL UNIVERSITY LONDON

Brunel
UNIVERSITY
L O N D O N

© SALLY TRUSSLER

If you are considering, studying, or just have completed an undergraduate degree in Theatre, Drama or Performing Arts, you will probably have encountered this old question: 'Theatre, huh? What're you going to do with that?'

I completed a BA in Theatre and English in 2004, and 'what I have done with it' includes: working in theatre marketing; running a theatre company; directing; working as an actor in musical theatre, film and TV; being a stand-up comedian; training as a professional wrestler; teaching; completing a PhD and becoming a lecturer and researcher at Brunel University, London. So perhaps 'what can I do with this degree?' is not the right question.

Instead: start with you, not with your degree. Think about what you enjoy, and what you are good at. Employers look for graduates who are able to hit the ground running and are already equipped with skills – and the confidence to use them. According to targetjobs.co.uk, employers are looking for skills such as: creativity, problem solving, teamwork, communication and emotional intelligence (to name a few). Look at this list and think how your degree, your experience within the messy and chaotic world of the theatre might help you develop these. Theatre students don't merely learn these skills, they live them. After all, theatre is something we do. When you're putting together a production or performance project with a group, you're already demonstrating that you have the ability to 'cope with pressure or change'; to 'self motivate and to motivate others'; to 'research'; to 'plan and deliver a project'... the list goes on.

Think direction, not destination. This means just starting somewhere (ideally in a job that plays to your strengths) and having faith in your ability to make smart decisions as you go along. But allow yourself to be surprised as well.

201

Graduate Profile: Dana Segal, BA Modern Drama Studies

'It's almost too difficult to articulate the value of my degree in theatre. Since graduating from Brunel University in 2012, I've been a reviewer for The Stage, I've produced and directed an Edinburgh Fringe show, I've worked as the Youth Engagement Officer at the Roundhouse, in arts marketing... yet today I find myself working as an arts fundraiser. I always knew I wanted to work in the arts, but never knew my 'final destination.' In a way this was a blessing in disguise. I made sure to open myself to any opportunities available and with lots of hard work, enthusiasm and passion, paved my way into a rewarding job that is having a significant and tangible impact on the industry I love so much.'

Brunel is a world-class university based in Uxbridge, West London. Brunel graduates enjoy an excellent employment record, and there will be a strong focus throughout your study on the development of your employability skills: **www.brunel.ac.uk**

"Think direction, not destination. This means just starting somewhere and having faith in your ability to make smart decisions as you go along. But allow yourself to be surprised as well"

Internships

ELAINE FAULKNER, COMPANY STAGE MANAGER AT THEATRE ALIBI

In recent years internships seem to have been cropping up more and more, especially in the theatre industry. When well run and thought through, both by the company and the intern, an internship can be very satisfying and fruitful for everyone involved. However, there are pitfalls to watch out for as there is no legal definition of what an internship is and so the whole thing is open to interpretation. As the number of both high and low quality internships on offer has increased, so has the amount of conversation about what is and isn't acceptable. There are now some really great guides available for both the employer and the potential intern.

We ran the first Stage Management Internship at Theatre Alibi in 2010 for 11 weeks. It was so successful that we have offered one each year since, and this year have been fortunate enough to secure some extra funding which has enabled us to increase the contract to 6 months. The idea began, as I'm sure it does for many companies, as a wish for an extra pair of hands at a particularly busy time of year. Every autumn we start preparations for the spring show whilst the current show is still touring so, as Company Stage Manager, there are a lot of different demands on my time. I was also receiving quite a few requests for stage management work experience, which I find quite hard to accommodate and make worthwhile. We thought there might be a way to solve both problems together and came up with a Stage Management Internship. The plan was that the intern could help provide some much needed extra support and assistance for the busy times, but would also really benefit from working with an established company and experienced performers. We did some research on what makes a successful internship and made sure that we had time for a Health & Safety induction, specific training and feedback.

Every year we try to improve in any way we can and take on board any feedback, not just from the intern themselves, but also from other members of the company they have worked with. We have found it so mutually beneficial that every year we have increased the length of contract (as much as the budget would allow!).

An internship can be a really valuable and pivotal step in your career. Many of the people I've spoken to who are looking to do an internship have identified a gap in their training and/or experience and see it as a way to help fill it. It might be that they have decided later on, after completing their education, that stage management is the career for them or that their further or higher education theatre course was too varied and they need to focus on stage management a bit more. It can often be the next step for someone stuck in unpaid work that needs to kick starttheir career so they have consistent paid professional work. Whatever your initial reason, the right internship with the right company will be a great credit on your CV and an effective way to get your foot in the door of your chosen industry, helping you make lots of new contacts.

If you are considering an internship it's really important to do some research so that you can spot the good from the bad. Probably the most important thing to check is pay. If you are going to be working then it's the law that you be paid at least minimum wage and your working conditions must abide by the Working Time Regulations. The definition of working is to undertake specific tasks that contribute to the work of the company. I would be very suspicious of any internship that doesn't require you to work and/or is unpaid. The only times it is ok not to be paid is if you are a student on a Work Placement as part of your course or have decided to volunteer with an organisation that's a registered charity. Some organisations also offer Work Experience, but this is usually only for a maximum of a couple of weeks and would be a mainly shadowing role and you would always be under supervision. For more details visit **www.gov.uk/national-minimum-wage-work-experience-and-internships**

However, it takes more than wages to make a high quality internship. When considering applying for an internship, read any information available carefully and don't be afraid to ask questions if anything isn't clear. There should be a balance between opportunities to learn and tasks to complete. For this to work, it's important that someone at the company has been designated as the manager or supervisor of the intern. At the very least they are a specific point of contact, but when an internship is working at its best they are a good manager and mentor who will continue to provide support after the contract has ended. A good company will fully induct you into their team, introducing you to everyone and making sure to go through Health & Safety policies. You might be able to find extra info, feedback and reviews if the company has run internships previously by having a search on the internet or asking the company directly (but do check their website first or you'll just look disorganised).

Once you've found an internship that you think will work for you, it's important that you submit a good application ... on time. There's a lot of competition out there so you need to make sure you stand out. You can find lots of advice about writing your CV on the internet (and in this handbook!) so do a little research and see what will work for you. Everyone has different thoughts and opinions so it's worth finding someone you trust in the industry to tell you what they think. My main advice or putting your CV together is to make sure it's clear. By that I mean both in format and in content. For example, it can be quite confusing if someone uses abbreviations for organisations that I don't know as it makes it hard to gauge what sort of experience a particular credit was. Also, I would expect somebody applying for an internship to be able to keep their CV to one page, two as an absolute maximum.

However, I find the area people let themselves down with most is the cover letter. Check if there's a word count and stick to it. It's ok to be under, but the word count is a good guide to what the employer is expecting to receive from you so just writing 'Please find attached my CV' when the guide was 500 words probably isn't a good idea. The cover letter is a real opportunity to sell yourself and let a bit of your personality shine through. Use it to write about why you want that particular job with that particular company. When applying specifically for an internship, I think it's important to say where you're at in your career and why the internship is the perfect next step for you. Part of that is demonstrating an awareness of the things you still need to learn. It really helps the employer imagine how you could fit into their programme. It's ok to reference any particularly important or relevant experiences, but make sure you're not just repeating your CV. Do use the letter to clear up any gaps or anomalies on your CV. For example, it's really worth mentioning a six month gap on your CV that looks like you weren't doing anything, but actually you were teaching drama to disadvantaged children abroad. Not only is it a relevant and interesting experience, but it will make you memorable and will be something to talk about when you hopefully get an interview.

And finally, before you meet a company, make sure you know what you hope to gain from the internship, including how it's going help your future career. Think about any specific training opportunities you could benefit from, especially if none have been mentioned so far. Don't be afraid to ask questions- a well organised and well intentioned company will be happy to answer your (well thought out) questions and intelligent questioning might even work in your favour.

*Theatre Alibi creates exciting new work for audiences of all ages and tours it nationally and internationally. The company also tours its children's shows to primary schools and community venues in its home region, the South West: **www.theatrealibi.co.uk***

Getting Into The Industry

Joe Stathers-Tracey, Senior Lecturer in Multimedia and CAD at LIPA

Getting into 'The Business' can seem daunting at first but we've found our graduates have had a great amount of success by following a few basic principles. If you're studying on a technical or design course you will be prepared for job applications or for building a freelance career, but you'll also have a couple of extra things behind you.

If you don't do a degree or training course you may have to make up some of this work on your own to compete, or to know where you're going.

Highlight your experience: A good course will give you a range of responsibilities in your chosen field, and the chance to work on some ambitious productions alongside performers in your institution, or on external professional shows. Make sure you credit everything you do on your CV and keep it up to date (this includes your StageJobsPro profile!). There are never enough backstage students to cover all the work that needs doing so volunteer for other work that you're not getting marked on to build up your skills. List your practical abilities as well as your projects so that a prospective employer can see what you can do.

If you aren't surrounded by other students then volunteer or get as much casual work as you can at local theatres to add to your list.

Exploit your contacts: Get to know all the people around you and work hard to show what you can do. Many of our graduates get work from people they knew at LIPA, or from other graduates that they haven't met but who appreciate the value of the training they've had.
We've also had really good recommendations from employers who have employed LIPA graduates before and so are happy to see others as they know the standards we set.

If you don't graduate from a recognised course then be friendly to everyone you work with and make sure they know your name. Follow people you are interested in when you see reviews online or read show programmes. See lots of shows and research the places you'd like to work and the people you want to work with. Remember names, hold onto business cards, have an electronic contact list or keep a notebook so that you don't miss an opportunity.

Use your placements wisely: Most courses now have a placement built in, and sometimes it's a stretch to leave it when an employer wants to keep you on and pay you, but remember that completing your degree will set you ahead of the game in the future, especially in seeking a more senior post later on. We have lots of offers from big companies and festivals to use our students, as well as a lot of activity based in Liverpool and the North West, so there will be plenty of chances to work outside your assessed modules and also pick up extra projects for experience or even hard cash.

If you don't take a course with formal placement modules then look for upcoming events near you and volunteer. Be specific about what you can do and when and it will be much easier for someone to decide to take you along.

Exploit your staff: In a place like LIPA all the staff still work in the industry, and will also bring in some professional contacts of their own to talk to you from time to time. Ask them if they need help on one of their projects, or if they can put you in touch with people you'd like to work with. See how they built up their careers and follow their example.

If you don't have formal 'teachers' then everyone you work for and work with has passed on their knowledge in some way (setting a good or bad) example. Learn from this, but also don't be afraid to get back in touch to ask questions or for suggestions about what to do next.

Build up your part: Lots of our design graduates who now design their own professional shows have started out as assistants to leading UK designers. A busy professional doesn't want to make fifty 1:25 model chairs so many employ graduate assistants to do the fiddly details of modelboxes after they've created the initial concept. A lot of technical departments will expect you to start at the bottom, even if you've been the LD for a couple of shows in your final year, so don't think that you're above rigging and prepping gels. We do find that a lot of our graduates have risen up to responsible positions quite quickly, partly because they've had to carry shows before they graduated.

If you haven't had more senior experience don't panic, because there will always be a need for crew and assistants in busy show productions. Learn gradually and develop your career as you go.

"We do find that a lot of our graduates have risen up to responsible positions quite quickly, partly because they've had to carry shows before they graduated"

Keep in touch: This means both staying sociable and knowing what your friends are doing now, but also keeping an eye out on the industry. See how things are changing, who is becoming successful, and what new technology is coming out. See shows and stay in love with the theatre or the music business – be excited! Facebook is great for checking in with people, and also for asking for favours when you need extra crew yourself, or needs digs whilst you're on tour. Keep regularly checking other websites, even whilst you're employed, as you may need to get the next job lined up before you finish this one. Stage Jobs Pro is a must.

Anyone can do this so there's no excuse for slipping behind. Theatre is a very sociable business, and social media make it much easier to keep in contact.

Pay it forward: A lot of our graduates come to us first when they need help on their own productions, and we have Facebook groups and email lists to pass on offers to current and ex-students. When you have an opportunity to help someone else up the ladder use the networks you already have to support your fellow alumni – you will have a better idea of where they are coming from than a total stranger with no references. Staff are usually happy to pass on information about people who you never met at the same college, and they will recommend the best people for the job.

Get back in touch with old colleagues and see if they know suitable people. They may release current staff for one project or know someone good who passed through their venue.

It's a good chance to catch up and also say what you're doing now.
The Liverpool Institute for Performing Arts opened in 1996, and was co-founded by our Lead Patron Sir Paul McCartney and Mark Featherstone-Witty (LIPA's Principal). Today LIPA is an acknowledged part of the UK's higher education provision for the performing arts, recognised and ranked alongside institutions a lot older: www.lipa.ac.uk

Funding Your Training: Useful Links

Student Loans
The Student Loans Company **www.slc.co.uk**
Student Finance Wales **www.studentfinancewales.co.uk**
Student Awards Agency for Scotland **www.saas.gov.uk**
Student Finance Northern Ireland **www.studentfinanceni.co.uk**

Scholarships & Bursaries
Scholarship Search **www.scholarship-search.org.uk**
BBC Performing Arts Fund **www.bbc.co.uk/performingartsfund**
Dance and Drama Awards **www.gov.uk/dance-drama-awards**
Student Cash Point **www.studentcashpoint.co.uk**

Help, Guidance & Support
Direct Gov – Student Finance **www.gov.uk/student-finance/overview**
Direct Gov – Professional and Career Development Loans **www.gov.uk/career-development-loans/overview**
Money Saving Expert **www.moneysavingexpert.com/students**
Drama UK **www.dramauk.co.uk/funding**
Prospects **www.prospects.ac.uk/money.htm**
NUS – Money and Funding **www.nus.org.uk/en/advice/money-and-funding**

A-Z of Drama Schools & Universities

There are so many many institutions offering training across the UK that it's really worth taking the time to do your research and find the course that's best for you.

To help you make a start, we've made a list of the 20 most commonly attended institutions by Stage Jobs Pro members. The following is by no means an exhaustive list and there is more information on course providers at **www.stagejobspro.com/uk/college.php**.

In addition to Undergraduate and Postgraduate courses, do keep in mind that many of these institutions also run a wide variety of short courses and diploma programmes – you can find out more via their websites.

We've also included the number of SJP members who have attended these institutions. These figures are correct at the time of going to press.

ARTS UNIVERSITY BOURNEMOUTH
WALLISDOWN
POOLE
DORSET
BH12 5HH
WWW.AUB.AC.UK
SJP MEMBERS: 337

Arts University Bournemouth, established in 1885 as a specialist institution, is now a leading University offering high quality specialist education in art, design, media and performance across the creative industries. We remain passionate about our subjects and continue to encourage curiosity, risk-taking and adventure in exploring and pushing subject knowledge and its boundaries. The University provides staff and students with a well resourced environment in which to practise to the highest professional standards.

BRISTOL OLD VIC THEATRE SCHOOL
1 – 2 DOWNSIDE ROAD
BRISTOL
BS8 2XF
WWW.OLDVIC.AC.UK
SJP MEMBERS: 410

Professional vocational training for actors, designers, technicians and directors.

EAST 15 ACTING SCHOOL
HATFIELDS
RECTORY LANE
LOUGHTON
IG10 3RY, UK
WWW.EAST15.AC.UK
SJP MEMBERS: 283

One of the UK's most innovative acting schools, East 15 has been providing professional training for those wishing to work in theatre, film, TV, radio and related fields for over 50 years.

GOLDSMITHS, UNIVERSITY OF LONDON
NEW CROSS
LONDON
SE14 6NW
WWW.GOLD.AC.UK
SJP MEMBERS: 507

We're a small campus community with a global reach, bringing learning to life through powerful conversations and personal connections. Proud to nurture the best and the brightest minds, we're looking at the world through our own lens.

GUILDHALL SCHOOL OF MUSIC & DRAMA
SILK STREET
BARBICAN
LONDON
EC2Y 8DT
WWW.GSMD.AC.UK
SJP MEMBERS: 405
The Guildhall School of Music & Drama is one of the world's leading conservatoires and drama schools, offering musicians, actors, stage managers and theatre technicians an inspiring environment in which to develop as artists and professionals.

GUILDFORD SCHOOL OF ACTING
STAG HILL CAMPUS
GUILDFORD
SURREY
GU2 7XH
WWW.GSAUK.ORG
SJP MEMBERS: 393
GSA has built an international reputation for excellence in training for actors and technicians in all areas of theatre and the recorded media.

LIVERPOOL INSTITUTE OF PERFORMING ARTS
MOUNT ST
LIVERPOOL
MERSEYSIDE
L1 9HF
WWW.LIPA.AC.UK
SJP MEMBERS: 415
The Liverpool Institute for Performing Arts opened in 1996, and was co-founded by our Lead Patron Sir Paul McCartney and Mark Featherstone-Witty (LIPA's Principal). Today LIPA is an acknowledged part of the UK's higher education provision for the performing arts, recognised and ranked alongside institutions a lot older.

LONDON ACADEMY OF MUSIC & DRAMATIC ART
155 TALGARTH ROAD
LONDON
W14 9DA
WWW.LAMDA.ORG.UK
SJP MEMBERS: 426
LAMDA has been fuelling the performing arts for over 150 years. We deal in excellence, passion, talent and imagination. A world leader and pioneer, the Drama School offers exceptional vocational training to talented individuals – enabling them to become outstanding actors, stage managers, technicians, directors, designers, musical directors and movement instructors, regardless of their background, educational qualifications or economic circumstances

LONDON COLLEGE OF FASHION

ST. JOHN PRINCE'S STREET
LONDON
W1G 0BJ
WWW.ARTS.AC.UK/FASHION
SJP MEMBERS: 799

London College of Fashion's rich heritage, and responsiveness to changes in design practice, has positioned it as a leading global provider of fashion education, research and consultancy.

MOUNTVIEW ACADEMY OF THEATRE ARTS

CLARENDON ROAD
LONDON
N22 6XF
WWW.MOUNTVIEW.ORG.UK
SJP MEMBERS: 617

Mountview is one of the UK's leading drama schools, with a long-standing and international reputation for providing the highest quality training to actors, musical theatre performers, directors and theatre technicians.

NOTTINGHAM TRENT

BURTON STREET
NOTTINGHAM
NG1 4BU
WWW.NTU.AC.UK
SJP MEMBERS: 407

We're one of the largest and most popular universities in the UK, because we are committed to giving you the best possible student experience. We've invested £350 million in our staff, facilities and buildings over the last 10 years.

ROSE BRUFORD COLLEGE

LAMORBEY PARK
BURNT OAK LANE
SIDCUP
KENT
DA15 9DF
WWW.BRUFORD.AC.UK
SJP MEMBERS: 1081

Set in beautiful, protected parkland, just 25 minutes by train from the heart of London's West End, the Rose Bruford College campus clusters around the Grade II listed Lamorbey House and grounds with modern, purpose-built facilities, including a 330-seat theatre-in-the-round, a 100-seat flexible theatre, two black box studio theatres, spacious rehearsal rooms, recording studios, computer laboratories, design and production workshops, a unique drama library and well-equipped study areas and a café-bar.

ROYAL ACADEMY OF DRAMATIC ART

62-64 GOWER STREET
LONDON
WC1E 6ED
WWW.RADA.AC.UK
SJP MEMBERS: 562

The Royal Academy of Dramatic Art (RADA) offers vocational training for actors, stage managers, directors, designers and technical stage craft specialists.

ROYAL CENTRAL SCHOOL OF SPEECH & DRAMA

ETON AVENUE

LONDON

NW3 3HY

WWW.CSSD.AC.UK

SJP MEMBERS: 1278

Central's mission is to place students at the centre of its work. Central develops practitioners and researchers who shape the future of theatre and performance across the UK and beyond.

ROYAL CONSERVATOIRE OF SCOTLAND

100 RENFREW STREET

GLASGOW

G2 3DB

WWW.RCS.AC.UK

SJP MEMBERS: 397

The Royal Conservatoire is Scotland's national centre of professional vocational training in performance arts. Our location is the heart of Glasgow; our orientation is the contemporary international scene. We are leading the way as one of Europe's top conservatoires, offering a rare breadth of artistic disciplines.

ROYAL WELSH COLLEGE OF MUSIC & DRAMA

CASTLE GROUNDS

CARDIFF

CF10 3ER

WWW.RWCMD.AC.UK

SJP MEMBERS: 565

The Royal Welsh College of Music & Drama, the National Conservatoire of Wales, and part of the University of South Wales Group, competes alongside an international peer group of conservatoires and specialist arts colleges for the best students globally, enabling students to enter and influence the world of music, theatre and related professions.

UNIVERSITY OF HULL

HULL

HU6 7RX

WWW.HULL.AC.UK

SJP MEMBERS: 315

The University of Hull is providing a cutting-edge educational experience for over 18,000 students a year. The academic portfolio contains 50 disciplines across the arts and humanities, business, education, health, the sciences and the social sciences.

Training

UNIVERSITY OF LEEDS

Leeds
LS2 9JT
WWW.LEEDS.AC.UK
SJP members: 396
The University of Leeds is one of the world's top 100 universities and part of the Russell Group of leading UK universities.

UNIVERSITY OF SALFORD

The Crescent
Salford
M5 4WT
WWW.SALFORD.AC.UK
SJP members: 289
The University of Salford is a friendly, vibrant and pioneering University. We continually invest in our campus, facilities and industry partnerships to enhance your student experience and provide opportunities to develop the skills needed to succeed in your career.

WIMBLEDON SCHOOL OF ART

Merton Hall Road
London
SW19 3QA
WWW.ARTS.AC.UK/WIMBLEDON
SJP members: 358
Wimbledon College of Arts has a rich history as one of London's leading specialist art colleges. Our Fine Art and Theatre and Screen courses encourage practical experimentation as a way to learn the skills needed for a successful career in the arts.

Chapter 3
Life as a Theatre Professional

Managing Your Career Online

Despite some very old traditions, the theatre world has fully embraced the power of the web. No longer do employers have to store folders full of paper CVs and covering letters. Using the web they have access to thousands of theatre professionals' CVs at the push of a button and last-minute jobs can be filled in hours.

With the use of powerful search engines, they also now have the ability to find theatre crew and staff with specific skills, experience, driving licences and work permits quickly and easily.

Not just to the benefit of employers, online jobs and networking services have taken massive strides at breaking down the exclusivity of the theatre industry. Details of vacancies can now be shared and communicated on the web to theatre professionals from all across the UK. For those wishing to take control of their career, online jobs services can be a godsend and are probably the most important tool for anyone intending to make a successful theatre career.

The main use of the online service is to find and apply for work, to network and to promote yourself but creating an excellent online profile comes with its own do's and don'ts. Here are Stage Jobs Pro's Top Tips for making the most out of our service:

1. **First impressions still count** – Being online gives you access to the world from your living room sofa. There is nothing more satisfying than sitting in your pyjamas with your bowl of cereal and at the same time being able to apply for a West End theatre job. However you are not 100% free from judgement. We remain a vain bunch and first impressions do still count. Instead of the focus being on you the attention turns to your online profile. So make sure it is crisp and clean. The biggest turn-offs for employers are an out of date or half complete profile, giving off the impression of a lack of interest and commitment. A poor profile can do more damage than not having one at all. If you are going to have a profile online, make sure you are committed to maintaining its appearance!

2. **Be Interesting and Busy** – All sites will allow you to write a section 'About You'. This is your chance to introduce yourself as a person and is the part of your profile where you can be creative and write something interesting. It should be engaging, informative and coherent. It should tell people what you do well and what you want to do more of in the future. Be specific, state certain skills that you have, mention areas of the industry you enjoy and explain why. However, do not waffle (one or two paragraphs are fine). Things to include can be: current role, background, experiences and any additional skills that make you stand out.

3. **Be Contactable** – There is quite often the debate about how much information you put online, however the whole point of an online profile is to let people know who you are and how to contact you. At Stage Jobs Pro we see some of our best jobs come through as urgent requirements. The Internet is fast, but a telephone call is still quicker. Employers in a hurry are not willing to send an email and then wait. They will look for a profile with a telephone number and make the call. As a security measure, at SJP we only allow telephone numbers to be seen by employers, but we still see so many profiles missing this information and hence missing some great opportunities.

4. **Be Literate** – In a time when jobs get high numbers of strong applicants, the employer is looking for any little excuse to help whittle the numbers down to a short-list. Spelling and grammar errors, so simple but yet such a common mistake are a sure fire way of excluding yourself from the running. No excuses – get it right!

5. **Be Professional** – With great power comes great responsibility. Remember you are being watched at all times online. SJP, personal websites, Facebook, Twitter, Linkedin all give prospective employers access to your history. If you want to blow off some steam or rant and rave, do it over a beer with your friends. Don't publish it on the web. Many people have learnt the hard way. Don't make the same mistake. A trend we have seen happening a lot recently is for many professionals to separate their professional presence online from their personal one i.e. creating an open access web page, Facebook page

and Twitter account to promote their professional theatre activities to the world, but also maintaining a separate personal online presence accessible by only a very selective group of friends!

As a final thought, being online is a great way of getting your foot through the door and has completely changed the way the industry works, giving people transparency and access to jobs across the globe. But remember, it will never replace the impact you have from an actual face to face meeting or a good hearty handshake!

Applying for Jobs
AMBASSADOR THEATRE GROUP

Sell yourself
Tell us why you are interested in the job you are applying for and what you can bring to the role. Fill in as much of the application form as you possibly can. Don't leave the supporting statement blank. Supporting information is your opportunity to tell us why you are right for the role. Even if you think you might not have the skills and experience you imagine we are looking for, consider what skills and experiences you do have that could be relevant and transferable and tell us why you might be suitable.

Make sure all information is relevant
Make sure you carefully read the job description and person specification and show us what skills and experiences you have that are relevant to the role.

Make sure your application is well presented
Your CV or application form is your first introduction to your prospective employer and first impressions count. Grammar, punctuation and spelling are still enormously important in creating a good first impression and presentation is key. Check, recheck and read again before you send your form off or get someone else to look through it with fresh eyes. A good application will be remembered even if you don't necessarily have the right skills we're looking for at the time. If the format of the form is an issue for you, tell us. Better that we find a way around it than think you haven't tried.

Double check the application details
If we've asked you to complete an application form, don't send in your CV. Likewise, please don't put on your application form, 'please see CV...' If an application form is requested, then it's part of the application process.

Do your research
Send your application to the contact specified in the advert, and spell their name correctly. If you're sending in a speculative application, make sure the role you put yourself forward for is potentially available at the theatre. As

an example, we get a lot of applications for wardrobe departments across the country, but virtually all our theatres are receiving houses meaning they don't operate with that department. If in doubt, pick up the phone and ask.

Ambassador Theatre Group Ltd (ATG) has grown to be the world's number one live-theatre group with a total of 40 venues in Britain and on Broadway and an internationally recognised award-winning theatre producer with co-productions in New York, across North America, Europe, Asia and Australia. In addition to jobs, they offer internships, apprenticeships and a graduate scheme, more information about which can be found at **www.atgtickets.com/blog/theatre-internships-work-experience** *and* **www.atgtickets.com/blog/atg-graduate-scheme**

"Even if you think you might not have the skills and experience you imagine we are looking for, consider what skills and experiences you do have that could be relevant and transferable and tell us why you might be suitable"

Women Working Backstage

SORCHA HUNTER, PRESS AND MEDIA MANAGER AT THE PLACE

W̶e talked to two Stage Managers who have worked in one of the busiest contemporary dance venues in the UK.

We asked two stage managers who have been part of the technical team at The Place about how they got into the industry and what they think is the most common misconception about the job. Carly Hook is the Technical Stage Manager for Richard Alston Dance Company and Sam Wood is currently the Stage Manager for Hofesh Shechter Company. Both Sam and Carly worked in the Robin Howard Dance Theatre before going on to their current roles.

The Robin Howard Dance Theatre is a 288 seat contemporary dance venue situated in The Place, which is a purpose-built centre uniting dance training, creation and performance in the heart of central London. The Place is also home to London Contemporary Dance School, Richard Alston Dance Company, several youth dance companies, recreational dance classes, and pioneering learning, teaching, outreach, and professional development projects.

When did you decide what career path you wanted to take?

"My interest in the theatre started back in school where I did drama and enjoyed helping to produce shows. For my work experience I contacted the Tricycle Theatre, and then from school I went on to study theatre practice and lighting at University. On leaving university a good friend suggested I start work as a casual technician at The Place. I learnt so much in those three years of freelance work, and it has led on to working in different areas of the organisation. I'm now about to start my second tour with the Richard Alston Dance Company." **Carly**

223

Life as a Theatre Professional

"I studied dance at university and knew that I wanted to work within this industry, but was always unsure in what capacity. In my final year of university I did a week's work experience at The Place. It made me want to learn more about all the different production elements that go into making a dance piece; lighting, sound, costume etc. When I graduated in 2010, I asked if I could return to The Place and help out. I've been working as a casual technician in between tour dates ever since." **Sam**

What does your typical day involve?

"On a fit-up day on tour we arrive at a new venue, unload our trailer of lighting equipment, dance floor and costumes, before starting to rig the lighting with the help of the in-house crew. If we're lucky we squeeze in a mid morning tea break before laying the floor and flashing through the rig. After lunch we'll focus the lights and prepare the stage for the arrival of the dancers the following day." **Carly**

"A show day involves doing technical and dress rehearsals, keeping the company running to schedule as we often have strict time constraints, and then ensuring the smooth running of the show." **Sam**

Which organisations/resources do you think are helpful for people entering your industry?

"Websites such as Stage Jobs Pro email you the latest opportunities. However, I believe, that contacting the companies, venues or organisations that you want to work for and asking for work experience, or if they have any internships or openings is a good way to get started." **Sam**

"I'm a current member of BECTU, the theatre technicians' union and I would recommend joining the SMA, the stage management association. You can't expect to sit back and the work to find you, every job builds your personal network and that is what gets you work." **Carly**

What is the one thing you wish you'd known at the start of your career that you know now?

"How much it would take over my life, the hours are very unsociable, but I do enjoy it." **Sam**

"If you find the thing you love to do, it will never feel like work. I adore what I do, running a show fills me with adrenaline and joy." **Carly**

What I the most common misconception about your job?

"That technicians are big burly men who shift equipment around; I think that a good and efficient technical team consists of a range of skills and qualities. Within the technical team we all have our strengths and weaknesses." **Sam**

The technical team at The Place is a mix of full time staff and regular freelancers who have a variety of backgrounds. From speaking to Sam and Carly the advice that came across strongest for anyone wanting to pursue a backstage career is the importance of supporting any training with hands-on experience, and not being shy about contacting people to ask about potential ways to get involved. Find out more about The Place and any job opportunities here: ***www.theplace.org.uk/about***

"If you find the thing you love to do, it will never feel like work. I adore what I do, running a show fills me with adrenaline and joy"

Working in a Receiving House

REBECCA KEABLE-CROUCH AND EVE D'ATON, SOHO THEATRE

We have both received formal training in technical theatre and stage management. This gave us a good basic knowledge of all areas in our chosen industry. Drama school also provided us with contacts and resources to find work within the industry. For many graduating the next step would be to become freelance or join producing house theatres around the country.

We both went into freelancing in respective positions with many different companies and theatres in the country. Freelancing has many advantages including choice of companies to work with, a larger allowance of personal time and a larger allowance of creative input in the production process. A disadvantage would be being self employed creates a lot more professional pressure with regard to being your own boss, the financial responsibilities and finding and continuing good relationships with companies.

We both believe this is the reason that more and more theatre technicians are seeking roles in receiving theatres. Receiving houses have many benefits including a regular income, continuity in terms of knowledge of venue but with the advantage of a larger turnover of productions and opportunities to progress further up the professional ladder. The reality of such work comes as surprise to many people joining this part of industry. We both work longer hours; usually starting 8 or 9am and finishing around midnight most days. A lot of productions are touring; leaving us the challenge of refitting sets, lighting plans and sound equipment to fit our specific venues. We have had to develop a wider range of professional skill sets to accommodate new challenges we encounter on a daily basis; i.e, equipment we may not have used in previous employment, carpentry skills, retrofitting of outdated kit from visiting companies to a modernised system. There is a lot of emphasis on continuing to improve upon and update this skill set for future endeavours.

Soho Theatre is also a very unique receiving house as it functions as a year-round festival-style theatre. Three venues run at least two different performances in rep every night, seven days a week. A lot of the shows are new writing and are being performed for the very first time, meaning many areas of the performance are in flux and constantly being improved upon or altered technically. As house technicians we have to keep up with this demand and be available to make adjustments successfully at short notice. We both agree that it takes a certain type of 'adrenaline junkie' technician to work, thrive and enjoy such an environment!

Bang in the creative heart of London, Soho Theatre is a major new writing theatre and a writers' development organisation of national significance. With a programme spanning theatre, comedy, cabaret and writers' events and home to a lively bar, Soho Theatre is one of the most vibrant venues on London's cultural scene: ***www.sohotheatre.com***

"A lot of the shows are new writing and are being performed for the very first time, meaning many areas of the performance are in flux and constantly being improved upon or altered technically"

Starting in the Middle

JOHN ROBINSON, WHO MOVED INTO BACKSTAGE WORK IN HIS MID 40S AFTER A CAREER AS A CONSULTANT IN SAFETY CRITICAL COMPUTER SYSTEMS.

Let's get the obvious comment out of the way first, this was no mid-life crisis, and there was certainly no Ferrari involved. However, I did attract more than a hint of shock and disbelief when I decided to turn my back on a 20 year career as a computer consultant to pursue a career in backstage work.

Although I may not have been aware of it at the time, the foundations had been laid in my childhood, when I accompanied my cinema organ-playing Mum to a local cinema. These backstage visits, which gave me the opportunity to clamber into the organ chambers and explore what at that age seemed to be a warren of corridors, fueled a passion for theatrical spaces which stays with me to this day. It took a life changing event many years later, however, before I finally translated this into action.

It was October 2003, the place was Trinity Arts Centre in Gainsborough, and my partner, guitarist and singer songwriter Julie Ellison, had just finished a storming set. The audience had lifted the roof off the place and I was left with the conviction that her career as a performer really should move, in a manner of speaking, centre stage. A year later, at the age of 44, I had retrained as a sound engineer, gained experience in a recording studio, and started a new life as a touring sound engineer and stage manager for a show which we were to tour for the next five years.

I was fortunate to have access to a one year training programme from an excellent, local authority funded, music technology training centre. Admittedly, I did significantly raise the average age of any group of musicians and engineers I worked with, but that never seemed to pose any problems and I quickly discovered that I possessed many skills that were readily transferable to my new working environment. Whilst I expected my existing technology skills would help me get up to speed with the digital technology of audio workstations and digital sound desks, the business and people skills acquired over 20 years of self-employment also provided a firm foundation for my new career.

Some career changes are voluntary, some enforced. This first move was certainly voluntary, and well planned. The second was anything but voluntary, as health problems meant that my partner, Julie, could no longer tour. In some respects I was faced with a harder decision this time around.

I had to decide between returning to consultancy, or to seek other employment in theatre or music.

In the end, it was a chance event that nudged me in the right direction. Trinity Arts Centre had remained a special place to me. It is, after all, the theatre in which I took that first life-changing decision. So, when I saw an appeal for technical volunteers in the theatre's brochure, I got in touch. A couple of emails later, I found myself, back where it had all started, ready to contribute my sound engineering skills, and ready to learn about lighting.

It wasn't long before paid opportunities began to crop up and, again within a year, I was starting to generate income through a variety of stage management, re-lighting and sound engineering jobs. Since then I ve been really fortunate to have worked in some iconic theatres, including modern venues such as The Lowry, and Frank Matcham masterpieces such as Buxton Opera House, as well as being part of the UK's largest walkabout theatre event (the Dukes Theatre s summer production in Lancaster's Williamson Park).

"Volunteering brings its own challenges, not least of which is deciding how much time you can give freely, and at which theatre or event"

The second time around it is volunteering, rather than training, that has built the foundation for my career change. Volunteering brings its own challenges, not least of which is deciding how much time you can give freely, and at which theatre or event. There is no doubt that volunteers keep many venues open, and in doing so they often help to keep the paid staff in work. However, there is a world of difference between this and a volunteer whose time boosts the profits of a commercial venue, whilst displacing paid staff. It can be a tricky call to make, but I can say that, at Trinity, I have given a lot but gained far more than I put in, and I have not displaced a paid member of staff in the process.

Certainly, ten years on, I would find it harder to justify taking a year out to retrain than I did at 43. Of course, training is an ongoing process, and I attend training events on specific technologies, topics or products, whenever I can. Thankfully there is a wealth of training available, sometimes at low or no cost. In the last year I have had hands-on training on DiGiCo sound desks and expanded my skills in sound design, but I also continue to volunteer. Although paid work has reduced the amount of time I can offer, and must take precedence, I still do what I can and I still gain experience every time. And that experience is important. The feedback from employers is that experience is very highly valued, often taking precedence over training or qualifications.

Age is sometimes a barrier. For example, I have lost count of the number of times I have seen the phrase '18-30' or similar when opportunities for training or support are advertised, but I ve also lost count of the number of times a venue technician has been critical of the recent graduate who refuses to sweep the floor. Whether this is the fault of the graduate, or the institution from which they have graduated, is perhaps debatable, but there is no doubt that a more advanced age, and the life experience that goes with it, can also be a positive thing.

Age also brings an increasing sense of urgency, a need to fast-track, to move forward without too much delay. I simply don t have the time I had when I was 20. That means keeping focussed on my personal goals and avoiding any unnecessary, or unproductive, diversions.

Life has many roads, many twists and turns, u-turns and detours. But I am happy that there is a moment in every show, usually sometime between beginners call and LX2 (it varies according to my role) when I know that there is nowhere else I would rather be.

John Robinson is a freelance sound engineer, theatre technician and technical stage manager. His website is **www.acoustyistics.co.uk**

Alternative Sources of Work

The beauty of pursuing a career backstage is that the skills you develop aren't just limited to working in traditional theatre environments. The following are just a few areas of work open to you as a trained theatre professional.

Working in the Leisure Industry

<small>ANDREW SUGG, BOURNE LEISURE</small>

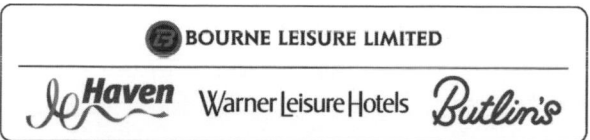

Where do technically gifted/trained/minded people find employment that gives them a foundation to grow and flourish within the entertainments industry? No doubt a question asked by many, and one to which that people looking to get into the industry add several additional factors: a job that provides stability and an opportunity to display skills and creativity.

Having over fifteen years experience exploring different avenues in the entertainment world, including amateur theatre, the West End and working with a renowned UK supplier to the entertainments industry, I have found a place that many have overlooked as it is not seen as part of mainstream entertainment: the Leisure Industry!

The Leisure Industry provides a variety of entertainment to thousands upon thousands of people year in year out, and is a great place for technical people to work and make a career. There are many sectors of the leisure industry including theme parks, cruise ships, museums and holiday resorts, all of which have a need for technical people.

Bourne Leisure, the company which owns Butlins, Haven and Warner Holidays, understands the importance of technical support when it comes to providing great entertainment and continues to evolve each of its brands to ensure the guests receive a well-delivered experience. It is not widely known that each year Butlins recruit on average sixty technical support team member across our three resorts (Bognor Regis, Skegness, and Minehead). The teams are made up of Stage Managers, ASMs, Lighting Technicians, Audio Engineers, AV Engineers, Crew and Wardrobe professionals.

So, what can the Leisure Industry offer?

Butlins have a range of technical support teams – each differing in experience, with the opportunity to learn new skills whilst progressing others. Most training takes place within the team but with strong links with industry manufacturers and suppliers Butlins is committed to progression. At Butlins our teams experience a vast range of genres of entertainment – one that is rarely matched. Our teams could be working on comedy, live music, West End style productions, children's shows, top-named artists, game shows, circus, to name but a few – and all of this can be in a single day.

Bourne Leisure appoints technical teams across its three brands (Butlins, Warner and Haven), each of which with its own structure and job roles, but with the same goal of delivering the best for their guests to ensure entertainment is enjoyed by all.

So to answer the question, I believe there is no better place to be exposed to a wide range of entertainment, with the built-in support of a team with a varied background of experience and the opportunity to be hone skills, learn new ones and be creative.

"I believe there is no better place to be exposed to a wide range of entertainment, with the built-in support of a team with a varied background of experience and the opportunity to be hone skills, learn new ones and be creative"

So is the Leisure Industry viable for a career?

At Bourne Leisure we see our technical teams develop all the time – some team members stay with us for many years and others leave to seek pastures new, such is the nature of the business! As with any business we never want to say goodbye to good people, but when our staff move on it is with the knowledge that they learned a huge amount with us and developed relevant industry skills and experience.

"My name is Matthew Ross and I am an AV Technician within the entertainment team at Butlins Skegness. My role within the department consists of maintaining and operating the camera equipment before and during our shows, creating videos and logos and building, repairing cleaning and upgrading computers, laptops, TVs and projectors. The technology involved in AV is diverse and constantly changing, it's hard to keep up with the amazing advances in what we can produce and create.

AV gives us the opportunity to add a wow factor for our audiences by using graphics and effects through the screens. With each passing year more and more shows are being run by the AV side of the industry. This could involve videos or tracks combined to be queued and played, or having control of several cameras at the same time and having the option of blending computer graphics over live camera feeds. It's brilliant for us to have the opportunity to use our imaginations and when your idea works the feeling is amazing. Many of my most rewarding moments have been when a quick thought of an effect to use during a show has turned into something you would see broadcast in pre-edited films or TV programmes.

I started in the entertainments business as stage crew with no previous experience or qualifications, just wanting a change from bar work. Three years on and I have discovered so much about the business and myself, not to mention learning more than I ever did at school – and I still have a passion for my work.

During my time I have worked with many stars from Katy Ashworth of I Can Cook on Cbeebies, to David Guest and his Legends of Soul show. It is an absolute honour to work alongside people of their stature. There is no repetitiveness in the business, every day is different and there is always something to do to keep you on your toes. I can honestly say that I love my job and hope more people wish to be a part of our big-hearted business."

Bourne Leisure is the UK's number one leisure business. Operating three of the most successful holiday brands – Haven Holidays, Warner Leisure Hotels and Butlins – they have been providing holidays for millions of families since the 1960s. You can find out more at
www.leisurejobs.com/employer/bourne_leisure.

Working in Schools

LUKE GILLIVER

Job Role overview

My current position at Bootham School York is officially a 'Sound & Light Technician'. However, my responsibilities and duties extend well beyond the scope of my initial Job Description. You could call me a 'Multi skilled Theatre Technician'.

My main duties are divided between supporting the academic Drama department and working on all aspects of school performances and events, as well as helping to manage and maintain the facilities.

The position is full time with flexible hours as required, including weekend and evenings as well as early mornings. Excess hours during busy periods are offset in quiet times and during school holidays when working hours will reduce (subject to the demands of holiday events and external lettings).

A little about me

My ambition was always to work in the entertainment industry. I originally wanted to work as a recording technician in a studio, but after a short spell in one for a work experience placement I soon realised I thrived more in the live arena, and so it was then I started looking for courses and pathways into the industry.

I joined the University of Derby on their BSc (Hons) Sound, Light and Live Event Technology course. This was a great course and provided me with endless opportunities to access the wider industry and network, as well as providing me with the training and tools to go on to be successful in this area. The great thing about this course was the flexibility of it, the wide and diverse topics covered and the high standard of teaching from all the staff.

During my final year, I did what I thought was normal, and started panicking relentlessly about what I was going to do at the end. I joined Stage Jobs Pro and started applying for nearly every job that came up that was a resident in a venue somewhere. One particular job cropped up for a 'Sound & Light Technician' in York. It turned out to be in an independent school. Having a link already in York and my hometown being not too far away, I decided to apply and, after a day of interviewing, I was successful against the other five candidates (all whom on the face of it seemed older, and, presumaby, more experienced). This was the first practical interview I'd ever participated in, and involved a series of simple troubleshooting tasks, a

Q&A with a panel and a 10-15 minute teaching slot with GCSE students. Perhaps it was my vast experience of working in schools (primarily my old ones), my delivery of the lesson utilising modern technology, or the knowledge of skills I demonstrated from both university and my work at various theatres that gave me the edge. Either way, I was in.

My First Days
Having joined the Sound & Light department (i.e. me), my first major job was to find out what everything did, the kit available, where all the various controls for everything were and so on. The major downfall here was that everything was hidden beneath a great pile of rubbish, clutter and mess! You can imagine the disregard for tidiness that 11 – 18 year olds have when it comes to this.

It was important that I first got a grasp of the equipment we had, so I developed an inventory database to account for everything (and to this day I'm still stumbling upon 'new' equipment found in store cupboards). I then had to develop and implement new systems of working. This included updating and renewing risk assessments and method statements and reviewing with the school's H&S Advisor the procedures we had in place.

"I originally wanted to work as a recording technician in a studio, but after a short spell in one for a work experience placement I soon realised I thrived more in the live arena"

Day to Day
• Taking venue bookings from staff for spaces and equipment (projectors, laptop, sound requirements)
• Liaising with estates and domestics staff regarding new bookings
• Liaising with staff in the Drama department with regard to supporting the examination candidates
• Liaising with other staff with regard to the possibilities of using of technology in lessons
• Teaching and tutoring small groups of technical theatre drama candidates for GCSE, AS & A2

- Sound, Light, Stage, AV, Video, Show Control, IT, Automation and Live (online) Video Streaming
- Running extra curricular 'activities' after school for Y7 – Y13 in the area of 'Stage Production Skills'
- Preparing Risk Assessments and all paperwork associated with performances and events
- RAs, Method Statements, LX Plots, LX Designs, SFX Plot & Design, Stage & Set Design
- Realisation of designs for lighting, sound and AV ready for shows/events/rehearsals, often to tight deadlines and turnaround times
- Set design and construction on-site, including painting
- Stage Management and overall Technical Manager of ALL events held in Bootham
- Liaising with external bookings of the venue and the Business Development Manager in-house
- Memorial services, external theatre workshops, external venue lets over summer
- Research, source and hire of external equipment for events, arranging courier deliveries for equipment
- Repairing damaged or faulty equipment (current task of repairing Soundcraft LX7II)
- Upkeep of department equipment database (in progress) and repair logs
- Management and administration of department budget and submission of budget requests (annually) and purchasing
- Arranging trips to external venues and exhibitions (current trip to Leeds, PLASAFocus industry event)
- Upkeep of venue equipment and arranging periodic test and inspection of equipment to meet with LOLER, Fixed Wiring
- Installation, PAT (PAT moving to in-house)
- Maintaining and repairing faults with classroom IT (sound, projection) across the school

The expected

At various points throughout the year it's also necessary to work closely with the Drama Department on their termly production and work as the Technical Manager or Stage Manager to oversee the project. This has included working with external theatre companies (Imitating the Dog, Pilot Theatre) and producing a variety of productions. This is where the challenges lie, in providing solutions to make the director's designs a reality in a realistic and safe way. This has ranged from constructing a raked seating system, to mounting four projectors to project four different images of four different surfaces along with the programming and infrastructure behind that control. It also falls down to me to arrange any hires of equipment that are required and beating down the prices.

Beyond the Drama department, every other department can see a use at some point for your specialist knowledge and skills. Our Art department creates some wonderful art pieces that are, let's say, a little tricky to display and so enlist my help. A 10-15ft Man made of only woven cardboard and masking tape ... need I say more?

There are times also where knowledge of installation systems is advantageous to aid the other departments in school (particularly IT) with the troubleshooting of their classroom AV systems.

With other events throughout the year there's never time to sit and relax. With discos, music concerts, fashion shows, cabarets, mini-day festivals and more, there's always something to be preparing paperwork for and planning.

"Passing on the knowledge to the next generation is a vital way of sustaining the industry for years to come"

Teaching
From a teaching perspective, it falls to me to guide and teach GCSE and A Level students who opt for Technical Theatre / Design elements on a one-to-one basis. Passing on the knowledge to the next generation is a vital way of sustaining the industry for years to come. Making sure that these students get a good broad understanding at this age will certainly aid them with their studies in the future and in any work they go into.
As well as this, introducing the concept of technical theatre to younger students (school years 7 – 9) can really inspire and shed new light onto an area that they perhaps haven't realised even really existed before. As part of the teaching syllabus there are also several theatre trips that you get to be a part of, about which you can then feed back any specialist technical aspects of the performances back to the students. This provides them with a varied outlook on the show, and also introduces them to looking at performances from multiple 'angles'.

Special Projects
It's been a pleasure to be involved in the design specification team for a new Art Music and Performance building being developed on site. This has been an outlet for me to network with players in the consultancy, construc-

tion and architectural fields, as well as share ideas and information with these parties. Further to this, I have now been given the task of producing a full technical specification for two new Drama conversion spaces within the school.

Time Off
Now, not every school is the same, but don't assume that because you work in a school you get the summer holidays off! I'm personally on a Full Time contract with annual leave allowance. So while the students are away there's always work to be done, including maintenance, inspections, auditing, stocktaking, budget requests, tidying, re-organising and cleaning.

Exam time you're thinking, everyone's busy doing exams. Well yes, that's true, but in most schools, the exam hall is their main hall (in our case our Assembly Hall), so your venue becomes unusable for 6 weeks. Don't go booking that holiday just yet though – if you have Drama Exam candidates, they need to perform. You need to prepare a performance space for them (somewhere) and you need to help with their exam or moderated performance – setting it up with your technical candidates and often recording the pieces as well as evidence.

"When you see children running a show seamlessly with the skills, tools and knowledge that you have imparted to them, it is a tremendous feeling of success"

What do you need?
A head for planning. Planning, planning, planning. A school is a dynamic place where everything is more important that everything else (depending who you speak to).

Organisation. Students don't put anything back. Find a place for everything, and make sure that everything is in its place. It makes accounting for everything so much easier.

Patience. 'Never work with children or animals' is what they say. Some would argue that these are one and the same. Either way they are great to work with, they just take a little controlling (some more than others) but when you see them running a show seamlessly with the skills, tools and knowledge that you have imparted to them, it is a tremendous feeling of success.

Knowledge. You really do need to know your Profile from your Fresnel, your Speakon from your Powercon. Schools are a vulnerable venue. They are seen by companies to have money to spend on their product, which is of course the best thing since sliced bread. It's vital that you keep an ear to the ground and look and listen at what's going on to protect your establishment. The school relies on you to know what you are doing, and know what others are too.

Communication. You need to talk and liaise a lot with a lot of different people. Without this key skill, you won't survive.

A funny bone. You will drive yourself into the ground if you can't have a laugh. Laughing allows you to make it through the most stressful of days. An understanding partner. This job can dominate your life at times. There are weeks where management decide to have an event on every night (Christmas usually) that needs some sort of tech. Production weeks can be extremely long and hard work. Without an understanding partner, you could find yourself alone.

Sign off
Being a venue technician in a school is just so varied, and it isn't without its challenges. You're often working with people without any appreciation of the technical aspects and demands that theatre or live events have, and it can be frustrating. But stick with it because the rewards and satisfaction can't be beaten.
*Luke's website is **http://freelance.lukegilliver.co.uk**.*

Working on Cruise Ships
WENDY HERON, CROWN RECRUITMENT

I am the director of Crown Recruitment who are the Preferred Hiring Partner for Royal Caribbean International & Celebrity Cruises Ltd. I have worked with the cruise line for almost 20 years and as an ex crew member myself I have an in-depth knowledge of what is involved with cruise work.

If you are considering a theatre career at sea this should give you a guideline of what is expected from a crew member on board a ship. Cruise ship entertainment has changed dramatically over the past few years and you may be pleasantly surprised at the career options and the training programmes on offer. Generally speaking we promote from within so if you have completed your degree and are looking for an entry level stage staff role then this may be of interest to you.

Working in the cruise industry. We don't have a 'season': the ships sail every day of the year and therefore we recruit year round. Positions are available for Stage Technicians, Sound Techs, Light Techs, Broadcast Techs and Riggers. Our venues onboard range from theatres with a capacity of 800 to 1300 seats, to medium and small size lounges. Programming varies from Broadway productions, to club jazz bands, piano and guitar soloists. Some of our ships even feature ice skating productions and an AquaTheater with performance pools, diving platforms and other water features.

"Our venues onboard range from theatres with a capacity of 800 to 1300 seats, to medium and small size lounges"

Sound and Light Technicians. To work as either a Sound or Light Technician, one must have two years experience in live productions. Sound Technicians must have experience with both analog and digital boards, and be skilled in all aspects of live audio from microphone and monitor placement to front of house and monitor mixing. Light Technicians must have experience operating and programming with intelligent lighting on a variety of lighting desks, paired with the ability to troubleshoot plus repair and maintain moving light fixtures.

Stage Staff. Stage Staff must have at least two years experience assisting with live stage or concert productions, including stage equipment breakdown, repair and assembly. Completion of high school or equivalency is required, and training in the field is preferred. The experience does not need to be paid, it can be part of your degree course.

Rigging Specialist. Rigging Specialist (automation technician) applicants must have a minimum of three years experience in the field. In addition, a working knowledge of theatrical rigging, plus the ability to operate and program on automated rigging systems is a must. An ability to repair and provide maintenance of systems is also required, and completion of training or equivalent stage and arena rigging courses is preferred. Riggers will usually be sent to Las Vegas for Foy training prior to joining at the company's expense.

Broadcast Technicians. Broadcast Technicians must have a minimum of three years television broadcast experience in producing, directing, shooting and editing. Experience in editing on linear and non-linear production systems and in multiple formats is required, and knowledge of satellite uplink & downlink procedures is preferred. Finally, troubleshooting abilities are required, and educational training in the field is preferred.

"Cruise ship entertainment has changed dramatically over the past few years and you may be pleasantly surprised at the career options and the training programmes on offer"

Your prospects. Career progression for entry level technical stage staff is good and candidates can be promoted within their first contract to higher level positions. The Rigging Support Stage Staff are sent to Las Vegas for Foy Operator's Certification with Flying by Foy. This position is a stepping stone role to Rigging Specialist working alongside a team of specially trained flyers and many of Royal Caribbean ships include the Centrum

WOW show involving three different shows with flying. The Centrum Wow project takes an under-utilised vertical space in the centre of the ship and turns it into an Aerial Spectacular show running from 4 – 15 minutes combining different styles of dance with circus-like acrobatics and feats of amazing strength leaving the audience in awe every time. You won't find this type of entertainment on any other cruise line.

Other requirements for crew applying to work on board include proof of a clear criminal background check and passing a medical with an approved clinic. Applicants must be over 21.

*Royal Caribbean International produce world-class entertainment with the best equipment, performers and technicians. If you are interested in being a part of this team please submit your CV to **shipjob@aol.com** for the attention of Wendy Heron.*

Social Media for Stage Production

CARON LYON, FREELANCE DIGITAL PROJECTS MANAGER AND COLLABORATION COORDINATOR AT PCM PROJECTS

In 1994 I graduated as a Stage Manager from Bretton Hall gaining a Bachelor of Arts Degree in Theatre Crafts. A year later the course had been renamed to Theatre, Design & Technology. The course hadn't changed but the predominance of specialisms (lighting design, sound engineering) and the emergence of technology (computerisation, projection and automation) was to irrevocably change the skillset and necessary knowledge foundation demanded of production and technical teams in the entertainment industry. Twenty years later and its the Stage Managers' turn to advance and profit for the shifting change.

As a Stage Manager I worked throughout the UK in Sub Rep (Leicester, Sheffield & Chichester), Toured to No.1 touring houses, arts centres, village halls and outdoor venues nationwide, spent a season at Butlins and several years in London Fringe performance spaces gaining experience as Stage Manager, DSM, ASM and production assistant. I operated lights, sound, called cues, acquired props, paged doors, assisted with costume changes and relit shows.

Analog has given way to digital. Bluetooth, Wireless, Wifi and Mobile are not only commonplace but getting 'smart'. Productions can be operated after being intricately programmed and are increasingly automated to such an extent that the only manual involvement is the pressing of a button.

Design, Creation and Operation are distinct roles. Human decision making, timing, planning, judgement are still the realm of stage management and the digital shift has taken place around them.

In 2002 I found myself needing to move sound effects to MiniDisc from a computer after downloading from the internet. This began my journey, 'phono to USB' that was to lead me to discover Social Media, in awe of how pre production and rehearsal communication was going to benefit and how staying connected after a contract ended would become a firm reality. I could see props resourcing and production promotion changing forever.

Discovering Digital

Producing paper props was my first encounter with IT using photoshop and paint packages in the late 90's. I had been using an electronic typewriter and photocopier to write up and distribute rehearsal notes and company calls. The noticeboard and the pigeonhole post was 'the' most effective and accepted method of communication. It wasn't Facebook and Twitter that excited me but email, then Dropbox, Evernote and Bambuser. The ability to share notes without printing, to make changes without reprinting, recording live and having a live reactive audience. I didn't get my first email address until 1996 and social was a long way off. Facebook and Twitter weren't in my tool set until 2007. I hadn't sent my first instant message until 2006.

Pilot Theatre, Second Life and Live-streaming

After several years I retrained as a web designer in order pursue a creative career and to make it possible for me to live at home. My heart always lay with theatre and performance, and the internet opened up a new world of resources. For a short time I worked on an R&D project with Pilot Theatre as their Virtual Stage Manager in Second-Life exploring the capabilities of virtual exhibition space and a pre-production audience engagement arena. Facebook emerged on the scene as an audience engagement location. Not many of my colleagues had even heard of it. I was plunged in to Twitter after being presented with it as a team communication tool; it was the digital water cooler for chatter, links, notes, messages and questions. I discovered a community of digital pioneers at ease with this new teamed-up social interaction, making me feel at the time I had missed the party invite and was playing catch up.

"Theatre people, especially the production creatives including Stage Managers, are inherently good at 'social'. Communication is a key talent"

I now realise its like that for everyone when social media first makes it onto their radar. Social Media has exploded into society's consciousness and has quickly produced a generation with no memory of a world before the web and, even more recently, a generation with no memory of a world before Facebook. That has happened not just in my lifetime (I'm 40) but in twenty years: that's just half of my life time. How long before there is no generation with a living memory of a world without the internet?

2014-15 is set to be dominated by 'the Internet of Things'. Affordable 3D printing is on the verge of becoming the next big phenomenon, yet for many in the theatre industry the age of Social Media is still a baffling trend that many hope will disappear as a passing fad.

The influence of Social Media on stage production is its use to communicate, inform, record and document. In pre and post production social media platforms, tools and services excel. Theatre is a collaborative process. Theatre people, especially the production creatives including Stage Managers, are inherently good at 'social'. Communication is a key talent. The pre Facebook generation are at ease with the tools they need to do their job, up skilling and adapting with necessity.

"Perhaps, therefore, ideal stage managers not only need to be calm and meticulous professionals who know their craft, but masochists who feel pride in rising above impossible odds." Peter Hall

Paper and Show Time
As the Peter Hall quote suggests, Stage Managers need to be calm and meticulous professionals. This also means in this connected digital world being confident that the infrastructure is reliably operational. A clipboard and paper will never run out off power. Multiple copies can be cheaply reproduced and positioned at locations of choice. Only transfer to powered devices with the certainly you will always have access and enough battery remaining.

"Don't add technology to the way you do things, Change the way you do things when you know what the technology can do." Marcus Romer

Going Social – Media, Networking and associated Technology
Many production areas and career professionals in theatre can benefit from the application of the various social strands available online.
Here are the seven I work to develop with organisations and industry professionals. It is vital to acknowledge the bigger picture:

1. Industry Connections and Job Seeking
2. Company Management & Coordination
3. Staying informed
4. Career Development

5. Promotions and Funding
6. Measuring relevance and influence
7. Production Collaboration

The greatest hurdles to adopting digital working are access to compatible technology, reliable internet connectivity and an accepted set of platforms with best practice procedures to gain access in place. Stage Manager, Company or Production Managers can be at the heart of this digital nexus adopting a digital toolkit, embedding process, documenting and determining accepted best practice and taking the the collaborative lead. Social Media mastery is a career skill asset.

Top 10 platforms, tools and services essentials for your toolkit:

Social Media – Photos, Audio, Video, Text shared via links posted to media specific platforms

Instagram – http://instagram.com
Instagram is a fun and quirky way to share your life and work with digital platforms through a series of pictures. Snap a photo with your mobile phone, then choose a filter to transform the image, tag it and post it. The team at Instagram imagine a world more connected through photos.

AudioBoo – http://audioboo.fm
Audioboo is a tool for audio producers to record, upload and share audio. The Audioboo team believe in the power of the spoken word to inspire, inform and connect people across the globe.

A 'boo' is made up of any clip of audio, a picture, a location, a title and a description. Broadcasters, Newspapers, Sports networks, Podcasters, Educators and Community Organisations all use 'boos' to increase audience reach. They can easily share audio on Facebook, Twitter and other platforms and embed playlists onto their sites as listen again players. Audioboo also have a highly active and engaged visually impaired community for whom the platform functions as a social network.

Bambuser – http://bambuser.com
Bambuser is a simple-to-use live video streaming service that allows users to quickly and easily capture, share and watch live video broadcast from mobile phones or computers. Bambuser also enables instant sharing to the world's favorite social networks including Facebook, Twitter, Tumblr, and many more.

Social Networking – Establishing, maintaining and developing opportunities via online platforms

Facebook – www.facebook.com
Facebook's mission is to give people the power to share and make the world more open and connected.

Linkedin – http://www.linkedin.com
LinkedIn is the world's largest professional network with 225 million members in over 200 countries and territories around the globe. Their mission is simple: connect the world's professionals to make them more productive and successful. When you join LinkedIn, you get access to people, jobs, news, updates, and insights that help you be great at what you do.

Twitter – http://twitter.com
Twitter helps you create and share ideas and information instantly, without barriers. Forums and industry site members areas are also an excellent source of networking for sharing best practice, advice and job vacancies. Social Technology – Tools and Applications available providing connectivity for the whole company to a central data resource enabling real time notifications and updating of common documents. (production schedules, rehearsal notes, setting lists, cue sheets, research, company calls etc)

"The greatest hurdles to adopting digital working are access to compatible technology, reliable internet connectivity and an accepted set of platforms with best practice procedures to gain access in place"

Dropbox – www.dropbox.com
Dropbox is a free service that lets you bring your photos, docs, and videos from anywhere and share them easily. Dropbox was founded in 2007 by two MIT students tired of emailing files to themselves while working from more than one computer. Today, more than 200 million people use Dropbox to always have their stuff at hand, share with family and friends, and work on team projects.

Evernote – www.evernote.com

Evernote's goal is to help the world remember everything, communicate effectively and get things done. From saving thoughts and ideas to preserving experiences to working efficiently with others, Evernote's collection of apps make it easy to stay organized and productive.

Google Drive – http://drive.google.com

Google Drive lets you store up to 15GB of your stuff for free, access them from anywhere, and collaborate with others.

Group.me – http://groupme.com

GroupMe is the best way to chat with everyone you in your company or working on your production. It's absolutely free, whether you're talking to a department, or texting with one person. Best of all, it works on nearly every phone, via push or SMS. With GroupMe, it's easy to reach anyone, anytime, anywhere.

Caron has created professional social networks for Arts Council England, the Federation of Entertainment Unions and Audiences Europe:
www.pcmcreative.com/social-media-consultation.html *|*
www.twitter.com/pcmcreative *|* ***www.linkedin.com/in/pcmcreative****. For further insights in developing your toolkit and skillset register for PCM & SJP associated workshops and surgeries:* ***http://bit.ly/sjppcm14***

Crossing Borders: Life as an International Theatre Director

TEUNKIE VAN DER SLUIJS

The question theatre professionals are asked the most, think (or should think) about the hardest, and are likely to be worst at answering, is: 'what do you do?' You'll encounter it in every theatre job interview, see it on every application form, and have to answer it for every funding bid – not to mention hear it from bemused outsiders and concerned relatives. It is the question I find most challenging to answer, as at least half my work will be invisible to the asker: I spend about half the year working in the UK, and the other half internationally in continental Europe or the US. What are the rewards, challenges, and opportunities for contemporary theatre directors, or theatre professionals of any kind, aspiring to an international career?

The same but different

In conversations with peers, I realised how many British directors define their work by the repertoire they do, answering the question 'what do you do?' with 'new writing' or 'classics', while their European counterparts will talk about the aspects of society, life, or their artistic practice that they want to question through their work. To me, working internationally provides an opportunity to interrogate changing lives in a changing Europe, inspired by the perspectives that writers from outside the UK can bring, or by the reverberations of big political questions – like the Palestine-Israel conflict with the play Yasser, or more recently with an Anglo-Dutch co-production to stage an adaption of French film La Haine set in the aftermath of the London riots. Perhaps working internationally was a natural career path, having grown up on the European mainland but trained in Britain, or maybe it's because the directors I find most inspiring have branched out beyond their countries: Ivo van Hove, Katie Mitchell, Declan Donnellan, Romeo Castellucci, Robert Lepage, Thomas Ostermeier. Working between countries, between cultures and between languages has widened my perspective and given me an angle I would not have found otherwise.

I won't deny the practical reason behind the path I followed. Working in more than one country provided me with just enough work to not have to do anything but theatre since I left drama school. Historically, the level of pay, the availability of public funding and the working conditions have been more favourable in Europe, although a lot has changed in the past years due to austerity measures. And I like being an outsider: following my own independent path, bringing something from the UK to Europe and the US that doesn't exist there yet, and vice versa.

I was lucky that the first show I directed professionally, fresh out of drama school on the Edinburgh Fringe, got picked up by theatres in Chicago, the Netherlands, and eventually London. Shortly after, I took part in Old Vic New Voices' US/UK exchange, establishing contacts which have been beneficial to this day. I went on to the trainee director scheme at the Orange Tree Theatre where I focused on international repertoire, then to assistant and staff director positions and eventually to directing my own work. I can't tell whether working abroad half the year has halved the speed of my career development – maybe it has, but it is good to remember that comparisons to the career paths of others can be a quick recipe to make yourself feel miserable.

"It is good to remember that comparisons to the career paths of others can be a quick recipe to make yourself feel miserable"

A world of difference

To explain what you encounter when you work internationally, it is helpful to understand the fundamental difference in the function of theatre in Britain and the US on the one side, and continental Europe on the other. The role of the director in Anglo-American theatre has traditionally been one of subservience to the playwright because of the centrality of text, preferring directors to be educated craftspeople rather than artists. In Europe, the director is seen more as an auteur who gives the writing an equal, not a leading position in the myriad of elements of a theatre production. This creates different aspirations: in Britain, directors will largely keep a playtext intact, but look for links or relevance to the present. In Europe, directors are more likely to think the present through with the aid of theatre from a need to rigorously exorcise what troubles, moves or traumatises them in our world. There are different theories as to how this came about, but I believe the relative political stability of Britain led to pragmatism, whereas Europe's tumultuous past of changing borders and allegiances led to continual re-investigating of identity and beliefs. Stable

Britain produced a rich language. Unstable Europe and horrific experiences of abuse of words for political power produced a need for exorcisms transcending the word by embracing the visual, the physical, the aural, the spatial, et cetera.

It led to practical implications on the processes of theatremaking. British theatre is rehearsed largely in pragmatic ways: four week periods to tackle the challenges in staging the script, only bringing elements into the rehearsal room when they are needed, from deciding which samovar should be pulled from the prop store to seeing the actors in costume not before the dress rehearsal. In Europe, the role of conceptual dramaturgy is bigger (even the notion that a dramaturge is fundamental to a rehearsal process is alien to most British theatre), and more time is given to montage, the painstaking process to edit a show together out of all its contributing disciplines, miles removed from the British technical rehearsal which largely favours practicality over artistry. Actors' concerns stay reassuringly similar, however: they will the same questions and the same insecurities whether you work in London, Chicago, Amsterdam or Oslo.

Some tips for taking your work across borders
1. Thoroughly examine why you would want to do this. Sure, travelling is nice, but comes at a cost to our planet, your wallet and your family life. What, in your work, makes an international aspect not just a bonus, but a fundamental aspect of it?

2. Be sensible, be sensitive. British theatre can be seen as old-fashioned in Europe; European theatre can be seen as extravagantly experimental in Britain. What works in one culture, and how one culture works, might not apply to another. But the tension between the two can create wonderful results. And never assume that everyone everywhere will just (want to) speak English.

3. School yourself. See as much as you can. Go to the Barbican's BITE season, the LIFT, MIF and EIF festivals. Go abroad. It is easier and cheaper to go that play in Berlin, or that festival in Serbia than our parents' generation could ever have expected. The internet allows you to read trade papers, reviews and, increasingly, plays from all over the world.

4. Be prepared to do a lot of administration. International tours and co-productions require a mind-boggling amount of paperwork, money, funding applications, tax forms, and bookkeeping.

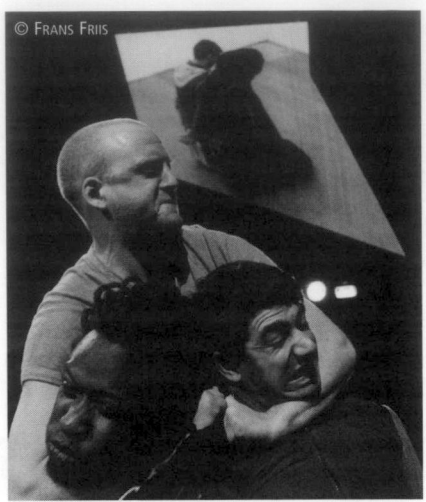

© Frans Friis

Akwasi Ansah, David Beynon and Danny Rahim in HATE after the film La Haine, directed by Teunkie Van Der Sluijs, Rozentheater Amsterdam, 2012

5. Get organised. Develop a system to keep yourself efficient and up to speed. Mine is David Allen's Getting Things Done (Penguin, 2002), but find the one that works for you.

6. Don't expect to get rich, do it for the long game. Sure, overnight success would be nice, but is a very rare exception. Staying power and stamina are worth more than that one hit.

7. Join training and support networks, like Old Vic New Voices, Young Vic's Genesis and others.

8. Learn how to pitch. Stephen Bayley & Roger Mavity's Life's a Pitch (Corgi, 2009) has many helpful tips.

9. Join international organizations like the International Network for Students in Theatre Directing (insted.eu), International Young Makers in Transit (iyme.eu), the International Network for Contemporary Performing Arts (ietm.org) or others.

*Teunkie Van Der Sluijs is a director and translator, artistic director of Anglo-Dutch company Studio Dubbelagent and resident director at the National Theatre of the Netherlands & ImagineNation's collaboration Theater Amsterdam. You can find him on Twitter at **@teunkie** and at **teunkie.com**.*

Using Film in Theatre: Can these Two Mediums Contribute to one another?

KARL FALCONER, ARTISTIC DIRECTOR AT PURPLECOAT PRODUCTIONS

S am Mendes was once asked when he was going to make a 3D film. He told the reporter that he's been making them for years: it's called theatre. A constant line of enquiry to actors and directors working across mediums is which grabs their interest more: theatre or film? The expectation clearly is that one is subservient to the other; the magic of live theatre can never be replicated on a cinema screen, whereas the mind-boggling effects of a Hollywood blockbuster are far superior to anything playing on Broadway. The people who ask these questions and make these assumptions clearly haven't taken a step back to consider who they're questioning. I'm sure the likes of Kevin Spacey or Ian McKellen aren't so strapped for cash that they're accepting work that they believe to be 'less interesting' than others. The constant response is that there is huge enjoyment to be gleaned from both, and actually, the subtle but important differences between these two very different platforms is a huge benefit to their own skills as an actor or director.

One of the first things you're told as a director is that you have to watch films. And theatre. And read books. Listen to music. Paint a picture. Open yourself up to as many varied and expressive types of art as possible, soak it all in like a sponge and filter through the bits that you like. Why then is the modern theatre scene so afraid of cross-medium experimentalism? I'm not talking here about the idea of filming a piece of theatre, in ways increasingly being adopted by schemes such as Digital Theatre and NT Live. The issue of whether a piece of theatre should be watched in a cinema, and whether it should be accessible after the production has closed are very important, but very different debates. What I want to draw attention to is the use of film within theatre. I am convinced that both mediums can lend to one another, both as an actor and a director, and that if we wish to see a real, tangible development and revolution in these mediums, we need to not be afraid to experiment in such ways.

Our very first theatre production was the Greek Tragedy, 'The Trojan Women'. It is a very dense story on the face of it, riddled with history and backstory and more strange character names than you could shake your copy of the Iliad at. We join the action the day after the fall of Troy, as our protagonist Hecuba rises from the ashes of her fallen city, her family, her community, her army, slaughtered. A series of atrocities are left for Hecuba to endure during the course of the play, not least the heartless butchering of her baby grandson, and the final burning of her city. It is epic theatre in the grandest sense and drama that I warrant could rival any blockbuster epic currently showing at your local multiplex. But our first challenge, as an actor or director, is how to communicate the weight, the gravitas and the depth of everything that has come before. How to communicate the scale of the might of Troy and the relentlessness of the ten year war in a converted club with seats for thirty people?

My solution: film. A five minute video projected onto part of the set, we wrote and filmed our own prologue in which to contextualise the piece that was about to follow. Of course, this could open up the floodgates to an awful lot of frankly dire pieces of improvised drama: ridiculous scenes of men in home made togas running around someone's garden trying to communicate the might of the Trojan army. It shouldn't be approached lightly but should be treated with the same approach and professionalism as the theatre piece itself. It needs to match the style, it needs to genuinely be beneficial, complimenting the production and not just feel like a hastily glued on extra. Get it right, and it can be fantastic. Get it wrong and be prepared for the negativity.

"I have seen a handful of productions that have incorporated film in this way, all of which added extra depth and character development to what isn't, or perhaps can't be, presented on stage"

I have seen a handful of productions that have incorporated film in this way, all of which added extra depth and character development to what isn't, or perhaps can't be, presented on stage. It's not limited to a form or genre either. Two of the productions in question were Alan Bennett's 'The History Boys', and Robert Farquhar's 'Dead, Heavy, Fantastic', a new comedy set during a night out in Liverpool. 'Dead, Heavy, Fantastic' in particular, made hugely effective use of the multimedia to bring the show to life in a dynamic and adrenaline filled way, which was brilliantly fitting of the subject matter. The Liverpool Everyman became a nightclub, and high octane, vivid video inserts overlayed on top of the action helped to link scenes and locations together brilliantly. Sit up set designers: the AV inserts also solved the need for sets! The Everyman is a thrust stage, limiting set design to a degree, which needed to become a nightclub, a terraced house, a club cellar, an A+E department, even an airport at one point. The careful placement of three separate, high end projectors, which were synced to cast a panoramic throw along the back wall, were routinely used to project images and video to extend the sense of location further. One scene takes place in an apartment high above the city. Cue a beautifully filmed long-shot of Liverpool's skyline at night. Another scene was set in a car. Two actors with seats, one of them holding a steering wheel. Behind them, a video, probably filmed from the back of a van. Add some lighting and a few sound effects and you're there, with them, totally engrossed by the action.

But what about projector screens, I hear you cry. Yes, having the whole back wall available to project onto is perfect. But your carefully thought out video insert in the middle of 'Private Lives' is going to take something away from the set when you have to place a 10ft wide projector screen in the middle of the stage. True. The solution? That most hideous of phrases: think outside the box. Literally. I saw a fantastic production of 'Richard III' once which demonstrated the use of AV perfectly. Lady Anne has just been wooed by Richard; overcome with her own emotion she produces a hand-kerchief from her pocket. Holding it out in front of her, boom! The lights dim and a piece of video is played out, projected onto the handkerchief. There are a couple of basic rules when it comes to projection but there is also a huge amount of flexibility. Companies such as The Wooster Group really should be applauded for their innovations in areas such as this. Project onto your actors. Project onto the floor. Don't project at all; have a TV on stage. Loads of TVs on stage. Make a point of it. Don't make a point of it. See its potential as a storytelling device.

We have used film lots to convey backstory. In our production of 'Titus Andronicus' with the RSC we wanted to really solidify the central relation-ship between Titus and his daughter as the key focus of the production. We filmed her 18th birthday, mock 'home-video' style. We bought copious amounts of cake and soft drinks (note: Ribenna is a great filmic substitute for red wine!) and told the cast to just be themselves. The footage we got was pretty average – but when we edited that with our soundtrack, we ended up returning to the visual motif of the video about four or five times throughout the show. The naturalism really balanced out with the stylised, highly tense drama occurring on stage, all the while backing up the tragedy that was happening to Titus and his family. The same clips, which meant nothing at the start of the night, were cueing an awful lot of tears by the time we closed the show with them three hours later.

This really is an unexplored, and hugely exciting ballpark, that I would encourage anyone working in theatre to start to consider. It can be a lot of work: having to fit filming days into your rehearsal schedule is a bit of a game changer for some old timers. But the fact is that theatre needs to be a game changer: it's increasingly competing against movies and against the iPhone generation who would struggle to sit through anything for 3 hours. And I don't blame them. In fact, I'm on their side. If I'm going to invest 3 hours of my time, not to mention the price of a ticket, you'd better make it worth it. Hold my interest. Try new things. There is an awful lot of theatre in England today that is too safe. Theatre that reinforces the boring, stuffy stereotype that all of us working in the industry have a right to fight and reform. The country doesn't need another amateur production of The Crucible, for the love of God, grab hold of a barely performed Elizabethan tragedy and figure out how you're going to do it. Film within theatre is ultimately one more tool in your arsenal of tricks for telling your stories. Sometimes it'll be perfect, sometimes it'll be the last thing you need. But if you want to make theatre that engages and that stands out, you'd be silly not to look into it.

Virgin Media Shorts finalists, PurpleCoat have worked with Stephen Fry and the RSC, receiving support from the likes of Sir Ian McKellen and Shane Meadows. They have performed across the country as parts of the World Shakespeare Festival, the 24/7 Theatre Festival and the International Youth Arts Festival. They are entirely self-funded, starting 5 years ago with £100.
www.purplecoatproductions.com I **facebook.com/purplecoat** I **twitter.com/purple_coat**

Working in Theatre: The Things We Forget

SHARON D.CALCUTT

I've been a stage manager for the past twelve years – it's the best job in the world, but it's not without challenges. These are my golden ten, they keep me grounded, good humoured, and more than anything, sane. I wish I had written this list at the start of my career. I now keep it as a go-to list to remind myself, my students, and anyone who finds themselves snapping and becoming the theatre grouch. It's easy to forget why we do it in week three of an endless and tedious tech when all you need is a shower and a good night's sleep. We've all been there, and we are all in this together.

1. **It's not rocket science.** I still spend a lot of my time explain to non theatre folk what it is we actually do. I settle for this, which my father seems to be able to grasp. 'I make sure everything is in the right place at the right time with the right person. Nothing happens without my overview and I keep everyone warm and safe'. When you break it down like that it is very straight forward, however complex the demands of the show.

2. **It's not life or death.** We are not saving babies or curing cancer. It's entertainment. The show will always go on, because we make sure it does. Take your job seriously, of course – however remember that whilst it feels just awful to make a mistake you will only do it once, and you will learn from it.

3. **Take responsibility.** There is no such thing as 'It's not my job'. If you don't know how to do something take it upon yourself to find someone who does. You are never too big to sweep the stage. You will be asked the impossible and be expected to step up to the mark. Have confidence that you can do it, and back that up with creative know-how. Be proud of your work. Make it proud of you.

4. **We are all on the same side.** Actors, directors, technicians, stage management, and wardrobe – we all want to create excellent theatre. We are all doing the best we can with invariably a tiny budget and no time. There is no 'Us and Them'. Be patient with people. Their interests are the same as yours.

257

5. **Be nice to everyone.** A smile can make someone's day. Be socially aware, look for opportunities to be kind. Move through the world with generosity and grace. That is what will be remembered.

6. **There is no 'right way'.** There are many standardised ways of doing things. Try them all, Find out what works for you. Training just gives you a toolkit of techniques; it's up to you how you use them.

7. **Always be prepared for everything.** Think ahead, be ready. Preempt requests. Do your presets the night before. Always have a pencil and paper, safety pins and a multitool. Write things down, however good you think your memory is.

8. **Know your worth and read your contracts.** Know the industry rates, what should and shouldn't be included in your contract and work out where your limits are. If in doubt ask, and don't be afraid to query points and negotiate before you sign. A contract has to work for both parties.

9. **Know your craft.** Inside out. Do your research on theatre history; know the historical and cultural influences that lead to theatre being where it is now, and where every show you do sits along that line. It will make your work richer and more informed.

10. And lastly – It's meant to be fun; and it is. That's why we got into it in the first place. Theatre really is the most amazing place to work.
Sharon was going to be a musician and then... she got caught up in theatre and never looked back. A decade on she is a well regarded stage manager in the industry. She works closely with the SMA, writes for The Stage and teaches the next generation in London's leading drama schools.

"You are never too big to sweep the stage. You will be asked the impossible and be expected to step up to the mark"

A-Z of Useful Organisations

ASSOCIATION OF BRITISH THEATRE TECHNICIANS (ABTT)

WWW.ABTT.ORG.UK

The ABTT is a charity and a company limited by the guarantee of its members. We campaign to provide education at all levels in the technical subjects connected with the theatre and theatrical presentation. We also contribute to appropriate regulation, guidance and training for the theatre industry.

ASSOCIATION OF LIGHTING DESIGNERS (ALD)

WWW.ALD.ORG.UK

The Association of Lighting Designers is the professional body representing all those who work or are interested in the creation of lighting design for live performance and events in the United Kingdom and around the world.

ASSOCIATION OF SOUND DESIGNERS (ASD)

WWW.ASSOCIATIONOFSOUNDDESIGNERS.COM

The Association of Sound Designers is a professional association representing the interests of sound designers and others in the UK theatre industry. Our function is to connect the widely dispersed sound design community, to educate and promote high standards.

ASSOCIATION OF STAGE PYROTECH-NICIANS (ASP)

WWW.STAGE-PYRO.ORG.UK

The ASP is a UK administered organisation for people working with stage pyrotechnics.

THE BROADCASTING, ENTERTAINMENT, CINEMATOGRAPH AND THEATRE UNION (BECTU)

WWW.BECTU.ORG.UK

BECTU is the UK's media and entertainment trade union; sectors covered include broadcasting, film, independent production, theatre and the arts, leisure and digital media.

CREATIVE CHOICES

WWW.CREATIVE-CHOICES.CO.UK

Creative Choices is dedicated to helping you develop your career in the creative and cultural industries.

CREATIVE & CULTURAL SKILLS

WWW.CCSKILLS.ORG.UK

Creative & Cultural Skills is the licensed Sector Skills Council for the UK's creative and cultural industries, including craft, cultural heritage, design, literature, music, performing arts and visual arts.

DIRECTOR'S GUILD OF GREAT BRITAIN

WWW.DGGB.ORG

The Directors Guild Trust and the Directors Guild of Great Britain work together to train, promote and celebrate directors and directing across all media: film, television, theatre, radio, opera, commercials, music videos, corporate film, multimedia and new technology.

DRAMA UK

WWW.DRAMAUK.CO.UK

Drama UK provides a unique link between the theatre, media and broadcast industries and DRAMA TRAINING PROVIDERS IN THE UK.

EQUITY

WWW.EQUITY.ORG.UK

Equity is the UK trade union for professional performers and creative practitioners. As a leading industry organisation, Equity is known and respected nationally and internationally for the work we do with, and on behalf of, our members working across all areas of the entertainment industry.

GET INTO THEATRE

WWW.GETINTOTHEATRE.ORG

Get Into Theatre belongs to a series of practical resources for young people interested getting into the creative and cultural industries.

IDEASTAP

WWW.IDEASTAP.COM

IdeasTap is an arts charity for young, creative people at the start of their careers.

NASMAH

WWW.NASMAH.CO.UK

NASMAH is a professional, social and educational organisation. We encourage the highest standards in the craft of media hair and make-up, and work hard to promote our members.

NATIONAL SKILLS ACADEMY

WWW.NSA-CCSKILLS.CO.UK

We help young people realise their potential and find rewarding work in the creative industries.

PLASA

WWW.PLASA.ORG

PLASA is the lead international membership body for those who supply technologies and services to the event, entertainment and installation industries. As a pro-active trade association, it looks after the interests of its members and seeks to influence business practices and skills development across the industry.

SOCIETY OF BRITISH THEATRE DESIGNERS (SBTD)

WWW.THEATREDESIGN.ORG.UK

The Society of British Theatre Designers is a professional organisation run by designers for the benefit of designers. It was created to benefit theatre designers and their profession and to explore and further the role of the designer within the arts today.

STAGE MANAGEMENT ASSOCIATION (SMA)

WWW.STAGEMANAGEMENTASSOCIATION.CO.UK

The SMA is the national organisation for stage managers and those interested in stage management.

STAGE TECHNOLOGIES

WWW.STAGETECH.COM

A long-term promoter of stage engineering in the world of performance, Stage Technologies has evolved hand-in-hand with and been a key developer of this exciting market.

THE THEATRICAL GUILD

WWW.TTG.ORG.UK

The Theatrical Guild is a national charity supporting those that work in theatres.

Chapter 4
Putting On Your Own Work

From Idea to Stage

RICHARD DARBOURNE, PRODUCER AT RICHARD DARBOURNE LTD

So you know you've got a great idea and you want to get it on stage. You've finished your training and you've spent some time interning at your local theatre (if not, why not?) but you don't know where to go next.

Progressing in the theatre industry is all about you and your idea having credibility. Approaching a venue or a producer with just an idea is not enough and here are a few tips as to what you can do to get started:

Choosing a venue.
Every venue is looking for good work. Identify which venue you think might be suited to the piece you want to stage. Go and see a show there and try to meet with one of the theatre staff. What sort of work are they looking for? How many people do they seat and at what ticket price? Might they have a dark evening when they could give your idea some time on stage? Can they lend some rehearsal space to develop your idea? If not then can a local school or drama group?

Choosing the right team.
Your work is only likely to get on stage if there is a reason why people will buy tickets to see it. Is that the title of the piece, or the director attached to it, or the author, or the people starring in it? Or is it due to the subject matter and could it play in a certain town or at a certain time (such as the centenary of World War One, or the eve of the Rio Olympics?). If you've written it then who would you want to direct it? Where did they last work? If you wrote an email to that venue they will likely forward it to their agent. Or who was the Assistant Director? Could you write to them first? You might be surprised how often those you admire in the industry reply to offer advice. The more you have thought your project through the more they are likely to respond.

How are you going to raise money?

Whether you are a writer, a director, an actor, a designer or a stage manager you need to have thought about this question. Even a modest Edinburgh Festival show can cost around £20,000 (once you've fed and housed everyone and paid the venue and printed your flyers) and you cannot expect someone else to find this amount. They may be able to meet you halfway but have you looked into bursaries, foundations, charitable groups and fundraising events to make your project a reality?

What are you going to do in the meantime?

Even the most successful directors, producers and artists admit that this is a lifestyle and not a job. It can take years before you are able to sustain yourself by doing what you love doing. In the meantime how are you going to cover your bills? If you have a degree then tutoring is often a possibility but others have done carpentry, to driving vans or making picture frames. There is no shame in having to subsidise yourself through other means but you should try and find something that enables you to pursue your goals and not take up all your time so you are exhausted when it counts.

Believe in yourself: but don't just blindly believe in yourself.

Think, this is my idea and, therefore, how can I go about achieving it? Good luck.

*Richard Darbourne Ltd (RDL) is a commercial theatre producer and events producer based in London: **www.richarddarbourne.com***

"There is no shame in having to subsidise yourself through other means but you should try and find something that enables you to pursue your goals and not take up all your time so you are exhausted when it counts"

Arts Festivals & Fringe Theatre Q&A

Q. What is Fringe Theatre?

Fringe Theatre is independent, non-mainstream theatre. It is often low-budget and less predictable than larger, mainstream productions. Fringe Theatre as a term encompasses both Fringe venues – small theatres, or places that aren't traditionally performance venues but will host performances anyway such as pubs or cafes – and semi-professional theatre companies.

Fringe Festivals are events where a particular town, city, or region will host lots of Fringe theatre performances within a short space of time. Fringe Festivals are notable for allowing any performers (amateur or professional) to apply and with any kind of theatrical content (within reason). This means a wide variety of productions are showcased. Usually the only restriction with Fringe Festivals is that the available venues and performance slots are greatly outnumbered by the applicants, so performers have to be refused due to limitations of space and time.

Q. What are Arts Festivals?

Arts Festivals are similar to Fringe Festivals, in that they are usually a series of performances in various venues in a small area. Arts Festivals can programme performances belonging to a variety of disciplines – theatre, dance, poetry, visual arts – or may just specialise in one subject, such as the Brighton Early Music Festival.

The level of performers also varies between festivals – some arts festivals will only have famous, high-calibre performers, and a great deal will be expected from each performance. Other smaller festivals may give amateur musicians/theatre companies/comedians the chance to perform, and some solely focus on young people. Some arts festivals can be a great chance for a small theatre company to perform when they're building up experience, but it is necessary to find an appropriate arts festival – appropriate in terms of experience, genre, and budget. An extensive list of arts festivals can be found at www.artsfestivals.co.uk.

Q. How does it all work?

When applying to Arts and Fringe Festivals, it's usually necessary to contact the festival organisers and submit an application to perform. However, make sure you check the organiser's website where there will be clear guidelines on the application process – when performing at the Edinburgh Fringe, for example, you apply directly to specific venues. Whoever you're applying to, it's usually worth applying early, as fringe festivals are very popular, and venues can get booked up quite far in advance.

If you want to stage a performance at a fringe theatre, you'll need to decide on a theatre that you want to perform at, contact the theatre, and negotiate booking costs and other considerations with them.

Q. What are the advantages?

Because Fringe Theatre and Arts Festivals are often focused on small scale, non-professional performance, there is a much greater scope for a variety of productions. They can also potentially attract a much larger audience and media attention than a company might have had back home. A successful performance at a fringe festival has launched the careers of many performers and theatre companies, and can often lead to UK tours or future performance bookings. They're also a great place to network with other like-minded people in a wonderfully creative and exciting environment, and watch productions and shows you otherwise not get a chance to see.

How To Get The Most Out Of A Fringe Festival

BRIGHTON FRINGE

Brighton Fringe is the largest arts festival in England and one of the largest fringe festivals in the world. It sets out to stimulate, educate and entertain a wide audience by providing a showcase for all art forms. It is also a completely open access festival, which means anyone can put on an event and be included in the brochure and website listings on payment of a fee. No artistic judgment or selection criteria are imposed on participants, enabling the development of both new and established work to attract fresh audiences, press and promoters.

Taking part in any fringe festival can be a life-changing move. It is important to be clued up and knowledgeable about why you are taking part and how participating in a fringe could lead the way to other experiences. Do your research and find out about the various different services fringe festivals can offer. For example, Brighton Fringe is an organisation that nurtures fringe arts all year round. The organisation connects local artists and organisations to promote their work, to develop professionally and to meet other artists, promoters, venues and businesses. It also works closely with festivals world-wide and international networks (e.g. World Festival Network and World Fringe Alliance) to support fringe productions in their touring, fundraising and professional development.

If you are thinking about taking part in Brighton Fringe or any other fringe festival here are some top tips that will help you make the most of your experience.

So you've got an event, but before approaching venues, ask yourself the obvious – why do I want to take part in a fringe festival? A fringe event is a business opportunity; it can be high risk and a financial return can never be guaranteed. For this reason it is important to set clear, achievable goals and objectives. Think about why you are participating; is it to try out new material? Reach audiences? Make money? Or perhaps you want to get a review before Edinburgh? Chances are that it is a combination of some or

268

all of these things. Before you take part, make sure to plan out every step of your fringe journey – include short and long term goals. Think practically about how you will go about achieving them.

Be honest with your audiences – do not over-promise or over-egg your event. When putting publicity together, try to think about audiences and their expectations. In all communication it is important to be clear and honest to ticket-buyers. For example, don't advertise your show as being the best time of someone's life, when it may not be. Words are precious in a fringe environment, so be concise and use them wisely.

Use the advice and resources provided by Participant Services. The team at Brighton Fringe work throughout the year to make sure that participation in the festival is accessible. If you have a query or require information that isn't available in the Participant resource-bank online, contact the team by email: **participantservices@brightonfringe.org**. There are also some great online resources from the folks at Broadway Baby and Fringe Review, these websites have their own participant areas that give advice on marketing, flyering and making up press packs.

Sell yourself silly and take every opportunity to promote your show! Take part in Fringe City (Brighton Fringe's outdoor showcase every Saturday during the festival) and go to the workshops and networking events that take place leading up to and during the festival. As part of your registration

fee you will also have access to the Brighton Fringe flyer licence, which will allow you to flyer anywhere in Brighton & Hove (flyering is not permitted in Brighton & Hove without a licence). The Brighton Fringe Arts Industry office also organises networking events during the festival, which are good places to meet bookers, venue programmers and agents.

Think outside the box! Yes, Brighton Fringe is a market place, like any other fringe festival, but this doesn't mean that you can't approach the experience with creativity and imagination. Do what you do best and be inventive! But remember to be realistic about your aims and how you will achieve them.

Hear from past & present Brighton Fringe Participants...

Jessica Cheetham -Spun Glass Theatre, Participant 2012 & 2013:
'Brighton Fringe helped our career in a few crucial ways; securing a great review from Total Theatre, establishing Spun Glass Theatre as a local company and as a springboard to running Scratch Sessions, a monthly performance event in partnership with The Old Market. The advice that I would give anyone who wants to take part in Brighton Fringe is go for *shorter runs and more traditional performance times than you would in Edinburgh as the audiences keep their day jobs! Also, take full advantage of*

Fringe City every Saturday – it's always packed with people happy to take flyers and hear about your show.'

Doug Segal – Brighton Fringe Participant 2011, 2012 & 2103:
'Brighton Fringe was the springboard for the career I have now. I took my first show along in 2011 with zero expectations and found myself with a hit. The thing I like most about Brighton are the audiences – they are bright, articulate and great fun to perform for.'

Paul Gunn, Brighton Fringe Participant 2012, 2013:
'My advice to others...? Building a performance career is a 'slow burn' as they say. It will not happen overnight and success must be measured in small achievements.'

Brighton Fringe Managing Director Julian Caddy knows a thing or two about surviving a fringe environment. Prior to becoming Brighton Fringe MD he co-founded and co-ran Sweet Entertainments Ltd ("Sweet Venues") with seasons at the Edinburgh Fringe Festival since 2003 and co-productions at the Adelaide, Avignon and Montreal Fringe Festivals since 2006. He programmed and presented more than 700 shows to audiences of over 250,000 people, he shares his thoughts on participating in a fringe below...

'Don't rush in. Approach fringe participation as a business and if you aren't absolutely sure that a fringe is right for you, don't do it. If you're serious about making a success of your work, you will need to have a long term plan to make the most of it. It's probably your hard-earned cash that you are using to bankroll your project so go and experience the environment, visit the venues, speak to as many people as possible before committing. Putting on your work right one year later is infinitely better than jumping in unprepared.

Once you've decided to take part, set a realistic budget and stick to it. Treat the marketing and promotion just as seriously as the work itself. Look for interesting ways to fundraise – anything from raffles, parties, crowdfunding, nepotism, local interest groups, and so on. Look carefully to see if there is any funding to be had for what you do. Think laterally. If at all possible, try to avoid reliance on credit. Overall, be totally committed and shameless at all aspects but inspire people rather than be annoying – there is a fine line. Remember that convincing an audience to fund you is a similar job to getting them to come and watch you. Enlist support on your team too, both admin and creative – don't try to do everything yourself, and besides, getting a second opinion is vital.

And enjoy it! It's a hard slog, so when the going gets tough (and it will), remember it's a well-worn path that you are taking and there is advice to be had from other participants, your venue and the Fringe Office at every step of the way.'

Have you got a show that you would like to include in Brighton Fringe? Contact them in the following ways: Email: Participantservices@brighton-fringe.org | Phone: 01273 764900 |
www.brightonfringe.org | **www.twitter.com/brightonfringe** |
www.facebook.com/brightonfringefestival |
www.facebook.com/BrightonFringeParticipants

"It's a hard slog, so when the going gets tough (and it will), remember it's a well-worn path that you are taking and there is advice to be had from other participants, your venue and the Fringe Office at every step"

A-Z of Arts & Fringe Festivals in the UK

This is by no means a fully comprehensive list of the many arts festivals that take place throughout the year in the UK, but it's a good introduction to the wealth of different events that take place each year. Why not check out local listings to see what's happening near to you? It's always worth contacting festivals around six months before they take place if you want to take part. Please note that the dates given are only the 2013 festival dates, and so may vary from year to year.

ABERDEEN INTERNATIONAL YOUTH FESTIVAL
WWW.AIYF.ORG
Over the years AIYF has hosted more than 25,000 young people from around the globe, making it one of the biggest and most successful gatherings of youth talent held anywhere in the world. AIYF brings more than 10 days of top class performances from around Scotland and the rest of the world.

ARUNDEL FESTIVAL FRINGE
WWW.ARUNDELFESTIVAL.CO.UK
Established fringe festival run alongside official Arundel Festival.

ASHBOURNE FESTIVAL
WWW.ASHBOURNEFESTIVAL.ORG
Ashbourne Arts and Ashbourne Festival celebrated their tenth anniversary in 2009. The company was granted Charitable status in July 2007 and its primary focus is to organise a two-week long Festival during June and July each year.

BATH FRINGE FESTIVAL
WWW.BATHFRINGE.CO.UK
Bath Fringe is a 17-Day festival of all the artforms we can find (and some that don't have names yet) in the Beautiful City of Bath, and with the collaboration of many of its Beautiful & Talented population.

BEDFRINGE
WWW.BEDFRINGE.CO.UK
Bedfringe is an event that celebrates the success of the Edinburgh Fringe and the fringe arts in general (new work and up and coming stars!)

BELFAST FESTIVAL
WWW.BELFASTFESTIVAL.COM
For over 50 years we've been lighting up the city with music, dance, drama, poetry, literature, comedy and visual arts. The festival attracts the biggest names in the world– everyone from Laurence Olivier to Jimi Hendrix has taken part.

BEWDLEY FESTIVAL

WWW.BEWDLEYFESTIVAL.ORG.UK

Festival featuring drama, comedy, music and visual arts, with a range of fringe events.

BRIGHTON FESTIVAL FRINGE

WWW.BRIGHTONFRINGE.ORG

Brighton Fringe is the largest arts festival in England... and one of the largest fringe festivals in the world. It sets out to stimulate, educate and entertain a wide audience by providing showcase for diverse art forms. Everyone can take part, in fact, whilst enjoying a friendly and supportive environment. And all this in an iconic city with unique cultural heritage.

BURY ST EDMUNDS FRINGE FESTIVAL

WWW.BURYFRINGE.COM

Bury Fringe is an independent project which seeks to merge artists of all kinds with an appreciative audience, and encourage the development and progression of existing and new creative projects within our community. The Bury Fringe welcomes performers of all ages and experience, from both the local area and across the UK.

BUXTON FESTIVAL FRINGE

WWW.BUXTONFRINGE.ORG.UK

Buxton Festival Fringe began in 1980 to run concurrently with the world-renowned Buxton Festival, with international opera and high profile literary talks at its core. The Fringe provides a showcase for performers and artists of all kinds in a variety of venues. Dance, drama, music, poetry, comedy, film, exhibitions and magic are just some of the forms that have appeared – we welcome all genres.

CAMDEN FRINGE

WWW.CAMDENFRINGE.COM

The Camden Fringe aims to give anyone the chance to perform and showcase their talents, from very experienced performers and companies to ambitious newcomers.

CANTERBURY FESTIVAL

WWW.CANTERBURYFESTIVAL.CO.UK

MONTH: OCTOBER/NOVEMBER.

Canterbury Festival is Kent's International Arts Festival, the largest festival of arts and culture in the region, and one of the most important cultural events in the South East.

DUBLIN FRINGE FESTIVAL

WWW.FRINGEFEST.COM

Dublin Fringe Festival is a curated, multi-disciplinary festival and year-round organisation focusing on new and innovative approaches to the arts.

DUBLIN THEATRE FESTIVAL

WWW.DUBLINTHEATREFESTIVAL.COM

MONTH: SEPTEMBER/OCTOBER

Established in 1957, Dublin Theatre Festival is an annual event that brings together artists, theatre-makers and audiences from Ireland and around the world.

EDINBURGH FESTIVAL FRINGE

WWW.EDFRINGE.COM

The Edinburgh Festival Fringe is the largest arts festival in the world and takes place every August for three weeks in Scotland's capital city.

GRASSINGTON FESTIVAL OF MUSIC AND ARTS

WWW.GRASSINGTON-FESTIVAL.ORG.UK

Grassington Festival has been providing a lively and enriching cultural experience to residents and visitors for 33 years with its combination of performances, visual arts and live music.

HEBDEN BRIDGE ART FESTIVAL

WWW.HBAF.CO.UK

An annual highlight for the Calder Valley, Hebden bridge Arts Festival brings the best national and international artists and performers to the area each summer for a celebration of comedy, music, dance, drama, literature, and visual arts.

LONDON INTERNATIONAL FESTIVAL OF THEATRE (LIFT)

WWW.LIFTFESTIVAL.COM

LIFT travels the world to bring global stories to London, transforming this city to stage, presenting unique cultural experiences and sharing the stories of the world with the culturally curious.

LLANGOLLEN FRINGE FESTIVAL

WWW.LLANGOLLENFRINGE.CO.UK

As well as attracting visitors from all over the UK, the Fringe continues to grow its local following and is achieving its aim to become 'the festival for the town in the town'.

MANCHESTER INTERNATIONAL FESTIVAL

WWW.MIF.CO.UK

Manchester International Festival is the world's first festival of original, new work and special events, and takes place biennially in Manchester, UK.

OXFRINGE

WWW.OXFRINGE.COM

Oxfringe is not for profit and is run for the prime purpose of promoting upcoming artists who are not yet established and to provide arts entertainment for the benefit of the community of Oxford and for audiences from further afield.

PULSE FRINGE FESTIVAL (IPSWICH)

WWW.PULSEFRINGE.COM

PULSE Festival is a part curated/part open application 10 day festival focusing on new and innovative approaches, offering a bright and inspiring snapshot of contemporary theatre and performance.

SALISBURY INTERNATIONAL ARTS FESTIVAL

WWW.SALISBURYFESTIVAL.CO.UK

From mid-May to early June each year, the beautiful historic city of Salisbury is transformed as people flock to the Festival, enjoying both ticketed events and free performances.

STRATFORD ARTS FESTIVAL

WWW.STRATFORDFRINGE.CO.UK

Fringe comedy, dance, theatre, poetry, and music in Stratford-upon-Avon.

Arts Funding

Putting on productions costs money. Lots of it. Hiring a performance space, costumes, props, and a cast and crew can be very expensive. Luckily there is arts funding out there to help – particularly if you're doing work that is innovative, groundbreaking, aims to be inclusive to minority groups, or which tackles a topical or social issue. Here's our basic rundown of what organisations can help and the right way to approach a funding application.

Arts Funding Organisations

The Arts Council (which has separate departments for Wales, Scotland, Northern Ireland, and England) is an organisation that gets government funding and money from The National Lottery, and then invests it into art-related projects – dance, theatre, music, art, and many other forms. You can apply for funding at **www.artscouncil.org.uk/funding/apply-for-funding**. Contact details for the Arts Council are provided below.

IdeasTap is a not-for-profit creative funding organisation, set up to help fund young people in the arts. They offer funding to arts projects, but also have a very informative section on Arts Funding at **www.ideastap.com/Funding**

The BBC Performing Arts Fund provides financial and other support to individuals and groups who would otherwise not be able to perform. More information can be found at **www.bbc.co.uk/performingarts-fund.**

Other Funding Options

For smaller projects it is also possible to fundraise independently. In recent years, crowd-funding websites such as IndieGoGo, Kickstarter, and RocketHub have become very successful, allowing people to raise money online. Good marketing is essential to fund your production in this way – what makes your work worth investing in? What can you do to encourage people to donate – could you make videos? Reward people for donating? How could you use social media to help spread the word? Making your company and production look as professional as possible will give people the confidence to part with their hard-earned cash.

It's also possible to fundraise in the real world – by holding special events such as concerts and charging for entry. This method of fundraising often depends on your ability to pitch your project to people, and is usually more effective if people are personally approached, rather than being emailed en masse. When raising money independently, it is important to be aware of your fundraising target, and it must be realistic.

Arts Funding: Useful Links and Websites

Arts Council England
www.artscouncil.org.uk

Arts Council of Northern Ireland
www.artscouncil-ni.org

Arts Council of Wales
www.artswales.org.uk

Scottish Arts Council
www.scottisharts.org.uk

Arts Council Ireland
www.artscouncil.ie

IdeasTap
www.ideastap.com

BBC Performing Arts Fund
www.bbc.co.uk/performingartsfund

Institute of Fundraising – Introduction to Fundraising
www.institute-of-fundraising.org.uk/guidance/about-fundraising

How 2 Fundraise
www.how2fundraise.org

IndieGoGo
www.indiegogo.com

Kickstarter
www.kickstarter.com

RocketHub
www.rockethub.com

We Fund
wefund.com

Sponsume.com
www.sponsume.com

We Did This
www.peoplefund.it/arts

Set Exchange
www.set-exchange.co.uk

Freecycle
www.uk.freecycle.org

Gumtree
www.gumtree.com

Deborah Williams: Applying to ACE

THIS ARTICLE HAS BEEN REPRODUCED IN ITS ENTIRETY WITH KIND PERMISSION FROM AUTHOR AMELIA FORSBROOK AND IDEASTAP

Applying for public funding can be an intimidating and competitive process, but you won't have much luck if you give up at the first hurdle. Deborah Williams, a Relationship Manager in the London theatre team at Arts Council England, reveals the efforts her team go to support and facilitate creativity, and explains why you should apply ...

At Arts Council England we advocate, develop and invest. We have "Achieving great art for everyone" as our 10-year strategic plan and our priorities are around excellence and engagement, enabling artists to create great work and ensuring everyone has access to fantastic artistic experiences. We're also creating things with digital in mind. Digital and the creative economy are areas that are quite new to the Arts Council so we're learning from the sector in some ways.

Essentially, I have two parts to my role. One is to work with National Portfolio Organisations, supporting them and putting together a funding agreement to help them to achieve our joint aims; the other side is working on Grants for the Arts. Here, I am part of panels that make recommendations on what projects to support. I also offer advice to potential applicants who come to us with enquiries. I'm a writer and performer as well and was once in the same position, thinking, "I have no idea what I'm doing, but I want to do this – and I'm going to!"

I don't think enough people aged 18, 19 or 20 submit applications. Get on our radar. Go to networking events and conferences, pick out a list of people from the Arts Council you would like to meet and introduce yourself so that we know who you are and we get an idea of what kind of projects you might be doing. I think it's good for us to be able to respond to what the sector is doing. We encourage conversations to take place to make sure people are heading in the right direction. This means that when applications come in, the knowledge is a shared knowledge and people don't have to try too hard to be seen and heard.

Sit down and take the time to figure the application process out. When you're trying something for the first time, it is going to be daunting. Find all the information you can on our website and if you find you need a little bit more support, you can ask specific questions. We want to make sure that as many people as possible are submitting good applications that best represent what they're trying to do and achieve.

It's great if you've got friends who have a particular kind of experience. Create networks and work with people who are happy to support you. If you are the artist and the focus of the project, then great, but if you can't do the producing or the accounting, find people who can. This will enable you to deliver the work to the standard and the quality that you want to deliver it to.

Top tips:
- Look at the Grants for the Arts web page to familiarise yourself with Arts Council's priorities
- Balance your books. Your income and your expenditure need to be the same.
- Request feedback if you need it. Deborah admits that her colleagues haven't as much time as they'd like to dedicate to this, but they can offer "a phone call, an email, or possibly a meeting."
- Your project may be great, but applying for Arts Council funding is a competitive process.
- Prepare to think about how you can improve and resubmit your proposal if it is unsuccessful.
- You don't have to come with a finished product. Grants for the Arts is also available for research and development work. The Arts Council acknowledges that creativity takes time to grow.

*This article has been reproduced in its entirety with kind permission from author **Amelia Forsbrook** and **IdeasTap**. IdeasTap is an arts charity set up to help young, creative people at the start of their careers, you can find out more and join at **www.ideastap.com**. You can check out Amelia's profile on Ideastap here: **www.ideastap.com/People/ameliaforsbrook***

"If you can't do the producing or the accounting, find people who can"

Starting Your Own Theatre Company

LINA JOHANSSON, JOINT ARTISTIC DIRECTOR AT MIMBRE

Mimbre, 2014, is a successful acrobatics theatre company producing shows that go onto National and European tours. We have an inspiring board, several employees and great freelance artists working with us. We even have our own Youth Company and we are supported as one of Arts Council's England National Portfolio Organisation. But, like others, we started very small.

Mimbre was set up by myself and two other optimistic acrobats when we graduated from Circus Space in 1998. We took any job we could find (I got up at 6 am every day and cycled across London on a rusty bike to sell sandwiches before our daily acrobatics training-pass), lived very frugally, saved up and went with our old teacher to the Circus Centre in Havana, Cuba to improve our skills. We came back with great tricks, no work, but a lot of determination. We took every chance to perform, pestered every contact we had, got side jobs to pay the bills and turned down some really good individual opportunities. We stuck together and put all our energy into creating our own thing. Slowly our company got recognised, grew and started getting support, but 'slowly' is the key word in this sentence! The honest truth; it is still bloody hard work! Running a company, even when it's a shared responsibility, never stops being stressful – but neither does it cease to be amazing! Below are a few things I would recommend you to think about if you are considering it:

Do you have the personality to run a company?
My advice if you are thinking of setting up your own company is to be really honest to yourself about what you are like and what drives you. Are you good at organising and dealing with administration? Can deal reasonably well with stress? Happy to take the lead and responsibility? Full of ideas and passionate about creating your own shows rather than being part of others? Happy to talk about your ideas and 'sell' your work? It is not for everyone

and you might want to go off and get more experience as a freelancer first, working with other people and companies and learn from that.

Have you found a good team?

Have you got the right people to set up a company with? You all need to be committed and be clear about each others' expectations and abilities. One person might be happy to scruff it for a year, but somebody else might have child support to pay and need to earn money immediately. Do you share values, do you want to create the same sort of work, or have you actually got very different ideas of what would be the perfect idea of 'success'? You need to compliment each other, you need to like each other (if you're successful you will be stuck together for a long time!) and you need to be prepared to share responsibilities.

Have you got a product or idea to sell?

This is where it gets very business-y, but some of this is equally useful for the arts. You need to have an inspiring idea of what you want to do. What is your Unique Selling Point, e.g. why is your Hamlet or trapeze act or clowning piece going to be different from others? To get support you need to have either a product, i.e. an existing piece of work, or a strong idea to pitch. It needs to stand out and you need to be passionate about it!

Be aware of what is out there

In business terms; 'build an awareness of the market'. In practicality:
- Go and see other shows, get inspired, think about how you would do it, but also think about how your company will stand out next to other companies that are out there.
- Think about what the different options are for the places where you can go and perform or get support.

© ERIC RICHMOND

- Try to find out what fees other people charge for a show/act/workshop similar to yours.
- Be aware of other people creating new work – are there many of you working on similar things, how will your work stand out?
- Be aware of the wider world. How do your ideas connect with what is going on in the world around us – art and theatre do not exist in a vacuum and it is more interesting, and easier to get support, if you can provide the context for it: what inspired you, how it connects etc.

"Ask people for help. Keep dreaming and be passionate about what you do!"

Build a profile for your company.
- Get 1 or 2 really good images – the best way of grabbing people's attention.
- Make business cards or a postcard with your new nice image on it and all the contact details on the back.
- Set up a webpage – you can build a basic one yourself on Wordpress or find a design student to do it as their project.
- Get a short, but nicely edited video of the work you have done or even just to describe your ideas. You can make basic ones with Window Media Maker, or as above – find a film student to make one for you!
- Find champions; people who will tell others about you – former teachers, other performers or companies, your friends and families, venues or festivals that have booked or given you support. Keep people informed about what you do and ask them to mention you to others!
- Use social media strategically. Facebook, YouTube and Twitter can waste a lot of time, so don't get obsessed, but do use them and other platforms as useful ways of getting people to hear about what you are up to – and get your new champions to like/retweet/link-in with you.
- Be seen – take as many opportunities as possible to perform, present and pitch your ideas, just in general to be seen and heard by people. Slowly people will start to recognise you and you never know in which context a really useful contact will be in the audience.
- Network. Go to conferences, festivals, events. Talk to people. Give them your card. They are unlikely to get back to you immediately but your name has entered their consciousness.

Finding support
This is possibly the scariest one. No one will just come and offer you money – you have to go and ask. And ask again. And again...
- Apply for funding and commissions. If you are starting with an idea you

need money to realise it. Arts Council's GFA (Grant For All) applications are really not as scary as they seem. And it gives you an excuse to approach venues or festival to pledge their support.

- Go to talk with venues, try to get rehearsal spaces for free or do a deal where you give something back in exchange – workshops against rehearsal space etc.
- Keep asking people for advice and help. Everybody loves the passion of people who are starting up and who are enthusiastic and full of dreams. If you ask you might be surprised about who will offer their support – especially directors, choreographers, designers and other companies who have all been there themselves. They will give you support in kind (i.e. not money but free advice or an offer to come in and help out on a show or give you their contacts etc). Once people have invested even a little they are more likely to champion you and support you again.
- Keep a look out for commission opportunities, especially programmes directed towards new companies.
- Look into local scheme for new businesses. Many councils have support initiatives for new companies and sometimes also small grants.
- If you have any rich family or friends see if they can support you or become 'Friends of' your new companies. Set up a support page on your website.
- Consider a loan – Prince's Trust has a variety of support for under 30s looking to set up their own business.

The money and legal stuff
None of this is as complicated as it first seems, but it is really worth going to one of the ITC workshops, or something run by a local business centre, that goes through the basics of the legal and financial side of setting up a company.

If you don't know how to use Excel then take a quick course or ask someone to show you the basics. This is essential, and making budgets and spreadsheets is really not as complicated as it seems. Keep track of who is putting in what if you are investing in your own money. Keep all receipts for things you buy – all of this is tax deductible. Become members of Equity and get their support!

Of course there is much more, but you will learn as you go and if you keep asking then you will get answers! Be focussed on your goals. Ask people for help. Keep dreaming and be passionate about what you do! Good Luck!

Mimbre is a local and international circus and street theatre company, producing innovative and extraordinary acrobatic performance work and promoting a positive, strong image of women: ***www.mimbre.co.uk*** *|* ***www.facebook.com/mimbre.acrobats***

Getting Your Show On At A Regional Theatre

Lisa Whitbread, Business Development Manager at the Stag Community Arts Centre in Sevenoaks

The overall aim behind the Stag Community Arts Centre, based in Sevenoaks, Kent, is to provide top quality experiences for our customers. Whether they are coming to see a production in the 450 seat theatre, stage their own show, watch a film or live West End, Shakespeare and opera in one of the two cinemas, hold a business meeting or run a community event, the whole ethos is about working hard to provide a good service and keep on providing excellent entertainment. There is a mix of shows staged at the Stag Sevenoaks from international ballet companies to some of the top names on the national comedy circuit. It also hosts local community theatre groups, dance schools, tribute bands, musicians and an annual professional pantomime.

At the Stag Sevenoaks, we have a booking fee to use the theatre. This means that we can offer a hefty 95% return on the ticket sales and we do not charge VAT. As a not-for-profit organisation, we simply focus on keeping the theatre running and as a result companies who come here enjoy a healthy profit on their successful shows. We are particularly popular with theatre productions, musicians, bands, ballets and comedians, who are looking to fill slots in their tour schedules and also those who want to test out a new production without having to 'sell' it to a venue in the hope that they book them.

Having your show on at a theatre can be an exciting, if not daunting experience and marks the culmination of the long planning process and the time, energy and money you've invested in getting this far. Of course there will be plenty more hard work to come in putting on your show, but securing a theatre marks a real moment in getting from page to stage.

Finding the right theatre for your show is crucial and you need to consider many factors. These include the venue's location, size, type of audiences, staging style, technical set up and facilities. You also want to find out as much as you can about how much you look to make on the ticket sales.

Some theatres offer a 'split deal' where whatever profit is made is split with you on an agreed percentage, others will offer a guarantee.

Of course programming is crucial to every theatre and they all want to stage shows which will be popular and attract audiences. Think about who your show would appeal to and ask the venues if they have hosted something similar before and how well it did. Also think about whether you want it to be an evening show or a matinee as this will affect the age groups you will attract. A show for very young children would not work in the evening for example, whereas an older audience might prefer the option of a matinee. We charge a daily rate to use the theatre so companies can stage both a matinee and evening performance for the one price. This can help keep costs down while doubling the profits so worth considering if that would work for you.

Your audiences need to be encouraged and you don't want them put off by the ticket price so think carefully about what you want (and need) to charge and budget accordingly. We encourage shows to set their own ticket prices at the Stag Sevenoaks to make it more flexible for them, so remember to ask the venue how the prices are decided. Set them too low and you may not make any profit; set them too high and you risk putting the punters off.

"An essential part of making your show a success is getting the publicity and marketing right"

An essential part of making your show a success is getting the publicity and marketing right. Many venues will have someone responsible for promotion so talk to them about what services they offer. The Stag Sevenoaks provides shows with a marketing package, within the booking price, which includes information in the What's On brochure, on the website, mail outs to customers, all day every day box office, online ticket booking and the local media and display space for posters and flyers. The level of support can vary enormously between different venues so be sure to check how your show can and will be promoted by the theatre. Research what marketing opportunities are available to you and spend wisely on those you feel will get the best results. Not everything needs to cost money, building a good relationship with the local media for example can be very beneficial, but be prepared to budget for materials such as posters and flyers. Eye-catching designs and quality printing can make a real difference to your ticket sales.

Top tips
- Be flexible – Have some dates in mind but be prepared to work around the theatre's existing programme.
- Do your homework – Research the venues, look on their website and call to have a chat.
- Pay a visit – This isn't always easy but if you can go and see the venue, walk round, ask questions and get a feel for the place.
- Be open-minded – Consider all types of venue and don't be put off by the different ways theatres work.
- Keep in touch – Make sure you let the theatre know when your next tour is going on the road. Building a relationship with the venues you know helps create long lasting partnerships.

The moment the lights come up and the audience are watching your show can be a truly magical experience. With the right approach and attitude to working with the theatres, you can be sure you'll give your production the very best opportunity to be a success. Good luck!

The Stag Community Arts Centre has the largest performance space in the South East, welcoming more than 25,000 people every month and working closely with theatre companies, promoters, musicians, businesses and local groups: www.stagsevenoaks.co.uk